MORE EQUAL THAN OTHERS...

MORE EQUAL THAN OTHERS ...

A Director's Guide to EU Competition Policy

WILLIAM PITT

DIRECTOR BOOKS

Published in association with the Institute of Directors

First published 1995 by
Director Books
an imprint of Fitzwilliam Publishing Limited
Campus 400, Maylands Avenue
Hemel Hempstead
Hertfordshire, HP2 7EZ

A division of
Simon & Schuster International Group

Typeset in 10/12pt
by Create Publishing Services, Bath

Printed and bound in Great Britain by
Hartnolls Limited, Bodmin, Cornwall

British Library Cataloguing in Publication Data

A catalogue record for this book is available from the British Library

ISBN: 0–870555678

1   2   3   4   5   99   98   97   96   95

CONTENTS

PREFACE

EU COMPETITION POLICY: THE DEVIL IN THE DETAIL

People of the same trade seldom meet together, even for merriment and diversion, but the conversation ends in a conspiracy against the public, or in some contrivance to raise prices.

Adam Smith, *Wealth of Nations*

Darksome statesmen

In the late autumn of 1993 a pall of gloom hung over Brussels. The depression was more than meterological, although the weather in the Belgian capital that autumn was unusually cold. On this occasion the main reason for the gloom was political; the newly renamed European Union seemed to have lost its way and each EU commissioner resembled the poet Henry Vaughan's 'darksome statesman, hung with weights and woe' who moved 'like a thick fog'.

Four years earlier it had all looked so different. By 1989, the single market programme had gathered what appeared to be unstoppable momentum. It was a goal on which everyone agreed, even the normally fractious British. The back cover of the English version of the EU-funded Cecchini report, 1992, *The Benefits of a Single Market*, summed it up: 'What is on offer,' the salespitch ran, 'is significant inflation-free growth and the creation of millions of new jobs within a single European market of over 320 million people.'

By the time the single market officially arrived, on 1 January 1993, the promises held out by the Cecchini report were looking decidedly tarnished. At the Edinburgh summit in December of the previous year, EU leaders had debated ways of kick-starting national economies that had apparently failed to respond to the single market stimulus. The creation of millions of new jobs seemed an illusion: instead, politicians in France and

Britain were trading insults over the decision by American multinational Hoover to transfer seven hundred jobs from Dijon in France to Cambuslang in Scotland. Social dumping had replaced Europe 1992 as the main preoccupation of politicians on both sides of the Channel.

Most dispiriting of all for the European Commission was the long, wearing process of ratifying the Maastricht Treaty on European Union. The planned ratification date of 1 January 1993 came and went. In May, the Danes approved the treaty (with various opt-outs) in a second referendum, but in Britain the Maastricht bill remained bogged down for months in party politics in the House of Commons. Conservative ministers sought to win over their party's Eurosceptics with the curious argument that monetary union as envisaged in the treaty would never be achieved in the proposed timescale anyway. In the end only a motion yoking support for Maastricht to support for the government enabled the bill to squeak through.

Some officials in Brussels claimed to have seen it all before, in the Euro-sclerosis of the early 1980s, when the need for unanimity among EU member states on every important issue meant that almost nothing was agreed. The log-jam was broken with the signing of the Single European Act in February 1986, which broke the power of the member state veto by introducing qualified majority voting for most European Union legislation.

On this reading, it is far too early to start writing obituaries for the vision of economic and monetary union (EMU) put forward in the Maastricht Treaty, which finally came into force on 1 November 1993. EMU may yet recover its appeal and come to galvanise businesses throughout Europe in the way that the single market programme once did: but as 1993 – the *annus mirabilis* forecast by the single market evangelists – slipped away, the chances appeared slim. The EU competition authorities themselves were not immune to the general malaise. One of the Union's proudest achievements in the competition field, the 1989 merger regulation, came up for review at the end of 1993. In early 1992 it had looked very likely that the regulation thresholds would be lowered to bring many more mergers under the Commission's scrutiny. A detailed survey carried out by the Commission in the spring of 1993 found the majority of European businesses appeared to favour reduction of at least one of the thresholds, but competition commissioner Karel Van Miert, aware that he faced insurmountable opposition from France, Britain and Germany, recommended no change.

That was in July 1993. Four months earlier, Philip Lowe, director of the Commission's merger task force, had explained the Commission's problem. The optimism of 1989, when the merger regulation was unanimously approved by the twelve EU member states, no longer obtained. 'There is a reticence', Mr Lowe said, 'to propose things which assume further integration and development [of the European Union].' This reflected 'hesitancy at national level over the political development of the Community as a whole'.[1]

Mr Van Miert put it more graphically in late August: 'It is not only the currencies that are floating today', he said. 'The Community is floating too.'[2] This mood of political uncertainty forms the backdrop to this book. It is debatable whether a guide to European competition policy is best written at a time of political euphoria in the

European Union or a time of political despondency. In the former case, the claims advanced for EU competition policy could be too grandiose; in the latter case too modest.

One thing is certain, however. Whether politicians are sunk in gloom or buoyed by elation, the businessmen and women of the EU still have order books to fill: and the way competition policy is administered from Brussels affects them profoundly, for good or ill. In the following pages we discover how.

EU competition policy: a tangled skein

The history of EU competition policy is a skein comprising three strands: economic, legal and political. Often the strands are so closely entwined that it is hard to distinguish one from the other, but the effort must be made: ignore one of the three strands and the evolution of EU competition policy becomes illogical, incomprehensible.

First, the economic strand. Directorate General IV, the competition division of the European Commission, both employs economists and retains economists as consultants to investigate competition cases. DGIV officials apply economic formulae to determine concentrations of market share, levels of state aid and the existence of predatory pricing. Detailed analysis of these formulae is outside the scope of this book, although references to such analytical tools as the Herfindahl–Hirschman Index or the Areeda/Turner test will not be left unexplained.

The second strand of EU competition policy is legal. Lawyers dominate the field. Two out of the past three EU competition commissioners, Peter Sutherland and Sir Leon Brittan, have been barristers: Mr Sutherland twice served as the Irish Republic's attorney general, the most senior lawyer in government. Commission officials often contrive to suggest that EU competition law and EU competition policy are one and the same thing.

They are not, though. Competition policy is competition law interpreted by politicians. Issues of competition policy are frequently contentious because they call into question the sovereignty of member states. The Commission's secretary general, David Williamson, admits that the political rows generated by competition issues take up more of his time than any other Commission activity.

Politics, then, the third strand of EU competition policy, should never be ignored. A company can hire the most adroit lawyers and the cleverest economists to help it avoid the Commission's displeasure, but if it ignores the Commission's political priorities, it may yet come to grief.

Consider the case of Nestlé, Europe's biggest food company, which in 1992 offered to pay FFr 15.46 billion for the French mineral water company Source Perrier. The purchase was not *prima facie* in breach of the 1989 merger regulation, still less of the Treaty of Rome. It did not leave Nestlé in a position to dominate the French bottled water market by itself: market dominance would only be possible if Nestlé teamed up with France's Groupe BSN. The merger regulation made no reference to oligopolistic dominance, and as late as April 1992 the Commission was pronouncing the question of its application to oligopolies 'open'.[3]

Three months later, the Commission approved Nestlé's purchase of Perrier on condition that it dispose of eight minor mineral water brands to a company other than BSN. Sir Leon Brittan, the then competition commissioner, claimed that this was necessary to dilute the duopoly that Nestlé and BSN would otherwise have enjoyed. David Hall, a partner at UK lawyers Linklaters & Paines, was not alone in seeing Sir Leon's decision as 'another example of Brussels pushing the boundaries further than anyone had anticipated from reading the text'.[4]

The Commission's task in interpreting the Treaty of Rome is sometimes akin to the task confronting the United States' Supreme Court in interpreting the US constitution. The world has moved on since 1957 when the Treaty of Rome was signed. New threats to competition, such as oligopolistic market dominance, have arisen. Powers vested in the European Commission under the Treaty of Rome have been interpreted in new ways.

A decade ago it would have been inconceivable that the French subsidiary of Brinks Mat, the US armoured delivery company, would complain to the Commission about unfair competition from La Poste, the French state-owned postal monopoly service, when La Poste started to make armoured deliveries. Article 90 of the Treaty of Rome gives the Commission the right to attack state monopolies on competition grounds when they encroach upon normal private sector activities. Since 1957 the Commission has had the legal right to ask whether La Poste was charging subsidised prices, but for many years after the treaty was signed, it would not have dared.

How to use this book

This book attempts to unravel the three strands in EU competition policy. It can be read in two ways: piecemeal or straight through.

For the reader seeking information on a particular aspect of EU competition policy – state aids, say, or merger control – I have sought to present the facts in a manner that is easily accessible. Each chapter should be intelligible on its own and not depend for comprehension on information available elsewhere in the book. This has inevitably resulted in some repetition; but a guide to EU competition policy should not be like a Russian novel, forcing the reader constantly to flick back to the first chapter to remind himself who the protagonists are.

The book is also designed to be read straight through. The characters involved are often colourful; the issues they confront are important for the future of Europe. I have dwelt in detail on the political ramifications of EU competition policy because I regard them as important and because I believe they command wider interest than economic formulae or judicial precedents. For this reason I have tried to avoid cluttering the text with long quotations from the EU treaties or from Commission directives, regulations and communications. Such texts have been relegated to the appendices: not because I consider them unimportant but because they would otherwise obstruct the flow of the narrative. Useful contact names and addresses can also be found in the appendices. On the same principle, checklists (where applicable) have been put at the end of chapters.

The one exception to this rule is the use of tables and flowcharts, which can often convey information more vividly than text. I have tried to use these wherever the prose risks becoming turgid with a surfeit of figures or procedural detail.

Shortly after I started work on this book, I was speaking to a friend who works as an insurance company analyst at a firm of US stockbrokers. 'What are you writing about?' he asked. I told him. 'Isn't that rather dull?' he enquired. I forbore to suggest that some people might consider his line of work rather dull too. Instead, I argued that an understanding of EU competition policy is essential to any understanding of the European Union's *raison d'être*. It is one of the pillars on which the Union is built. Moreover, if the Union is to develop as the Treaty of Rome intends it should, as an 'ever closer union among the peoples of Europe', competition policy will need to be rigorously and impartially enforced. Free and fair competition helps to cement relationships among the peoples of Europe: unfair competition risks sundering them.

This is not the only guide to EU competition policy. It is certainly not the definitive guide: like Heraclitus' river, EU competition policy is constantly changing. However, I hope that the book offers a refreshing introduction to the subject, whether the reader's preference be for a quick dip or more prolonged immersion.

European Community or European Union?

On 1 November 1993, the European Community officially became, for most purposes, the European Union. This created headaches for journalists and guidebook authors alike. Cynics observed that the Union was even less of a union than the Community had been a community. Journalists, though, faced a practical problem: should they reflect the spirit of Europe, which most saw as far from united, or should they respect the letter of the Maastricht Treaty, which asserted the existence of a union?

Guidebook authors faced a further conundrum. Should they backdate the creation of the European Union in the interests of simplicity? Or should the letters EC refer to events that took place before 1 November 1993 and the letters EU refer to events that took place after that date? And what about gradual processes that span both eras?

I have decided to use European Union and EU throughout this book. The only exceptions are references to the EC contained in direct quotations or reported speech pre-dating the birth of the Union. To readers who protest that the European Union is palpably not a union, I would reply: I agree, but the names of organisations frequently fail to reflect their true nature. To readers who complain that the use of EU before 1 November 1993 is anachronistic, I would reply: maybe so, but would you resuscitate 'the EEC' and 'the Common Market' as well? EU competition policy is complicated enough already without drawing attention to every change in the chameleon's skin.

Currency conversions

I have kept all references to currencies in this book in their original form and not attempted to convert them. The volatility of Europe's currencies at the end of 1993 would, in any case, have made conversion an unhelpful exercise.

For readers not used to Ecu transactions, the value of the Ecu against the main European currencies plus the US dollar and the Japanese yen on 29 December 1993 were as follows:

Ecu 1: pound sterling 0.7539
Ecu 1: US dollar 1.1278
Ecu 1: German mark 1.9342
Ecu 1: French franc 6.5819
Ecu 1: Japanese yen 125.86
Ecu 1: Belgian franc 40.232
Ecu 1: Dutch guilder 2.1667
Ecu 1: Danish krone 7.5569
Ecu 1: Italian lira 1913.5
Ecu 1: Greek drachma 277.64
Ecu 1: Portuguese escudo 197.08
Ecu 1: Swiss franc 1.6297
Ecu 1: Irish pound 0.7955
Ecu 1: Spanish peseta 159.44

NOTES

1. Interview with author, April 1993.
2. Press conference in Brussels, August 1993, quoted in *Les Echos*.
3. *XXIst Report on Competition Policy*, April 1992, annex III.A.7.35, page 394.
4. Quoted in the *Financial Times*, 23 July 1992.

CHAPTER 1

THE INSTITUTIONS OF THE EUROPEAN UNION

THE COMMISSION

Much criticised, little loved, rarely out of the headlines, the European Commission is the guardian of the European Union's sacred texts – the Treaty of Rome and the other treaties that have shaped the Union. It is not as powerful as some of its antagonists like to pretend: measures proposed by the unelected 'Eurocrats' are in fact regularly thrown out by the Council of Ministers, drawn from the elected governments of the EU member states. Nevertheless, in competition matters the Commission does wield impressive authority. The Commission acts as the Union's executive, policing implementation of the treaties and other measures enacted by the Council of Ministers. Where provisions in the Treaty of Rome are subject to exceptions, the Commission must determine whether the qualifying conditions have been met. Thus the Commission can outlaw a cartel under Article 85(1) of the treaty, but it may also permit a cartel that offers the advantages described in Article 85(3) of the treaty (see chapter 2). No other authority in the European Union has this power.

The Commission also administers the Union's budget, a difficult task in these straitened times. Sir Leon Brittan used to bite his lip when invited to comment on the resources available to his competition staff in Directorate General IV. His successor, Karel Van Miert, is more voluble, complaining about the tight spending constraints he inherited under the 1993 budget.

However, most of the flack aimed at the Commission derives from its duty under the Treaty of Rome to initiate EU policy. Commission proposals are drafted to be approved, rejected or modified by the Council of Ministers. Whenever jokes are told along the lines of 'The European Commission thinks carrots are a fruit', it is usually because the Commission has proposed a new piece of EU legislation in which carrots have been classed as fruit.[1] (Not always: many of the stories told about the bizarre antics of the polyglot Eurocrats are pure myth.)

The Commission is run by seventeen commissioners who are in charge of twenty-three directorates general. In 1993 Karel Van Miert was put in charge of Directorate General IX (DGIX, personnel and administration) as well as the much more important competition department, DGIV. He won his spurs as transport commissioner (DGVII) from 1988 to 1993. His predecessor, Sir Leon Brittan, used to run DGXV (financial institutions and company law) as well as DGIV. Sir Leon was thus able to preside over a remarkably successful liberalisation programme in EU banking and insurance markets. (The financial institutions portfolio later passed to Raniero Vanni d'Archirafi, one of Italy's two commissioners.)

Until 1993, commissioners' terms of office ran for four years. Under the Maastricht Treaty on European Union, they are to be extended to five years from the beginning of 1995. That leaves a two-year gap which Mr Van Miert and his sixteen fellow commissioners must fill. EU politics move at a different pace from national politics: whereas former prime minister Harold Wilson observed that 'a week is a long time in politics', Mr Van Miert argues that 'two years is not a long time' for an EU commissioner to get anything done.[2] (His reappointment in October 1994, just as this book was going to press, ensures that he will have rather longer to make his mark at DGIV than he at first envisaged.)

The periodic reshuffles of Commission positions rarely have much impact on the positions held by officials in the different directorates general. Almost all the senior and junior posts in DGIV continued to be occupied by the same people following the handover of control from Sir Leon Brittan to Karel Van Miert in December 1992. Claus-Dieter Ehlermann continued as director-general and almost all his adjutants remained as before. The only significant change was the retirement of Colin Overbury as director of the merger task force and his replacement by Philip Lowe.

Some continuity of policy is thus ensured, but it does not prevent the arrival of a new commissioner heralding important changes in the work of a directorate general's staff. The commissioner's job is to weigh the political implications of the findings his staff put to him. Under Article 10 of the Single European Act 1986, a commissioner must 'neither seek nor take instructions from any Government or from any other body'; but the political sensitivities of individual member states will be constantly on a commissioner's mind.

Commissioners are assisted in their labours by an inner circle of advisers known as the commissioner's cabinet (pronounced *ca-bee-nay* after the French). Cabinet officials tend to move around with their political masters: Mr Van Miert's have all accompanied him in his move from transport to competition. They are important people for two reasons: they have the ear of the commissioner, and they frequently attend crucial meetings in the commissioner's stead.

The division of cabinet responsibilities at DGIV is as follows: Philippe Renaudiere (mergers, regional aids and state monopolies), Pascale Wolfcarius (Articles 85 and 86), Marc Van Hoof (other state aids, sectoral and general aid schemes), and Gustaff Dierckx (international relations).

The division of labour at Directorate General IV

On 1 January 1993, Karel Van Miert inherited a staff of 407 at DGIV. This included secretarial staff. The most labour-intensive activity within DGIV, occupying 44 per cent of the staff full time, was investigation of cases under Articles 85 and 86 of the Treaty of Rome – the Union's main anti-trust rules. For each member of staff engaged in this field, there were nearly 9 cases awaiting investigation at the beginning of 1993 – 1,562 cases in all. This was a great improvement on a year earlier, when DGIV officials had confronted a backlog of 2,287 cases.

The division of labour at DGIV during the last year of Sir Leon Brittan's tenure as commissioner is interesting. Article 85 and 86 cases took by far the largest number of man-hours, followed by state aid cases (engaging 21 per cent of the workforce). Next came merger control cases (12 per cent), followed by clerical activities (11 per cent), and international relations (9 per cent).

Bringing up the rear, engaging only 3 per cent of DGIV's 407-strong workforce, were what the Commission calls Article 90 cases – cases involving the application of the competition rules to state-owned public service monopolies, like telecommunications, energy, and postal services. This is without a doubt the most politically controversial of the Commission's activities in the field of competition policy. Sir Leon Brittan's impressive rhetoric on the need to inject competition into these traditionally protected markets seems strangely at odds with the resources he devoted to the task in 1992.

Of course, such bald figures do not always tell the whole story. The officials within DGIV charged with investigating Article 90 cases can call upon assistance from other directorates general. Thus investigations into the import/export monopolies still enjoyed at the beginning of 1993 by six state-owned electricity companies were carried out in alliance with officials from DGXVII, the Commission's energy division.

It remains the case, though, that DGIV is grossly understaffed in some areas. For instance, in early 1993 only two officials were charged with the heavy responsibility of monitoring state aids to state-owned companies. Successive competition commissioners have spoken eloquently of the importance of this task. It is hard to avoid the impression that this politically contentious activity – the subject of a European Court of Justice action from France – had been shunted onto the backburner.

Full details of the structure of DGIV, including contact names, telephone and fax number for officials, are supplied in appendix 5.

THE COUNCIL OF MINISTERS

Under the Treaty of Rome, the Council of Ministers is responsible for enacting legislation put to it by the European Commission. Unlike the seventeen-member Commission, the Council is not a predetermined group of people, but a group of ministers from the twelve member states that changes according to the subject under discussion. Thus the important Ecofin [economics and finance] Council meetings will bring together the finance ministers of the member states, the Agriculture Council will comprise agriculture ministers, and so on. The meetings are chaired by a minister from the member state holding the presidency of the European Community, a responsibility that changes every six months. (Britain's last presidency, widely accounted a disaster in continental Europe on account of a series of much publicised disputes between Britain and her EU partners, ran from July 1992 to December 1992.)

Most matters considered by the Council of Ministers, including matters relating to competition policy, are enacted or rejected by a simple majority. Certain matters require a 'qualified majority'. This oft-used phrase is rarely explained, although it is far from self-explanatory. In the 12-member European Union, a motion to be carried by qualified majority must command at least fifty-four of the seventy-six votes available. Under the Treaty of Rome, Britain, France, Germany and Italy each hold ten votes; Spain holds eight; Belgium, Greece, the Netherlands and Portugal hold five each; Ireland and Denmark three each, and Luxembourg two.

This is the voting system that applied when the Council of Ministers came to decide whether the thresholds of the 1989 merger regulation should be lowered at the end of 1993. France was sceptical about the measure, which could have reduced the size of mergers investigated at EU level (see chapter 3) by more than half. The French government needed to win the support of just two other member states (providing one of them was a ten-vote heavyweight) in order to reject the measure. In the event, Mr Van Miert decided the odds were stacked too heavily against him, and declined to propose any changes.

The Council of Ministers is supported in its deliberations by the Committee of Permanent Representatives (COREPER), made up of the permanent ambassadors of the member states. This committee mulls over Commission proposals that are due to come up before the Council of Ministers, seeking compromises that will avoid a stalemate.

THE EUROPEAN PARLIAMENT

The European Parliament may be less vilified than the European Commission but it is the butt of just as many jokes – most of them aimed at its ineffectiveness.

The European Parliament has no power to initiate legislation, but it can and does debate and amend proposals put forward by the European Commission. In the unlikely event that it wanted to plunge the European Union into chaos, the Parliament could also exercise its right to dismiss the entire Commission on the strength of two-thirds of the votes of its 518 members.

The Commission's *XXIInd Report on Competition Policy*, published in May 1993, pays tribute to the 'lively attention to competition matters' shown by members of the European Parliament in the course of 1992. In particular, it proposed a range of amendments to the block exemption for insurance undertakings, most of which the Commission accepted (see chapter 6). Resolutions on the European steel industry and the British coal mining industry, both applicants for state aid, were also adopted and relayed to the Commission.

Lively the Parliament may be, but its effectiveness in persuading the Commission to change tack is more doubtful. Following the controversial de Havilland judgement in 1991 (see chapter 3), the Parliament asked the Commission to amend the 1989 merger regulation to enable certain industrial policy considerations to be taken into account in future judgements. The Commission refused.[3]

That does not mean that the European Parliament cannot be an effective means of extracting information from the Commission, or of bringing anti-competitive behaviour to the Commission's attention. In the course of 1991, MEPs submitted 169 written questions on competition policy to the Commission, and 75 questions for oral reply. In 1992, the tally was 141 written questions and 66 questions for oral reply.

If you run, say, a small business and believe you are the victim of predatory pricing by a bigger competitor, you would do well to inform your MEP. He or she may well have received similar information from other companies and thus may be better equipped than you to elicit a rapid response from the Commission.

THE EUROPEAN COURT OF JUSTICE

The complexity of some of the competition cases that come before the European Court of Justice (ECJ) can be mind-boggling. Take the so-called polypropylene cases over which fifteen European petrochemical companies were fined Ecu 56.8 million by the Commission in 1986. The petrochemical companies' appeal, when it finally came before the ECJ, assembled procedural documents four thousand pages long and supporting documentation twenty thousand pages long.[4]

Such cases resemble nothing so much as the famous Jarndyce and Jarndyce lawsuit that dragged on for decades in Dickens' *Bleak House*. It was perhaps as well that the polypropylene cases arose after the European Council of Ministers had approved the creation of a new court to handle, *inter alia*, competition cases. The old unicameral court of justice was becoming overburdened, so on 24 October 1988 the Council of Ministers agreed that a new court, the Court of First Instance, should be attached to the Court of Justice of the European Communities.

The idea was to improve the ECJ's ability to fulfil its demanding tasks as laid down in the Treaty of Rome. In relation to competition policy, the court's role is threefold:

1. It can review fines imposed by the Commission, using the authority of Article 172 of the Treaty of Rome.
2. Under Article 173 it can sit in judgement on the legality of Commission decisions.
3. Under Article 175 of the treaty it can oblige the Commission to act in accordance with the treaty in circumstances where it has previously failed to act.

The court thus wields fearsome power. Nothing is more likely to make the officials of DGIV sit up and take notice than the prospect of a legal challenge in the European Court of Justice. One of the reasons the 1989 merger regulation is hailed as such a success within the Commission is the scarcity of ECJ appeals it has generated – only four up to March 1993.

The court's power to review fines worked to the benefit of Britain's biggest chemicals company, Imperial Chemical Industries, in 1992. Fined Ecu 10 million by the Commission for its part in the cartel of polypropylene producers referred to above, ICI appealed to the Court of Justice. Its fine was reduced to Ecu 9 million in recognition of the extensive co-operation the company had shown in furnishing the Commission with information, both on its own behaviour and that of the other cartel members. The Commission had already reduced ICI's fine by 10 per cent as a result of this assistance, but the court concluded that this did not go far enough.[5]

The court's power to compel the Commission to pursue a complaint that it has rejected is less commonly exercised. This is because the process is so time-consuming. Bryan Harris, editor of the very useful periodical *Competition Law in the European Communities* describes such actions as using a 'judicial steamroller . . . for cracking an administrative nut'.[6]

Nevertheless the Court of First Instance did upbraid the Commission in 1992 for failing to act on a complaint over an alleged restrictive agreement between the French importers of five makes of Japanese car.[7] The agreement, concluded under the auspices of the French government, had sought to prevent the importation into France of other Japanese car models.

By far the most complex cases ever investigated by the European Court of Justice concern the legality of Commission decisions. The polypropylene cases fall into this category. The creation of the Court of First Instance has helped to spread the burden, but it remains heavy.

Immediately upon its creation, the new court was landed with a backlog of 153 cases that had built up at the Court of Justice. Around half of these were competition cases. In the course of 1990 a further 55 cases were brought before the new court, and in 1991, 93 new cases were brought. It has been calculated that, taking into account appeals from the Court of First Instance to the Court of Justice, the lower court saved the higher court the trouble of investigating over 75 cases in 1991.

Competition cases form the largest category of cases investigated by the ECJ, both upper and lower chambers. The court delivered 210 judgements in 1992, of which 112 were references from preliminary rulings from national courts throughout the European Union.

References for preliminary rulings make up a large proportion of the ECJ's caseload. They occur when national courts wish to clarify a point of EU law. The opinions handed down by the ECJ often prove valuable to the European Commission, helping to define the scope of the Commission's authority in competition matters. The ECJ has been known to hand down radical interpretations of Community law which, for political reasons, the Commission would never have dared propose. References for preliminary rulings are always addressed to the upper court.

The upper court is also the only forum in which cases brought against the Commission by member state governments can be heard, and vice versa. The French government in particular has proved very willing to go to court in recent years to defend its sovereignty against Commission incursions.

Thirteen judges sit in the European Court of Justice, each appointed for six years. They are assisted by six Advocates General whose task is to deliver an opinion to the court on the merits of the case in hand. An Advocate General's opinion is only sought in the more complicated cases: although judges tend, as a rule, to follow the line suggested in the Advocate General's opinion, they are not bound so to do.

Advocates General play no role in the Court of First Instance, which operates completely separately from the upper court. The Court of First Instance has twelve judges.

On 8 June 1993 the Council of Ministers decided that a wide range of cases currently handled by the Court of Justice should be transferred to the Court of First Instance. Under the Council of Ministers' original 1989 decision establishing the Court of First Instance, only competition cases and cases involving staff of the EU's institutions were to be heard there. The new rules provide for the transfer of all direct actions brought by legal or natural persons under EU law to be heard in the Court of First Instance.

The Council of Ministers hoped to leave the Court of Justice free to fulfil what it saw as the court's main task: to 'ensure a uniform interpretation of Community law and safeguard the institutional balance within the Community'.[8] This was threatened because the backlog of cases at the Court of Justice was once again beginning to mount up: the average period for preliminary rulings on references from member state courts rose from 18.5 months in 1991 to 18.8 months in 1992. The Commission is keen to encourage national courts to hear more competition cases (see chapter 5), but if the Court of Justice cannot give member state courts rapid guidance on points of EU law, that will not happen.

NOTES

1. Carrots are listed as a fruit in the amended definition for fruit set out in the Community's 1979 directive on jam. This was done in order to enable the Portuguese to continue using carrots in the production of jam.
2. Interview with author, 3 June 1993.
3. *XXIst Report on Competition Policy*, April 1992, chapter 4.I, section 1.3, page 317.
4. Bo Vesterdorf, 'The Court of First Instance of the European Communities after two full years in operation', *Common Market Law Review*, vol. 29, 1992.
5. *XXIInd Report on Competition Policy*, May 1993, chapter 2.11, section 1.1, page 190.
6. *Competition Law in the European Communities*, Bryan Harris (ed.), Monitor Press, June 1993.
7. *Asia Motor France and Other* v. *Commission*, judgement of 18 September 1992, case T-28/90, quoted in *XXIInd Report on Competition Policy*, May 1993.
8. Press release issued by European Court of Justice, 8 June 1993.

CHAPTER 2

THE COMMISSION'S HEAVY ARTILLERY:
ARTICLES 85 AND 86

CARTELS AND DOMINANT POSITIONS

'What is the basic idea behind the Treaty of Rome?' asked the British humorist Miles Kington in one of his vintage *Times* columns in the early 1980s. His answer? 'The idea, basically, is: when in Brussels, do as the Germans do.'

Miles Kington's interpretation may not command universal consent. Indeed, there may be people in Munich or Mannheim who would not even find it amusing. But no-one would deny the importance of the question. Nearly four decades after the Treaty of Rome was signed, its 248 articles influence the daily lives of over 369 million Europeans (the combined populations of the EU and EFTA countries, less Switzerland which failed to sign the European Economic Area agreement).

The Treaty of Rome gives the European Commission two principle weapons with which to fend off threats to competition: Articles 85 and 86. This chapter will gauge the firepower of these weapons. (The full text of Articles 85 and 86 is contained in appendix 1.)

Article 85 gives the Commission authority to crack down on 'all agreements between undertakings, decisions by associations of undertakings and concerted practices which may affect trade between Member States' and which threaten 'the prevention, restriction or distortion of competition'. We analyse these phrases in detail shortly, but for the time being suffice it to say that Article 85 bans cartels.

Article 86 outlaws the 'abuse by one or more undertakings of a dominant position within the common market or in a substantial part of it'. Again, the dominant position must 'affect trade' between member states and the gravity of the abuse will depend on the extent to which it affects trade. In a nutshell, Article 86 guards against abuses of monopoly, or near-monopoly, power.

The Commission is empowered to impose hefty fines on companies it finds to be in breach of Article 85 or 86. Under Council Regulation 17 of 1962, which defines the Commission's powers in relation to Articles 85 and 86, the Commission can levy fines up to 10 per cent of each culprit's turnover for the previous business year. (See Article 15, Regulation 17, in appendix 2.) Companies thus fined may appeal to the European Court of Justice for their penalties to be reduced.

Investigation of alleged infringements of Articles 85 and 86 still represents the biggest task undertaken by the 407 staff of Directorate General IV, the Commission's competition division. To be sure, the control of state aids (regulated under Articles 92, 93 and 94 of the treaty) has loomed larger as the single market has developed and politicians have recognised the need for a strategy to avoid a subsidy race among EU member states (see chapter 4). More recently the Commission has begun to turn its attention to the anti-competitive behaviour of state monopolies in areas like energy and telecommunications, but the relevance of Articles 85 and 86 remains undimmed.

THE NEED FOR EU-WIDE POWERS

Why do Articles 85 and 86 need to be policed from Brussels? Why cannot anti-trust agencies in the individual member states handle the job? There are two reasons. First, the cases investigated by the Commission usually span borders and it is by no means clear where responsibility for rooting out the abuse should lie. Second, Europe's anti-trust agencies vary enormously in terms of experience and resources: the British have been active in this field since 1965 and the Germans since 1967, but the Italians, Belgians and Irish have only had anti-trust laws for a few years.[1] The risk therefore arises that Articles 85 and 86 might be implemented unevenly across the European Union. This uneven application could prove a distorting influence on competition in its own right – the European Union would find itself adding to the problems it was trying to solve.

Both Articles 85 and 86 contain clauses suggesting the level at which a supranational authority should take charge. The practices outlawed are those that 'may affect trade between Member States'. In his last major speech as competition commissioner, Sir Leon Brittan defended this 'effect on trade' test as the 'logically correct limitation of Community competence' as far as Articles 85 and 86 were concerned. 'If an anti-competitive agreement or practice appreciably affects trade within the Community, the Commission is the authority best placed, in terms of linguistic resources and fact-finding powers, to examine the case.'[2]

In the case of Article 85, certain agreements between companies are not deemed significant enough to occupy the Commission's time. These are automatically approved under a 1986 Commission notice 'Agreements of minor importance'. The notice, which is described fully in chapter 7 on small and medium-sized businesses, generally permits companies with combined turnover of up to Ecu 200 million to co-operate without falling foul of the Commission. This does not, of course, guarantee them immunity from the scrutiny of national competition authorities.

BEYOND THE UNION – THE COMMISSION'S REACH

The biggest fine ever imposed by the European Commission for a breach of Article 85 or 86 was levied neither against an EU-based company nor against a company based in the European Economic Area, which from the beginning of 1993 adopted the European Union's competition rules lock, stock and barrel. It was foisted on a Swiss company, Tetra Pak (see case study on pages 17–18).

The principle that the Commission can attack non-EU companies for practices carried on by their subsidiaries within the European Union is well established in EU law. The principle was reaffirmed by the European Court of Justice on 27 September 1988 when it ruled in the so-called wood pulp case that agreements reached outside the EU could be penalised under Article 85 as long as they applied within the EU and had an anti-competitive effect on trade within the Union.[3] The Commission had fined, among others, wood pulp producers from Finland, the United States, Canada and Norway. (The fines were much later annulled by the court in a separate judgement on grounds unrelated to the Commission's jurisdiction.)

Companies in two of these countries, Finland and Norway, are now subject to the full force of Articles 85 and 86 under the European Economic Area (EEA) agreement between the European Union and the European Free Trade Association (EFTA).[4] These two core texts of EU competition policy have been reproduced, almost word for word, as Articles 53 and 54 of the EEA agreement. Responsibility for policing these measures is shared between the European Commission and a new European competition authority, the EFTA Surveillance Authority (ESA). If competition is distorted on trade within the EU, the European Commission handles the case – no matter where the culprits may be. As a rule, the ESA takes charge only where the effect on trade relates exclusively to EFTA member states. It remains to be seen whether the ESA will prove as tough – or tougher – in its treatment of anti-competitive behaviour than the European Commission has been.

THE 'EFFECT ON TRADE' TEST

The effect on trade test is, like all the clauses contained in Articles 85 and 86, open to varying judicial interpretation. It is worth glancing at some of the landmark cases in the application of this clause. The European Court of Justice (ECJ) has tended towards a very wide-ranging interpretation. Companies hoping to shelter behind legal niceties have been rudely disabused.

The classic definition of the effect on trade test was given by the ECJ as long ago as 1966. 'It must be possible to foresee ... that the agreement in question may have an influence, direct or indirect, actual or potential, on the pattern of trade between Member States.'[5]

Direct or indirect, actual or potential – these are broad criteria and, as the single market evolves, they will grow broader still. Under this definition it is quite possible to find agreements made within a single member state in breach of Article 85, because they hinder the competitive chances of firms from outside that member state. Brewers in particular have fallen foul of this definition, being found in breach of EU competition rules by virtue of exclusive sales agreements.[6]

Agreements which segment national markets can be just as offensive to the Commission as agreements that carve up international markets. The ECJ has even suggested to an Italian court that exclusive distribution agreements signed by Italian newspapers were anti-competitive at an EU level because they reinforced the partition of the EU market for newspapers along national lines.[7]

However, there has been some reaction against this ever narrower interpretation. Advocate General Trabucchi told the European Court of Justice in 1975 that EU competition rules concerned agreements which may result in a restriction of competition such as to be significant at Community level. He then defined significant as 'referring not to state frontiers or geographical areas but to the effect of the agreement on the product to which it relates, viewed not from the purely national standpoint, but from a wider standpoint which takes the ... Community economy into account'.

The merger regulation, which is discussed later, attempts to tackle this problem by laying down thresholds for mergers with a 'Community dimension'. However, the regulation does not deprive the Commission of its residual right to bring actions of its own against undertakings in EU member states under Articles 85 and 86.

UNDERSTANDING UNDERTAKINGS

Over the years, Articles 85 and 86 have provided hours of amusement to lawyers. Take the first section of Article 85, referred to above. In full it reads as follows:

> Article 85.1.   The following shall be prohibited as incompatible with the common market: all agreements between undertakings, decisions by associations of undertakings and concerted practices which may affect trade between Member States and which have as their object or effect the prevention, restriction or distortion of competition within the common market ...

The words 'following', 'prohibited' and 'incompatible' afford practically no scope for debate, so the first word the lawyers have seized upon is 'undertakings'. The word figures in Article 86 as well as Article 85; but what is an undertaking? Is it possible for a party to an alleged breach of Article 85 to elude its hunters by denying it is an undertaking?

Possible, but very difficult. In practice the Commission's net has been woven to a very fine mesh. An undertaking is defined as a person, whether legal or natural, carrying on independent economic or commercial activity.[8] An individual can also be classed as an undertaking according to this definition. Where a parent company issues orders to a subsidiary, the two are regarded as being the same undertaking, even if they have separate legal identities.

The European Court of Justice has made some exceptions. The British Royal Pharmaceutical Society, a professional association exercising disciplinary powers over its members, has been cleared of anti-competitive behaviour by the ECJ on the grounds that it is not an undertaking.[9] Likewise, a municipal authority granting an exclusive concession for funeral services escaped censure because it was not deemed to be an undertaking.[10]

In February 1993, the ECJ ruled that regional social security offices dealing with sickness, maternity and old age benefits could not be classed as undertakings. Two enterprising French citizens had claimed in a French court that they had the right to go to any private insurance company in the EU to pay their social security contributions. The court referred the matter to the ECJ which ruled that French social security offices were not 'undertakings' in competition with private sector insurers.[11]

Test cases have not always swung this way, though. Perhaps the most audacious interpretation of 'undertaking' was advanced by the ECJ in 1991, in a case involving a state-owned German employment agency. The case excited huge controversy in Germany, where it was claimed that the European Union was outlawing the state's right to grant exclusive rights to publicly funded agencies, deemed to be serving the public interest.

The case ran as follows. The German government conferred on the Bundesanstalt für Arbeit (BfA), a public corporation, the exclusive right to provide job placement services in Germany. The BfA was financed entirely through public funds, not by user fees.

Despite the BfA's legal monopoly, various private interests set up their own employment agencies for managers. The overburdened BfA turned a blind eye to this practice, although the contracts made by these private agencies were not enforceable under German law.

The German courts referred the case to the European Court of Justice in the hope of clarifying the legal status of the private agencies. The ECJ found that the BfA was in breach of EU competition rules because:

1. it was an undertaking;
2. its business, despite being publicly financed, was an 'economic activity', and
3. it held a 'dominant position' in the German market by virtue of its official monopoly.

The ECJ further found that the BfA was abusing its dominant position because it could not satisfy demand but would not waive its monopoly status. It was therefore 'limiting ... markets ... to the prejudice of consumers', a practice forbidden under Article 86(b) of the Treaty of Rome. Clearly, the ECJ had a point. The position of the private agencies that sprang up to meet the demand left unsatisfied by the BfA was intolerable. They should either have been told to stop competing with the BfA, or they should have been brought within the law.

The precedent set by the European Court's ruling is more questionable, though. If all publicly funded state agencies entrusted with exclusive rights are to be treated as undertakings subject to the full force of Article 86, how will government function? How will public service obligations be discharged if private sector companies can cream off the more profitable business held by state monopolies and defend their action on the grounds that the monopolies infringed their rights under Article 86 of the Treaty of Rome?

Surely this would leave hardly any scope for an EU member state to adduce social benefits in support of a monopoly service. Norbert Reich, professor of law at Bremen University in Germany, is not alone in warning that, in this way, 'public law relations are "privatised"; the State is regarded as interfering into private market relations even if they are confined to one member state.'[12] It is hard to believe that the signatories of the Treaty of Rome had this in mind back in 1957.

The next contentious words in Article 85 are 'agreements ... decisions by associations ... and concerted practices'. The words 'concerted practices' are included to ensure that no informal variety of co-operation among companies escapes the Commission's scrutiny. The phrase has been defined by the European Court of Justice as occurring when undertakings 'knowingly substitute practical co-operation ... for the risks of competition'.[13] No formal agreement need identify this change of tack.

Of course, the key words in the article are 'prevention, restriction or distortion of competition'. Any form of co-operation which does not have this as its object or its effect is permissible. It is usually only after an exhaustive investigation that a transaction can be cleared under this heading. Few agreements or concerted practices that cross the Commission's bows are flagrantly anti-competitive.

ARTICLE 86: DEFINING DOMINANCE

The most problematic words in Article 86 are 'dominant position'. What are the tell-tale signs of a dominant position within the common market?

Problems of defining dominance deterred the Commission from pursuing breaches of Article 86 for over a decade after the Treaty of Rome was signed in 1957. It preferred instead to concentrate on cartels that were clearly outlawed under Article 85. Even today, Article 86 decisions are far rarer than Article 85 decisions: in the course of 1991, for instance, only one company was fined for breaching Article 86.

The best definition of a dominant position available was supplied by the ECJ back in the early 1980s. It was:

> A position of economic strength enjoyed by an undertaking which enables it to hinder the maintenance of effective competition on the relevant market by allowing it to behave ... *independently of its competitors and customers and ultimately of consumers.* [emphasis added][14]

An earlier ECJ judgement had made it clear that a dominant position need not preclude competition altogether. All the Commission needs to prove is that the company in question can have 'an appreciable effect on the conditions under which that competition will develop'.[15] The dominant company must also be able to ignore such competition as exists, secure in the knowledge that this will do it no harm.

Clearly, one indicator of dominance is the market share of the company, or companies, in question. However, this can be a very misleading indicator: in many industries the pace of technological change means that today's market leader can be tomorrow's laggard. It would clearly be rash to penalise a software company, for instance, exclusively on the evidence of a high market share that could disappear within months. Instead, the Commission prefers to concentrate on evidence of abuse of a dominant position of the kinds demonstrated by Tetra Pak (see case study on pages 17–18).

ARTICLE 86: A QUESTION OF GEOGRAPHY

A further problem of Article 86 is deciding whether the dominant position held by one or more undertakings covers the 'common market or a substantial part of it'. As with Article 85 and its precondition that alleged restrictive practices must stand to 'affect trade between member states', the definition of 'substantial part' of the common market has proved elusive.

Unfortunately the European Court of Justice has not handed down any judgement of the kind given by the British House of Lords on 16 December 1992. Their lordships were asked to adjudicate on the meaning of 'a substantial part of the United Kingdom' as mentioned in the Fair Trading Act 1973. Specifically, they were asked whether South Yorkshire met this definition.

South Yorkshire represents only 1.65 per cent of the land area of the UK and, according to the latest figures available to their lordships, contained 3.2 per cent of the country's population. And yet the judicial committee of the House of Lords still found the Monopoly and Mergers Commission within its rights to interpret this as a substantial part of the United Kingdom.

If only Article 86 of the Treaty of Rome were as clearly interpreted. In practice the Commission is eager that member state courts should increasingly investigate cases of abuse of market dominance, where their effects are confined within the territory of a single member state. Clearly, the land area of France or Germany represents a 'substantial part' of the Community; but the Commission's new-found enthusiasm for subsidiarity has inclined it to back away from such cases (see chapter 5).

ARTICLE 85 IN ACTION

There is much more to Articles 85 and 86 than a few sonorous phrases. Article 85 gives five concrete examples of ways in which cartels can distort competition, and Article 86 lists four potentially grave abuses of market dominance.

Here follow the examples of anti-competitive conduct expressly forbidden under Article 85, together with some descriptions of how they have been interpreted in practice.

(a) Deals which 'directly or indirectly fix purchase or selling prices or any other trading conditions'

In March 1992, the Commission fined a group of French banks that were members of the Eurocheque system Ecu 5 million. Their offence was to charge French retailers the same commission for cashing foreign Eurocheques as they charged for payment by bank card. The Commission claimed this constituted price fixing.[16]

(b) Deals which 'limit or control production, markets, technical development, or investment'

On 18 March 1992 the Commission fined Dunlop Slazenger International, a subsidiary of the British conglomerate BTR, Ecu 5 million for restricting exports from the UK with the aim of protecting its sole distributors in other Community countries. The complaint against Dunlop, the EU market leader for tennis and squash balls, was brought by Newitt, a UK distribution company. Newitt claimed that Dunlop had suspended deliveries and then applied discriminatory tariffs to deter it from exporting the company's products.[17]

(c) Deals which 'share markets or sources of supply'

In May 1990 a Belgian dairy co-operative complained to the Commission about various clauses in the articles of association of Campina, a Dutch dairy co-operative. In particular, the Belgians were unhappy with the high 'resignation fee' imposed on Campina members who wished to sell outside the co-operative. The fee amounted to 10 per cent of the average annual milk price obtained by the member to the cooperative.

The Commission investigated the case and found that the resignation fee inhibited the economic freedom of Campina's members. The fee also denied Campina's competitors access to milk produced by the co-operative's members. In other words, it ring-fenced a significant share of the market. The Commission insisted that Campina reduce its resignation fees.[18] (By contrast, in October 1992 Sir Leon Brittan wrote to Britain's then agriculture minister John Gummer congratulating him on the UK government's plan to end the Milk Marketing Board's monopoly over the purchase and sale of milk in Britain.)[19]

(d) Deals which 'apply dissimilar conditions to equivalent transactions with other trading parties, thereby placing them at a competitive disadvantage'

In May 1991 the Commission fined the French cognac producer Martell Ecu 300,000 for withdrawing discounts from Gosme, a wholesale distributor of food, wines and spirits. Gosme had been exporting Martell cognac from France to Italy, undercutting the prices charged by Martell's exclusive Italian distributor. The Commission concluded that the discounts Martell had withdrawn from Gosme were originally given for reasons unrelated to whether the cognac was destined for French or export markets. They were bulk, promotional and other such discounts. The Commission decided that Martell had no right to penalise Gosme by withdrawing them.[20]

(e) Deals which 'make the conclusion of contracts subject to acceptance by the other parties of supplementary obligations which, by their nature or according to commercial usage, have no connection with the subject of such contracts'

In January 1991 the Commission found the French cosmetics company Société d'Hygiene Dermatologique de Vichy guilty of burdening its distributors with unreasonable 'supplementary obligations' of the kind prohibited here. Vichy was insisting its retailers should be dispensing chemists (except in France, where the authorities had already obliged Vichy to relax this condition and require instead that the retailer should hold a pharmacy diploma). The Commission argued that Vichy's demands went 'beyond what is necessary for maintaining quality and ensuring proper use of the product'.[21]

ARTICLE 85: INDIVIDUAL AND BLOCK EXEMPTIONS

All these contretemps could have been avoided if the apparent breaches of Article 85(1) of the Treaty of Rome had been covered by block exemptions authorised under Article 85(3). The European Commission does not approve block exemptions lightly, and their drafting commonly takes years, but in cases where the Commission would otherwise be bombarded with hundreds of requests for individual exemptions, block exemptions save time.

Block exemptions and individual exemptions from Article 85 derive their authority from the same source: clause 3 of Article 85 of the Treaty of Rome. Applicants must be able to show that their co-operation satisfies at least four out of five conditions:

1. It contributes to 'improving the production or distribution of goods', *or*
2. It contributes to 'promoting technical or economic progress', *and*
3. It does either 1 or 2 above 'while allowing consumers a fair share of the resulting benefit', *and*
4. The agreement must not impose restrictions on the participants beyond those which are indispensable to attain the above objectives, *and*
5. The agreement must not allow participants to eliminate competition 'in respect of a substantial part of the products in question'.

These are rather nebulous criteria. The best way to understand them may be to glance briefly at a couple of the block exemptions that, in the Commission's view, satisfy Article 85(3).

The first block exemption came into force in 1967. It dealt with exclusive dealing agreements and has since been split in two, with one exemption covering exclusive distribution agreements and the second covering exclusive purchasing agreements.

Exclusive distribution agreements possess many advantages for suppliers, retailers and customers alike. They offer economies of scale to suppliers, saving them the trouble of approving and dealing with numerous distributors. This can keep prices down. For small and medium-sized businesses, exclusive distribution channels are often the only means by which they can penetrate distant markets.

However, the block exemption relating to exclusive distribution agreements contains a number of conditions designed to remove its potential for abuse to the detriment of competition.[22] The effect of these conditions is to transform the block exemption's title into a misnomer: it does not truly guarantee 'exclusive' distribution rights. The main conditions are:

1. That the end user must be able to obtain the goods from some source other than the exclusive distributor.
2. That resellers should be able to buy the goods direct from the supplier and then export it to another market and compete with the supplier's approved exclusive distributor in that market. (Numerous companies have been found guilty of writing export bans into their domestic distribution contracts to avoid this happening, see Martell, above.)
3. Competing suppliers of goods cannot agree with one another to restrict imports into one another's territories through reciprocal distribution agreements.

The regulation will expire on 31 December 1997.

The block exemption governing exclusive purchasing agreements will also expire at the end of 1997.[23] Its shared parentage with the exclusive distribution exemption is obvious: reciprocal resale agreements are outlawed in the same way as reciprocal distribution agreements. However, there are some important differences:

1. An exclusive purchasing agreement may not cover more than one type of good.
2. Such an agreement may not run for more than five years. (This requirement may be relaxed as long as the contract can be quickly terminated.)
3. Special provisions relate to the sale of beer through tied outlets, and of petrol at service stations.

Since 1967 a host of new block exemptions have been incorporated into EU law. One of the most controversial of these, the block exemption governing motor dealerships, is described in chapter 6, as is the recent exemption sanctioning various forms of co-operation among insurance companies.

A full list of the block exemptions that now run throughout the European Economic Area under the EEA agreement is given in appendix 6. New block exemptions will be incorporated into the law of the EEA signatory counties (the EFTA countries excluding Switzerland and Liechtenstein) as they come into effect in the EU.

Case study
TETRA PAK – RECORD FINES FOR ARTICLE 86 BREACHES

Article 86 lists four forms of anti-competitive behaviour. These are all identical to those listed under Article 85. The only difference between the two articles is that clause (c) of Article 85(1) is not mirrored in Article 86: market sharing is not a vice often practised by companies that have achieved market dominance.

Fortunately we do not need to study several Commission investigations in order to grasp the variety of ways in which Article 86 can be violated. The behaviour of one company, the Swiss-based packaging firm Tetra Pak, will suffice.[24] (The case also illustrates the risks run by non-EU companies whose EU operations break the region's competition rules.)

In 1992 Tetra Pak acquired the dubious distinction of suffering the heaviest fine yet imposed by the European Commission. The Commission ordered the company to pay Ecu 75 million as punishment for a bewildering array of anti-competitive practices in a range of markets dominated by the company. Reading the Commission's account of Tetra Pak's misdeeds, a disinterested observer might be forgiven for wondering whether Tetra Pak's management had ever heard of EU competition policy. The Commission found Tetra Pak's infringements of Article 86 'involved almost all the aspects of its commercial policy'. Highlights included:

1. Exclusion of potential competition through unduly constraining exclusivity clauses in customer contracts. Only Tetra Pak cartons were allowed to be used in Tetra Pak machines for instance.
2. Ad hoc predatory pricing aimed at eliminating competitors. In Italy, for instance, Tetra Pak sold cartons for non-aseptic packaging at 34 per cent or more below their cost price in order to squeeze its main local competitor, Elopak, out of the market. (It almost succeeded: Tetra Pak's behaviour forced Elopak to close a new production plant.) The losses were made up from fat profits on European sales of aseptic cartons, where Tetra Pak enjoyed a virtual monopoly.
3. Marketing policy aimed at segregating national markets within the EU. The Commission found that Tetra Pak's pricing varied hugely. In some markets it was charging up to twice the price applicable in other markets for cartons and four times the price for packaging machines.

Following the Commission's investigation and fine, Tetra Pak promised to change its ways. It removed the requirement in its customer contracts that only Tetra Pak cartons should be used in Tetra Pak machines; it undertook to deliver cartons to independent distributors wishing to sell them, and it agreed not to exploit its dominance on the aseptic packaging markets to secure unfair advantages on the markets for non-aseptic packaging.

PRICING, PREDATORS AND PREY

The most egregious offence committed under Article 86 by Tetra Pak (see case study above) was probably predatory pricing. The Commission takes a very dim view of this, but its criteria for determining predatory pricing are far from simple. The classic economist's tool commonly used to identify predatory pricing in the United States, known as the Areeda/Turner test after its inventors, is apparently too blunt for the Commission's purposes.

The Areeda/Turner test states that predatory pricing occurs when a company is selling a product at less than the company's average variable cost. The variable cost is determined by dividing costs that vary according to output (such as labour and raw materials) by the company's actual output. According to the Areeda/Turner test, goods that are priced above the producer's average variable cost are *ipso facto* not priced in a predatory manner. This is where the inventors of the theorem part company with many competition authorities, including the European Commission.

An example of the Commission's more subtle analysis can be seen in its response to attempts by AKZO, the Dutch chemicals company, to squeeze a competitor, ECS, out of the European Union market for organic peroxides for the plastics industry. In 1991 the European Court of Justice found the Commission within its rights to fine AKZO for predatory pricing, even though the Areeda/Turner test might have left AKZO in the clear.[25]

The ECJ upheld the Commission's attempts to discern AKZO's intentions, rather than just applying an objective test based on the company's costs. Those intentions seemed pretty clear. AKZO held a dominant position in the EU market for organic peroxides, with a share in excess of 50 per cent. It sought to squeeze ECS out of this market, which ECS had only just entered, by offering special low price deals to the company's customers. Other organic peroxide consumers were not offered such low prices.

For businesses reviewing their pricing policy, the following conclusions can be drawn:

1. Under Article 86 of the Treaty of Rome, predatory pricing must be accompanied by market dominance.
2. The Areeda/Turner test is reliable to the extent that products that are priced at below the producer's average variable cost must have a predatory purpose. No other explanation will fit.
3. Discretionary pricing, to the prejudice of one particular competitor, is likely to be interpreted by the Commission as predatory, even if the product in question is being sold at above cost price.
4. If none of the above conditions are met, it will be very hard for the Commission to prove predatory pricing, whatever your competitors may allege. In every branch of law, culpable intention is notoriously hard to prove – and this certainly goes for predatory pricing. 'I don't suppose there will be too many office memos lying about the place', observed Sir Gordon Borrie, Britain's former director-general of fair trading, when News International lopped 15 pence off the price of the *Times* newspaper in September 1993.[26] Newspaper Publishing, owner of Britain's Independent newspaper, had complained to the Office of Fair Trading that News International was guilty of predatory pricing.

Tetra Pak was guilty of far more than predatory pricing: but before mocking Tetra Pak and its textbook violation of almost every competition rule in the book, companies should review their own commercial practices. Karel Van Miert is not the first competition commissioner to identify a kind of double-think among businesspeople. 'Quite often', he says, 'I am struck by the degree of contradiction in the attitudes displayed by heads of companies. Their [free market] ideology and their factual day-to-day line are quite far removed from one another and they just try to find ways to protect themselves.'[27]

For every Tetra Pak there is a host of companies found guilty of less blatant infringement of the competition rules. During the course of 1992 the Commission gave formal rulings on twenty agreements or practices under Articles 85 and 86. Of these, ten were found to infringe Article 85(1). In five of these cases, fines were imposed. On four occasions, the Commission granted the companies in question exemptions under Article 85(3). As for Article 86, four companies were found to have abused a dominant position during the course of 1992. Fines were imposed in all four cases.

ARTICLES 85 AND 86: A DEFENSIVE STRATEGY

So far in this chapter we have concentrated on identifying breaches of Articles 85 and 86. However, fending off the EU competition authorities should not be a fire-fighting exercise, with directors rushing from one blaze to another. Big companies in particular need a co-ordinated strategy to ensure they do not unwittingly breach Articles 85 or 86 – or any other competition provision of EU law.

The solution selected by many of Europe's largest companies is a competition law compliance programme. Law firms fall over themselves to offer such programmes to clients, suggesting that EU competition law is so arcane that only a skilled attorney can save a business from disastrous blunders. However, the key elements of a competition law compliance programme are quite simple. The headings of a typical programme for a multinational company with widespread European operations might run as follows:

PART A. Statement of corporate policy. Preferably a ringing declaration about the company's determination to comply with the letter and spirit of EU competition policy.

PART B. Implementation through:
  (i) Training
  (ii) An annual legal audit
  (iii) Contract drafting. All contracts need to be reviewed by an in-house lawyer versed in EU law.

PART C. A brief guide to EU competition law, Articles 85, 86, 92, 93, etc.

PART D. Practical implementation of the above with regard to:
  (i)   Contract drafting
  (ii) Relations with customers
  (iii) Relations with competitors
  (iv) Intellectual property rights
  (v)   Joint ventures
  (vi) Acquisitions

Of course, all the above will be to no avail if the company makes a conscious decision to breach EU competition law, but a compliance programme that is well understood throughout an organisation should at least ensure that inadvertent breaches of the law are avoided.

Compliance programmes may also prove their value in a different way. If your company is under investigation by the Commission for alleged breaches of EU competition law, one of the best investments you could make would be to buy a competition law compliance programme. Time after time the Commission has reduced fines imposed on companies for breaches of Articles 85 and 86 on the grounds that they are investing in a compliance programme to ensure that the offence is not repeated. For example, in 1991 Toshiba was fined the hefty sum of Ecu 2 million for writing an export ban into its distribution agreements relating to photocopiers: the Commission said the fine would have been still larger had Toshiba not shown a 'co-operative attitude', evidenced by its investment in a compliance programme for all its EU subsidiaries.[28]

CO-OPERATIVE JOINT VENTURES: SPEEDING UP THE PROCESS

In investigating abuses of Articles 85 and 86, the Commission has been known to move with almost glacial slowness. In December 1992 the outgoing competition commissioner Sir Leon Brittan decided it was time to do something about this. 'The challenge to the Commission', he declared, 'is ... to develop a rapid decision-making procedure, providing industry with quick decision-making and legal security.'[29] Quick decision-making was already guaranteed in the merger regulation. Sir Leon insisted that Article 85 and 86 cases should be investigated under similarly tough time constraints.

There are no time limits laid down for Commission decisions in Regulation 17, the measure adopted by the Council of Ministers in 1962 describing the procedures for implementation of Articles 85 and 86 (see appendix 2). It was not thought necessary. Just-in-time manufacturing was far in the future. Marketing strategies could be developed in months, not days. In addition, the Commission's workload was lighter, so delays appeared less of a risk.

Over three decades later the speed with which industry must react to market changes if it is to remain competitive has increased dramatically. If the Commission had continued to operate at speeds acceptable in 1962 it might well have ended up by damaging the European Union's overall competitiveness vis-à-vis the rest of the world.

Sir Leon offered to accept amendments to Regulation 17 imposing legally binding guidelines on the Commission if the EU member states granted him extra resources. However, he recognised this was unlikely and so offered to speed up Commission investigations of so-called 'structural' cases anyway.

Structural cases usually involve co-operative joint ventures which change the structure of an industry. They are reviewed under Article 85(1). (N.B. The distinction between co-operative joint ventures subject to Article 85(1) of the Treaty of Rome and concentrative joint ventures covered by the 1989 merger regulation is a fine one: details are given in chapter 3.) The process can be very slow: an investigation into European Vinyls Corporation, a co-operative joint venture between ICI of Great Britain and Enichem of Italy set up in 1986 to produce and distribute polyvinyl chloride and its raw material, vinyl chloride monomer, dragged on for years. 'It is unacceptable that companies should have to wait years before a decision is taken on a [joint venture] notification', said Heinz Kroeger, director of the company affairs division of UNICE, the European employers' federation, in early 1993.[30]

Sir Leon Brittan agreed. He had his own reasons for wanting to speed up the Commission's investigations. Anti-competitive joint ventures can be stopped quite quickly if nipped in the bud, but if left to develop, they are, he said, 'often difficult, sometimes impossible, to unscramble'.

Under the Commission's new self-imposed code of practice, the parties to major co-operative joint ventures will receive a letter from the Commission within two months of notification. This will either be a comfort letter or a warning letter.

A comfort letter should enable the parties to proceed, confident in the knowledge that the Commission has no objections. Such a letter does not guarantee that the Commission will not re-open investigations, but Sir Leon Brittan has promised that a comfort letter 'will only be withdrawn in the most extreme cases'. This may happen if any of the following obtain:

1. The main facts on which the letter was based change.
2. The parties breach an undertaking required by the letter.
3. The letter is based on inaccurate or deceitful information.
4. The parties abuse the exemption from Article 85(1) that has been afforded them (see below).

These are the same circumstances in which the Commission, having granted a formal exemption from Article 85(1), may revoke its decision. A comfort letter thus affords the recipient the same security *vis-à-vis* the Commission's position as a formal decision, which may take years to obtain.

A warning letter, by contrast, will help the joint venture partners identify threats to competition posed by their co-operation. Sir Leon described it as a significant innovation. A warning letter enables companies to confer with Commission officials at an early stage and try to hammer out a deal.

So far the reforms proposed by Sir Leon bear a strong resemblance to the mandatory deadlines contained in the merger control regulation (see chapter 3). The two month period during which the Commission debates whether to send out a comfort or a warning letter is akin to the 'first phase' of the analysis carried out by the mergers task force under the merger regulation. This lasts one month.

Thereafter, the procedures diverge. Under the merger regulation, the Commission guarantees it will make its mind up on 'second phase' cases (where serious doubts exist as to their compatibility with the common market) within four months. In Article 85(1) cases it makes no such promise. Instead, the Commission will act case by case, informing the joint venture parties how long it expects its second phase investigation to continue at the time it sends its warning letter.

The new system came into force in January 1993. It was widely welcomed by businesses, with two reservations. The first was that it was a voluntary system based, as the Commission put it, 'entirely on the principle of self discipline by the relevant Commission departments'.[31] The second was that the new timetable applied only to structural co-operative joint ventures. Nine months later, this remained the case: the accelerated timetable had not been extended to other Article 85 cases.

ARTICLES 85 AND 86: A CHECKLIST OF COMMON INFRINGEMENTS

Set out below is a checklist of commercial practices that, at one time or another, the Commission has ruled to be in breach of Article 85 or Article 86.

1. Loyalty discounts to longstanding customers or distributors.
2. Export bans or export restrictions included in contracts with distributors. (The temptation to do this can be strong when, as in the above case of Martell cognac, your product is sold at a far higher price abroad and unauthorised exports could push the price down.)
3. Predatory pricing and cross-subsidies from profitable lines of business to unprofitable ones. Naturally, all companies cross-subsidise to some extent. The acid test here is whether the cross-subsidies are designed to squeeze out competitors in the unprofitable line of business.
4. Unduly onerous demands on retailers. A luxury goods manufacturer, for instance, might be fussy about where its products are being sold. In 1991 the French crystal glass manufacturer, Compagnie des Cristalleries Baccarat, was forced to rewrite a clause in its standard contract with distributors which had stipulated that the place of sale was to be determined partly by the presence of other luxury shops nearby. The new clause said simply that other competing luxury products should be on offer at the place of sale.
5. Barriers to exit from market associations (see the Campina case above).
6. Pacts with competitors to share or pool technical facilities on an exclusive basis. For example, a group of airline operators could link up their computer reservation systems (CRS) and sell the combined package to travel agents. The Commission has ruled that a proposal to do just this (contemplated by, among others, Lufthansa, Air France, Iberia, SAS and American Airlines) would have reduced price competition between the CRS previously operated by the European airlines and that run by American Airlines.[32]
7. Price fixing. There is an important distinction between pooling resources in order to establish the correct cost of a product (excluding profit margin) and declaring that cost to be the minimum price that can be charged for the product. If, for example, a group of insurance companies wants to pool claims statistics for the purposes of determining appropriate premium rates, they must make it clear that the premium rates published are 'purely illustrative' and do not bind the insurers involved.[33]
8. Exclusionary rebates. Companies have been known to charge a certain price for a certain amount of their product and a far cheaper, discounted price for any surplus above this fixed amount. Such 'top slice' rebates have been used by companies that dominate a particular market to exclude would-be entrants.

NOTES

1. K.D. George, 'Lessons from UK merger policy', and E. Kantzenbach, 'Merger policy in

West Germany', pages 78 and 122 respectively, in *Mergers and Competition Policy in the European Community*, P.H. Admiral (ed.). Basil Blackwell, 1990.

2. Speech at the Centre of European Policy Studies, Brussels, 7 December 1992, 'The Future of EC Competition Policy'.

3. ECJ Case 56/65 *Société Technique Minière* v. *Maschinenbau Ulm* (1966) ECR 235.

4. The case, just one chapter in one of the lengthier legal sagas from the history of EU competition policy, is described in lawyers Allen & Overy's *Competition and Trade Law Review*, June 1993.

5. A good account of the sections of the EEA agreement dealing with competition is provided in a special bulletin published by Allen & Overy in October 1993 entitled *Competition Law under the EEA Agreement*.

6. ECJ Case 23/67 Brasserie de Haecht (1) 1967, ECR 407; ECJ Case 47/776 *de Norre* v. *Brouwerij Concordia* (1977) ECR 65.

7. ECJ Case 126/80 *Salonia* v. *Poidomani and Giglio*.

8. T. Anthony Downes and Julian Ellison, *The Legal Control of Mergers in the European Community*. Blackstone Press, 1991.

9. ECJ Case 266/87 *Regina* v. *The Royal Pharmaceutical Society of Great Britain, ex parte Association of Pharmaceutical Importers* [1989] ECR 1295 at 1327.

10. ECJ Case 30/87 *Bodson* v. *SA Pompes funèbres* [1988] ECR 2479 at 2516.

11. ECJ Cases C-159/91 and C-160/91.

12. Norbert Reich, 'Competition between legal orders: a new paradigm of EC law?', *Common Market Law Review*, vol. 29, no. 5, 1992, page 887.

13. ECJ Case 48/69 *ICI* v. *Commission* ['Dyestuffs'] 78[1972] ECR 619 at 615.

14. ECJ Case 322/81 *Michelin* v. *Commission*.

15. ECJ Case 85/76 *Hoffman-La Roche* v. *Commission*.

16. *XXIInd Report on Competition Policy*, May 1993, chapter 2.I.A, section 2.a.1, page 113.

17. *XXIInd Report on Competition Policy*, May 1993, chapter 2.I.A, section 1.f.11, page 94.

18. *XXIst Report on Competition Policy*, April 1992, chapter 2.I.A, section 1.c.1, page 83.

19. Commission press release WE/35/92, 8 October 1992.

20. *XXIst Report on Competition Policy*, April 1992, chapter 2.I.A, section 2.b.1, page 98.

21. *XXIst Report on Competition Policy*, April 1992, chapter 2.I.A, section 2.d.1, page 102.

22. Commission Regulation (EEC) No. 1983/83.

23. Commission Regulation (EEC) No. 1984/83.

24. *XXIst Report on Competition Policy*, April 1992, chapter 2.I, section B.a.1, page 109.

25. *XXIst Report on Competition Policy*, April 1992, section 2.II.11, pages 157–159.

26. Quoted in the *Financial Times*, 14 September 1993.

27. Club de Bruxelles conference speech, 6 May 1993.

28. *XXIst Report on Competition Policy*, April 1992, chapter 2.I.A, section 2.a.1, page 97.

29. Speech to Centre of European Policy Studies, Brussels, 7 December 1992.

30. Interview with author, 23 April 1993.

31. *XXIInd Report on Competition Policy*, May 1993, chapter 1.V, section 3.8., pages 78, 79.

32. *XXIst Report on Competition*, April 1992, chapter 2.I.A, section 1.i.1, page 94.

33. Commission Regulation (EEC) No. 3932/92. Block exemption for the insurance sector. See chapter 6.

CHAPTER 3

EU MERGER CONTROL: A PAPER TIGER?

THE MERGER REGULATION AND BRITISH BUSINESS

In relation to the size of its economy, Britain possesses far more giant conglomerates than any other EU member state.[1] Only the very biggest companies are directly affected by EC Regulation 4064/89 (the merger control regulation). Member states have resisted Commission suggestions that the net be cast wider, but there are good reasons why every British company active in the European market should nonetheless take an interest in the theory and practice of EU merger control.

1. The bigger the merger, the greater will be its potential impact on competition. The European Commission's merger task force may be all that stands between small businesses and bankruptcy if giant competitors exploit positions of market dominance created by mergers or acquisitions.

2. As the single market develops, the Commission is tending towards an ever broader interpretation of the geographical and product markets in which merger candidates are active. The broader the market, the harder it becomes to dominate it and distort competition. If this tendency continues, the Commission will be less and less likely to prohibit mergers or impose conditions upon merger candidates. Is this desirable?

3. EU merger policy interleaves with EU industrial policy in ways that may prove crucial for the future competitiveness of the Union. 'The question now is: what does Europe want?' said Pierre Suard, the then chairman of the giant French

telecommunications and engineering conglomerate Alcatel Alsthom, just after the merger regulation came into force. 'It remains to be seen whether Europe will permit the survival of companies big enough to confront the competition.'[2]

To date, Mr Suard's fears have not materialised. The merger regulation continues to enjoy remarkable popularity with European industry. It provides a 'one-stop shop' for review of the bigger mergers within the European Union. Before the regulation came into force, large-scale mergers could be reviewed simultaneously at both EU and member state level. Companies based in countries with weak or undeveloped competition authorities might get away with mergers that would be outlawed by more experienced or tougher authorities in other countries.

The merger regulation applies one rule to everybody. With a few exceptions (dealt with later in this chapter) mergers that have been cleared by the Commission under the regulation cannot be reinvestigated by national competition authorities. The participants are home free.

We shall examine whether the accolades of European business are justified at the end of this chapter. First we should glance at the merger control regulation's parentage, before studying in detail the theory and practice of the regulation itself.

A CHEQUERED HISTORY

The architects of the Treaty of Rome realised they were not omniscient. They regarded only the treaty's ends as unimprovable, not the means prescribed to achieve those ends. They therefore prudently included a clause in the treaty (Article 235) empowering the Council of Ministers to 'take the appropriate measures' to act in pursuit of the treaty's ends, even if the necessary powers were not supplied by the treaty. In so doing, the Council must act unanimously on a proposal from the Commission and must also consult the European Parliament.

One large gap in the Commission's powers under the Treaty of Rome relates to the regulation of concentrations caused by mergers or takeovers. Articles 85 and 86 of the treaty make no reference to mergers. There is a simple reason for this: the treaty's signatories did not want them to. In the late 1950s Europe was far more concerned than it is today about the puny size of its industrial companies when compared with the giant US corporations. (The Japanese threat had yet to materialise.) EU leaders did not want to discourage their companies from attaining the size necessary to compete with the Americans.

For industrial policy reasons, then, mergers were not restricted in Articles 85 or 86. The Commission's so-called Christmas memorandum of 1966 ruled out the application of Article 85 to industrial concentrations, and a landmark European Court of Justice (ECJ) ruling of February 1973 upheld the Commission's right to apply Article 86 to mergers only when the merger strengthened an *already* dominant position. The court thus ruled out the Commission's right to investigate dominant positions under Article 86 that had been *created* through mergers.[3]

These constraints upon the Commission led competition commissioner Peter Sutherland to develop what became known as the dual track approach to merger control in the mid to late 1980s.[4] On the one hand, he argued in favour of a new merger control regulation in order to remedy the deficiencies of Articles 85 and 86 in this field, and on the other he threatened that, in the absence of a new regulation, he would have to club companies with the blunt instruments at his disposal. Article 86 decisions in particular commonly took two or three years to reach: companies planning to merge scarcely wanted to wait that long.

It is Mr Sutherland (later to become director-general of GATT) who can claim the credit for eventually forcing EU member states to recognise that a merger control regulation was indispensable to an effective EU competition policy. The process had been a long one, even by the sometimes glacial rates of progress achieved by the Union in other fields. The Commission first submitted a proposal on merger control to the Council of Ministers in 1973. The merger control regulation was finally adopted by the Council over sixteen years later, on 21 December 1989. Its provisions came into force across the European Union on 21 December 1990. (This final delay was to give DGIV time to assemble a team to implement the regulation.)

One of the reasons the process took so long was the Treaty of Rome's insistence that new EU powers must receive the unanimous assent of the Council of Ministers. Achieving this was far from easy and the regulation underwent many changes, even in the final stages. Three compromises were reached.

At the insistence of the British in particular, the thresholds at which the regulation came into force were set very high. As late as January 1989 the Commission was still proposing a worldwide aggregate turnover threshold of Ecu 1 billion and an EU turnover threshold of Ecu 100 million per participant. In the event, the two turnover thresholds were set at ECU 5 billion and Ecu 250 million respectively.

At the insistence of the Germans, Article 9 of the regulation entitles the Commission to refer cases back to a member state where the threat to competition is posed within that member state's territory. In practice, cases are rarely referred back in this way – although the Germans have made a number of fruitless requests.

At the insistence of the French, a 'recital' at the beginning of the regulation mentions concerns other than pure competition concerns that the Commission should take into account. The Community's 'economic and social cohesion' is specifically mentioned. Thus while the regulation lays greater stress on pure competition criteria than comparable British legislation, it still undertakes to take other issues into account.

Colin Overbury, the first director of the Commission's merger task force, recalls that the regulation was finally adopted when France held the EU presidency.[5] Edith Cresson, who later went on to serve as a highly dirigiste, and not very successful, prime minister of France, piloted the regulation through the Council of Ministers.

Case study
NESTLÉ–PERRIER

On 17 July 1992 competition advisors from the cabinets of the seventeen EU commissioners met to discuss one of the most awkward cases to have crossed the Commission's bows in two decades. If the Commission swung one way, its chances of ever tackling oligopolies that threatened competition in the single European market would be much reduced. If it swung the other way, it might face a nerve-racking challenge in the European Court of Justice. The advice from the Commission's legal service was not entirely reassuring.

The case concerned bottled water and the terms on which it was sold in France, the biggest market for bottled water in Europe. The Swiss foods giant Nestlé proposed buying Source Perrier, the French mineral water company whose name, like Hoover or Aga, has become synonymous with its product across much of the globe. There was no risk that Nestlé might come to dominate the French bottled water market on its own – something clearly outlawed under the 1989 merger regulation. Instead, the Commission was worried lest Nestlé should acquire joint dominance of this market in alliance with BSN, the French foods group.

This was much more tricky. The words 'joint dominance' and 'oligopoly' are absent from the 1989 merger regulation. The regulation refers merely to 'concentrations' of power arising from mergers or takeovers. No attempt had previously been made to argue that more than one company could represent a concentration.

The meeting of cabinet advisors was crucial because commissioners do not generally study individual mergers in detail themselves. They rely instead on their advisors. Sources close to the Commission enable us to piece together the views expressed at the meeting.

Chris Jones from the cabinet of the then competition commissioner, Sir Leon Brittan, argued that the Commission must be seen to take a stand against duopolies. He pointed out that certain EU member states – notably Germany and Britain – already had such powers enshrined in their national anti-trust legislation. Andreas Strohm from Martin Bangemann's cabinet (industrial affairs) and Gerhard Hitzler from Peter Schmidhuber's cabinet (budgets and financial control) both agreed.

This was the view that ultimately prevailed; but the question of principle was only part of the problem. The practicalities were at least as awkward. The duopoly issue arose because Nestlé proposed selling one of its leading mineral water brands, Volvic, to BSN in order to quell fears that it might be acquiring near-monopoly powers. That would have left Nestlé with a 36.8 per cent market share and BSN with a 30.9 per cent market share in France.

The meeting agreed that the best way to reduce this concentration of market power would be to enforce the sale by Nestlé of various lesser mineral water brands to another company, creating a third force in the French bottled water market. There was a hitch, though: Daniel Jacob from Bruce Millan's cabinet (regional policy) wanted to know how this putative third force could be prevented from later selling the brands to BSN. Chris Jones replied that legally the Commission would have no powers to intervene.

Now, EU competition policy, like EU politics, is the art of the possible. The meeting of competition advisors broke up with the key elements of the Commission's decision settled. A few days later Sir Leon Brittan announced that the Commission was approving Nestlé's FFr 15.46 billion bid for Perrier on condition that eight of Perrier's lesser brands be sold to a buyer other than BSN. The advantage of this formula was that it enabled the Commission to demonstrate its abhorrence of duopolies, while giving

Nestlé no cause to challenge the decision. Sir Leon Brittan got his precedent; Nestlé got Perrier.

In other respects the deal was far from satisfactory. The Commission was meddling in the free market to an unprecedented degree. Any prospective buyer of Perrier's minor brands from Nestlé would have the Swiss company over a barrel: Nestlé had no choice but to sell. Worse still, competition lawyers complained that Sir Leon's precedent was far from water-tight. Future Commission rulings on oligopolies might still be challenged in the European Court of Justice.

Unice, the European employers' federation, doubts that the Commission's application of the merger regulation to duopolies or oligopolies would stick in a court of law. It would like to see the principle tested in the European Court of Justice.[6]

So the Nestlé–Perrier decision was, and remains, controversial. That is scarcely surprising. After all, the merger regulation, whence Sir Leon derived his authority in Nestlé–Perrier, is the child of controversy.

QUALIFYING TRANSACTIONS

Only companies contemplating mergers with a 'Community dimension' need contact the Commission. Under the regulation a merger is deemed to have a Community dimension where:

1. Aggregate worldwide turnover of the businesses concerned exceeds Ecu 5 billion, *and*
2. Aggregate Community (EU) turnover of each of at least two parties concerned exceeds Ecu 250 million, *unless*
3. Each party achieves more than two-thirds of its Community (EU) turnover within the same member state.

In addition, the Commission will normally clear a merger if the combined market share of the businesses does not exceed 25 per cent of the EU market, or of a substantial part of the EU market.

Philip Lowe, the mergers task force director, admits that these thresholds are 'necessarily rather crude methods of identifying target transactions'. They are, he says, particularly hard to apply in service industries, where two turnover figures are sometimes given. For instance, an advertising agency or insurance broker will charge commissions or fees on far larger sums passing through the firm's accounts. Is the turnover of an advertising agency the value of the space it fills, or the value of the commissions it receives for filling that space? The mergers task force has tended to opt for the latter.

Special turnover thresholds apply to banks, insurance companies and other financial institutions. Details of these are given in appendix 4.

The rules governing financial institutions are complicated and have given rise to some confusion in practice. So, too, have the apparently simple rules governing ordinary companies. Accor, the French catering and hotel group, found this out when it launched a takeover bid for Wagons Lits, the Belgian catering, hotel and tourism group, in late 1991.

The two companies did not, on the face of it, meet the Commission's criteria for a merger of Community dimensions. The aggregate consolidated turnover of the two companies, as recorded in their company accounts, fell below the Ecu 5 billion threshold. The Commission insisted, however, that the turnover from a group of hotels over which Accor had management responsibility, but only a minority equity stake, should also be included. This pushed the combined turnover of the two groups to over Ecu 5 billion.

Furthermore, it emerged that the only threat to competition posed by the merger was in France, where the combined company would control 89 per cent of the market for motorway catering and 69 per cent for light motorway meals. The Commission found this market dominance to be unacceptable and ruled that Accor should sell off all of Wagon Lits' French motorway catering facilities.

It is not clear what the French competition authorities would have done in these circumstances, but the attitude of Britain's Merger's and Monopolies Commission (MMC) to a similar issue – the 1987 merger between Little Chef and Happy Eater – proved far more relaxed. The MMC allowed the merger to go ahead, accepting the companies' argument that roadside catering had to be put into the context of catering services generally, rather than be regarded as a market in its own right.

Accor was perhaps unlucky. If the Commission had not boosted its turnover figure by including the hotel group over which it was deemed to have a 'right to manage', the case would never have been considered at EU level. Furthermore, if the assiduous Commission officials had not adopted a much narrower market definition than the British did five years before, Accor might have been able to keep its motorway catering business. This was a clear case of the Commission taking a tougher stance than the MMC.

NOTIFICATION

The Commission must be informed of proposed concentrations with a Community dimension within a week of any one of the following:

1. The conclusion of an agreement.
2. The announcement of a public bid.
3. The acquisition of a controlling interest.

This time limit cannot, in any circumstances, be extended. Nor can any of the three transactions listed above be put into effect until at least three weeks after the date of notification. It is important to remember that the three week period is a minimum period: the Commission can extend this time limit if it wishes to put the proposed transaction on ice while it makes up its mind.

The Commission encourages companies planning a concentration under the terms of the merger regulation to meet informally with merger task force officials beforehand.

This system of informal meetings is largely responsible for the high level of business satisfaction with the task force. Commission officials can be sounded out for information on likely obstacles to a proposed takeover or merger. Adjustments can be made before the wheels of the regulation grind into action.

A courtesy visit to the Commission beforehand can save time in another way. The formal application process is exhaustive, being designed to cover all conceivable types of 'concentration' that fall under the merger regulation. Discussions with DGIV officials can help weed out information that the Commission does not need. This is a process better achieved by discussion with DGIV than by guesswork on the part of applicants: the Commission can delay its investigation until it is satisfied it has all the information it requires.

The Commission can also fine companies that delay supplying relevant information. These fines can be quite steep: up to Ecu 25,000 for each day of delay. Failure to notify a concentration at all leaves the parties liable to fines of between Ecu 1,000 and Ecu 50,000. (This would be particularly unwise: multi-billion Ecu mergers are highly unlikely to go unreported in the press and DGIV officials are diligent newspaper readers.)

The formal notification process involves completing a form, called Form CO, giving full details of the companies involved in the proposed concentration and an account of the concentration's objectives. (The full text of Form CO is attached to the text of the merger regulation, appendix 3.)

Companies planning mergers or takeovers that are notifiable under the merger regulation should not underestimate the time necessary to fill in Form CO. The information sought by the Commission is very diverse: it is unlikely that any company would have all, or even most, of it readily to hand. Some of the statistics required will be straightforward, but most will be unique to the operation envisaged.

The process is likely to be expensive. American law firm Winthrop, Stimson, Putnam & Roberts likens completing a Form CO to responding to a 'second request' under the Hart Scott Rodino Act in the United States. In 1990, according to the lawyers, 'typical cost estimates' for complying with such a HSR second request were running at 'up to $1 million or more', including legal fees of between $150,000 and $600,000.[7]

In preparation for the rigours of Form CO, companies should arm themselves with the following information:

1. Basic details of the parties to the concentration (addresses, business descriptions, contact names, official representatives).
2. Details of the form and scope of the proposed concentration. This includes a breakdown of the economic sectors involved and economic and financial information on the merger, such as the parties' turnover (in Ecu), broken down by EU member state, for the last three financial years; pre-tax profits; numbers of employees.
3. Full details of the pre-merger structure of ownership and control covering the parent, subsidiary and associate companies.

4. Details of personal and financial links between each party concerned and all undertakings belonging to the same group.
5. Data on each of the relevant product markets affected by the merger for each of the last three financial years. This should be broken down by member state and other relevant geographical markets, market shares, turnover, prices, value, imports, exports and the most important aspects of business strategy.
6. Information on general conditions in each of the affected markets, including barriers to entry and vertical integration of the parties; research and development; distribution and service systems; the competitive environment; co-operative agreements; trade associations; and the worldwide context of the merger.
7. A description of the expected benefits to consumers and technical progress. This is important because it may incline the Commission to approve borderline competition cases on the grounds that their potential effect on competition is offset by other advantages.

A notification must be supported by the following documents:

1. The most recent annual reports of all the parties concerned.
2. The final or most recent versions of any documents required for bringing about the merger.
3. Copies of all other reports prepared for the purposes of the merger, from which information has been taken to provide information on the markets affected.
4. A list of any reports or studies prepared for the purpose of assessing the proposed merger with regard to competitive conditions, competitors and market conditions.

The Commission sometimes manages to make the Indian Civil Service look abstemious in its appetite for paper. It requires numerous copies of the notification: twenty copies of the completed Form CO must be supplied, together with fifteen copies of the supporting documentation. The Commission will send twelve of these copies to the member states upon receipt. (Martin Howe at Britain's Office of Fair Trading, stresses that the OFT 'checks every EC member regulation case, not just those involving UK companies'.)[8]

The information can be broken down into six classes:

1. *Legal.* This covers the description of the structure of the planned operation and its participants.
2. *Technical.* A description of the products involved, and of the markets for these products. Commission officials do their best to assemble a dynamic, rather than a static picture of the markets within which companies are operating. To do this they usually require up-to-date information on research and development in progress, and background information on the impact that technological changes have had on the companies' activities.
3. *Financial.* A description of the financial links that bind the enterprises, both internally and to one another. One company may be deemed to control another through a minority – and sometimes very modest – shareholding (although the

many-tentacled state-owned Italian bank, Mediobanca, got away with raising its stake in Italy's biggest insurer, Assicurazioni Generali, to 12.84 per cent from 5.98 per cent in late 1991).

4. *Economic.* A description of the structure and workings of the markets affected, and the role of the various key players in these markets. Such information may be readily available through the participants' marketing departments, but in industries where competitive advantage depends heavily on commercial confidentiality, it may be more easily said than done to provide reliable information about key players in the market.

5. *Commercial.* A description of the participants' relationships with clients and with suppliers.

6. *Strategic.* What is the purpose of the proposed concentration?

It will not always be clear who is best placed within a company to assemble all this information. Some companies, such as the French chemicals giant, Rhone Poulenc, have an in-house specialist in competition policy. Others may rely more heavily on external consultants or advisers. Either way, on the principle that negotiators should at least speak the same language, the person who presents the company's case to the European Commission should be a lawyer.

The most delicate part of the application process will, for most companies, be sections 5 and 6 of Form CO, headed respectively 'Information on affected markets' and 'General conditions in affected markets'. This will be particularly hard to provide when the markets in question are at the cutting edge of some new technology and are therefore evolving rapidly.

Much of the information contained in Form CO may be price-sensitive. Companies will understandably be nervous about disseminating such information around the European Union. They may also be worried that information gleaned from Form CO may be used by national competition authorities to bring anti-trust actions against the companies concerned, even if the Commission has approved the transaction. In a word, companies are concerned (and with good reason) about confidentiality.

BUSINESS SECRETS

The demands of confidentiality put the Commission in a very delicate position. On the one hand, it is under constant pressure from politicians and industrialists to explain its reasoning fully. An example is the declaration issued by the heads of EU governments at the Birmingham Summit, a largely unmemorable event that took place in October 1992. This called upon the Commission to 'complete by early next year its work on improving public access to the information available to it and to other Community institutions'.

On the other hand, the crucial information on which the Commission makes its decision may be price-sensitive. Companies will not want to divulge information to the Commission if they believe that their competitors will be able to use it to their advantage.

There is no obvious sword to hand with which to cut this Gordian knot. Instead, the Commission and its interlocutors must rely upon Article 17 of the merger regulation, which guarantees that information supplied by companies 'shall be used only for the purposes of the relevant request, investigation or hearing'. It also binds the Commission and the 'competent authorities of the Member States' (to whom all the relevant information is sent) to respect the confidentiality of 'information ... of the kind covered by the obligation of professional secrecy'.

DGIV undoubtedly takes Article 17 seriously, recognising that if breaches became known, it could lose the co-operation of companies overnight. A senior official has been appointed by DGIV to oversee internal security within the merger task force.

Form CO invites companies to submit confidential information separately from other information. Such information should be clearly marked 'business secrets'. Providers should explain why the information must not fall into the hands of third parties.

The Commission has many times shown its willingness to respect such information. For instance, when the Italian car-maker Fiat was attempting to purchase tractor manufacturer Ford New Holland, the Commission released on 12 February 1991 a very terse statement explaining that it had decided to let the merger go ahead, but not saying why. The reasoning behind the Commission's decision was not made public until May 1991, after the closing date of the agreement between the two companies.[9]

The parties to a concentration will have the chance to challenge the Commission's interpretation of what information is confidential, and what is not. Before it publishes its decisions, the Commission will send a draft to the parties involved. They can then argue that certain information should be withheld from publication, provided they can show it relates to their 'legitimate interest ... in the protection of their business secrets' (Article 20, merger regulation).

Nevertheless, confidentiality remains an issue that companies will have to consider before embarking on a concentration notifiable under the merger regulation. The information companies submit will be read not only by Commission officials but also by government officials in all twelve EU member states. The Commission itself will always be mindful of the need to show transparency in its reasoning. There are some rather comic examples of figures being left out of Commission decisions, where the surrounding text gives a pretty good idea of what they must have been.

The risk that information ferreted out of companies by the Commission might later be used by national competition authorities to bring an action against the companies concerned should not be overlooked. The Spanish competition authority has already attempted it. In 1990, the Spanish competition authority, the Direccion General de Defensa de la Competencia (DGDC), brought an action against an association of Spanish banks, the Asociacion Espanola de Banca Privada (AEB), on the basis of information originally supplied by the AEB to the European Commission.

The DGDC had sought information from the AEB on practices that it feared were restricting competition in the Spanish banking market in 1987. However, it had not got what it wanted and chose to rely instead on information obtained by the Commission in the course of a separate investigation. The banks had applied to the Commission for exemption from Article 85 of the Treaty of Rome (prohibiting agreements that distort competition within the common market) under clause 3 of Article 85 (see chapter 2). The Commission agreed and the agreement was cleared.

However, this did not satisfy the Spanish competition authorities, who launched their own investigation using the information the banks had supplied to the Commission. This gave the European Court of Justice the chance to affirm a principle which may be of value to companies finding themselves in a similar position in the future. The ECJ defined a 'professional secret' thus:

> A professional secret implies, not only the establishment of rules designed to prohibit the communication of confidential information, but equally making it impossible for bodies legally holding this information to use it, in the absence of express agreement, for a purpose other than that for which it was obtained.[10]

The ECJ accordingly found that the Spanish competition authorities had acted beyond their rights in using the information supplied by the European Commission. Commission officials were understandably relieved: had the court's judgement swung the other way, they might have found it much harder to obtain information in future.

One last problem with the confidentiality rules is that a company with something to be ashamed of might try to shelter behind them. Take the example of a company that tries to blow the whistle on a competitor for, say, rigging a market through a cartel. The aggrieved company gives the Commission its estimates on market shares and other indicators relevant to the alleged cartel. The company that has been challenged produces entirely different figures, which its competitor cannot inspect because they are held to be business secrets.

There is a way of getting round this problem. The complainant can offer to show the Commission its reasoning in reaching its estimates and suggest the company or companies it is criticising do the same. Commission officials can then decide which is the more plausible.

MARKET DEFINITION

The trickiest problem confronting Commission officials once they have learned of a proposed merger is to define the markets that will be affected. These fall under two headings: product markets and geographical markets. As a general rule, the narrower the market is defined, the more likely the Commission will be to detect trade-distorting market dominance within it. One of the most controversial competition decisions the European Commission has ever made arose because it identified turboprop commuter aircraft possessing between 40 and 59 seats as a distinct product market (the de Havilland case, see below).[11]

It is important for businesses to understand how the merger task force goes about defining relevant product and geographic markets. The Commission's final decision will invariably hinge upon these definitions. So will any hope that businesses may have of contesting the Commission's decision in the European Court of Justice.

Product markets

Product markets are identified by two tests:

1. *Substitutability.* A monster of a word that makes 'subsidiarity' look elegant. If another product cannot readily by substituted for the product in question, then the product in question occupies a clear market. There are two sub-species of this monster: demand-side substitutability (where consumers can shop around among comparable products) and supply-side substitutability (where other suppliers could quickly offer competing products).
2. *The competitive environment.* The second test applies not to the product itself but to the environment in which it is sold. Products occupying a single product market must compete with one another on an equal footing, or have the potential so to do within a short space of time. The Commission has accepted one year as representing a short space of time, although this may vary.[12]

Under the second test, virtually identical products sold in the same geographical region may not, in fact, belong to the same product market. Thus car components can be sold either to car manufacturers on the OEM (original equipment market) or to garages on the replacement market. A car battery sold on the OEM market will be subject to a range of competitive conditions from car manufacturers that will not apply to a battery sold on the replacement market.

Geographical markets

Geographical markets are no less slippery and hard to pin down than product markets. In the controversial Aerospaciale–Alenia/de Havilland case, the Commission's preferred geographical market was as broad as its product market was narrow. Aerospaciale and Alenia's proposed purchase of de Havilland was prohibited because it would give the purchasers *global* dominance of the 40–59 seater turboprop commuter aircraft market.

The Commission defined its understanding of a relevant geographical market in the regulation itself. 'The geographical reference market shall consist of the area in which the undertakings are involved in the supply and demand of products or services, in which the conditions of competition are sufficiently homogeneous and which can be distinguished from neighbouring areas because, in particular, conditions of competition are appreciably different in those areas.'[13]

The Commission's decisions on geographical markets make interesting reading. They can be seen as a verdict on the success of the single market. For some products the single market is a reality: for instance, the merger task force concluded in September 1991 that the relevant geographical market for car shock absorbers, sold either as original parts or replacement parts, was the European Union. By contrast, the task force concluded in January 1991 that the geographical market for telecommunications transmission equipment in Spain stopped at Spain's borders. The Spanish state-owned telecommunications operator, Telefonica, traditionally bought only Spanish and held minority stakes in its two major suppliers, Alcatel and Telettra (the merger candidates).[14]

The Alcatel/Telettra decision was particularly interesting because the grounds on which the Commission defined the relevant geographical market were not the same as the grounds on which it approved the merger. It defined the market as Spain because Telefonica traditionally bought Spanish; but it approved the merger (which left the merged group with an 80 per cent market share in Spain) because Telefonica seemed ready to buy abroad in the future.

In determining the geographical limits of a product market, the merger task force weighs a range of pros and cons. These are set out in Table 3.1.

Once the markets have been defined, the Commission's task is to decide whether the concentration under review holds a dominant position within those markets which would 'significantly impede ... effective competition' (Article 9.2, merger regulation).

Other competition authorities apply hard-and-fast rules to do this: in Germany, for instance, a market share of 33 per cent or more triggers a presumption of dominance.[15] By far the most popular yardstick, though, is the Herfindahl–Hirschman Index (HHI) used by the Department of Justice and the Federal Trade Commission in the United States.

The HHI of merging firms is calculated by squaring the firms' share of the relevant market and then adding these figures together. Thus a perfect monopoly created by a merger of two companies with market shares of 50 per cent apiece would yield an HHI

Table 3.1 *Factors considered in the analysis of geographical markets*

In support of a wider geographical market	*In support of a narrower geographical market*
Absence of barriers to entry enabling quick and easy transfer of supply (making a high market share in one member state irrelevant)	Existence of price differences
Absence of price differences	National suppliers holding high market shares. Appreciable differences in market shares in countries considered
Presence of the major suppliers in all member states	Low cross-border trade/imports
Substantial cross-border trade/imports	High transport costs/difficult transport
Low transport costs	'Just-in-time' deliveries/security of supplies
International/European buying policy/no strong national buying preferences	Import tariffs
Similar distribution systems throughout EEC	Legal/technical barriers to entry/national specification requirements/approval systems Language and cultural barriers

Source: European Commission

of 5,000. However, if one company held a 90 per cent market share and was planning to take over its only competitor (holding a 10 per cent market share), the resulting HHI would be far higher: $8,100 + 100 = 8,200$. This is because the index yields far higher values for large market shares than for the aggregate of smaller ones.

The US competition authorities derive three thresholds from the index:

1. Mergers yielding an HHI of below 1,000 are presumed inoffensive by the US competition authorities except in rare cases. Two companies with market shares of 22 per cent each could therefore merge without difficulties.

2. Mergers yielding an HHI of between 1,000 and 1,800 are usually exempt if the increase in the index created by the merger is 100 or less. If the increase is 100 or more, the competition authorities will investigate further.

3. Mergers yielding an HHI of 1,800 or more. Again, investigations will depend on the increase in the HHI created by the merger. If the increase is 50 or less, no challenge is likely. Between 50 and 100, the merger is deemed to 'raise significant competitive concerns'. Increases over 100 are deemed 'likely to create or enhance market power or facilitate its exercise'[16] and a detailed investigation will almost certainly ensue.

The European Commission does not lay down HHI thresholds, although they may be useful to firms planning to merge. The Commission is unlikely to be worried about mergers deemed inoffensive by the US authorities. For its part, the EU merger regulation merely notes that aggregate market shares of 25 per cent or less 'may be presumed to be compatible with the common market'. In practice market shares of below 35 per cent or 40 per cent are not usually considered harmful.[17] The Commission also stresses that much higher market shares may be inoffensive in rapidly evolving markets with low barriers to entry.

For the Commission, then, the character of the market commonly counts for more than the share held by the merging parties. Geographical markets are at least as dynamic as product markets. Colin Overbury, the merger task force's director until January 1993, says that the task force's market analysis became steadily 'more liberal' during his time at the helm. In other words, mergers were increasingly approved on the grounds that the markets affected were likely to become more open, even if they were not open already.[18]

Mr Overbury's comment implies the possibility that the Commission might approve mergers that pose a serious threat to competition, on the grounds that, some day, somehow, the markets affected might open up. What Mr Overbury calls the 'ultimate safeguard' against this remains the right of competitors to appeal to the European Court of Justice if they feel the merger task force has sanctioned an anti-competitive merger.

Martin Bangemann, the EU industrial affairs commissioner, has argued forcefully that the Commission should endeavour always to be forward-looking in this respect, favouring wherever possible the European single market as the relevant geographical market, rather than a portion of it. 'Current turnovers', he argues, 'are not necessarily relevant . . . It would be completely wrong to perpetuate current structures by judging border-crossing mergers by today's standards.'[19]

This perspective, which seems to be shared by the competition commissioner Karel Van Miert, leaves the merger task force in something of a quandary. How far should it ignore current business realities and instead judge mergers according to a prophecy of the single market that may eventually prove hollow?

It would be rash to place too much faith in the industrial affairs commissioner's views on how the competition commissioner should do his job, but businesses contemplating mergers that are likely to dominate narrow geographical markets would be well advised to spice their proposals with a little of Mr Bangemann's vision. It may find more favour with Mr Van Miert than it would have done with his predecessor, Sir Leon Brittan.

JOINT VENTURES

The merger regulation contains a big hole. Although it lays down certain principles relating to joint ventures, it fails to spell out exactly which types of joint venture are covered by the regulation and which are not.

The Commission decided that this omission necessitated another missive to member states, fully half as long as the merger regulation itself, explaining the difference between 'concentrative' joint ventures (which are covered under the merger regulation) and 'co-operative' ones (which are not). I have not included the text of the joint venture notice in the appendices on the grounds that these are quite long enough already.

Co-operative joint ventures are discussed in chapter 2. They fall under Article 85 of the Treaty of Rome, but not the merger regulation. They are not therefore eligible for the fast-lane treatment accorded to concentrative joint ventures. (However, under new procedures announced by Sir Leon Brittan in December 1992, the Commission has undertaken to issue either a comfort or a warning letter to the parties concerned within two months of their reporting a co-operative joint venture.)

What, then, is the difference between co-operative and concentrative joint ventures? The joint venture notice starts out by admitting that the issue is not a simple one, and warning that 'this notice cannot provide a definitive answer to all conceivable situations'. However, it does give a number of useful tips.

According to the merger regulation, there are two broad criteria which a concentrative joint venture must meet. It must:

1. 'Perform on a lasting basis all the functions of an autonomous economic entity', and it must
2. 'Not give rise to co-ordination of the competitive behaviour of the parties amongst themselves or between them and the joint venture' (Article 3, merger regulation).

These two criteria are usefully broken down in the explanatory notice on joint ventures. If the joint venture you have in mind meets the following conditions, it may be regarded as concentrative. The merger regulation will then apply.

Seven ways to spot a concentrative joint venture

1. The joint venture acts as an independent buyer and supplier on the market (independent, that is, of its parent companies).
2. The joint venture is not substantially dependent on its parents for the maintenance and development of its business.
3. The joint venture is equipped to carry on its business for an indefinite – or at least for a very long – time. It will need to be adequately funded, staffed and technically resourced to do this. Part or parts of the parents' business may well be transferred to the joint venture.
4. The joint venture is free to exercise its own commercial policy. Crucially, it must be free to adjust its competitive behaviour to serve its own economic interests.
5. The joint venture will, as a rule, not trade in markets where its parents are already active: it would be hard for it to meet condition 4 above were it to do so.
6. The joint venture will not influence the competitive behaviour of its parents in their markets.
7. The joint venture will not, as a rule, trade in markets that are upstream or downstream of its parents. This is likely to result in co-ordinated purchasing or sales policies between the joint venture and its parents, contravening condition 1 above.

Broadly speaking, the above conditions are likely to be met in two situations. First when two companies team up to create a joint venture to trade in a market where neither of them is currently active, and second when the joint venture's parents withdraw from a particular market in the interests of their joint venture.

The second of these scenarios occurred in 1990 when Mitsubishi agreed to acquire a 50 per cent interest in Union Carbide's worldwide carbon business. Union Carbide's entire interests in carbon and graphite markets thenceforth resided in the joint venture. At the same time, Mitsubishi undertook to withdraw from the joint venture's markets. The Commission accordingly classed the joint venture as concentrative: it was cleared under the merger regulation in January 1991.

Notwithstanding the Commission's efforts to explain the difference between co-operative and concentrative joint ventures, the distinction has been widely criticised. Jacques Lovergne, head of the mergers' bureau at France's competition authority, has described it as 'unnecessarily complicated ... and a source of legal uncertainty for companies'.

He is not alone. Nor is he alone in arguing that the merger regulation's thresholds can create anomalies when applied to joint ventures. Suppose two large companies (with joint global turnover of more than Ecu 5 billion and EU turnover of more than Ecu 250 million) were to set up a very modest joint venture, with a turnover of only a few dozen million ecu. The joint venture, notwithstanding its small size, would be eligible for investigation under the merger regulation.

ONE-STOP SHOPPING

As already mentioned, under the merger regulation the European Commission operates as a 'one-stop shop', or what the French more aptly call a *guichet unique* (single ticket office), for large-scale mergers possessing a Community dimension. Article 21.2 of the regulation grants the Commission sole competence to rule on the transactions covered in the regulation. It also denies member states the right to apply their national legislation to any concentration with a Community dimension.

There are, however, two exceptions, included at the insistence of Britain and Germany. They are commonly known as the English and German clauses.

Article 21, inserted at the insistence of the British, gives member states the right to take 'appropriate measures to protect legitimate interests', as long as these interests do not conflict with other provisions of Community law. These interests are described (although not exclusively defined) as including 'public security, plurality of the media and prudential rules'.

Public security relates to mergers in the defence sector, which member state governments might wish to review on other than purely competitive grounds. Plurality of the media is included to ensure that the Commission cannot approve, say, a newspaper merger on purely economic grounds that a member state might wish to oppose on democratic grounds – because it reduced the range of published political opinions. Lastly, prudential rules relate to such things as capital adequacy ratios for banks or solvency ratios for insurers.

Mergers between major national defence contractors are usually reviewed differently from other mergers. The normal standards of transparency required by the task force are likely to prove too rigorous for companies engaged in such sensitive activities. For instance, companies planning mergers that are notifiable under the regulation are required to give detailed information on both buyers and products. In the case of companies manufacturing defence systems, national governments might not be happy about such information being relayed to eleven other governments by DGIV.

Article 223 of the Treaty of Rome gives member states the right to withhold information 'the disclosure of which it considers contrary to the essential interests of its security'. Accordingly, the Commission does not insist on a full Form CO notification in mergers between defence contractors that are bound by confidentiality agreements with member state governments.

As for 'plurality of the media', the concrete example often given for the extra scrutiny this clause (21.3) affords to member states is the newspaper merger provisions of the UK's Fair Trading Act 1973. A merger between two British newspaper publishers could be rejected by the British authorities, even if approved by Brussels, for reasons that would have nothing to do with normal competitive considerations.

These three examples are the only ones actually written into the regulation, but they are not the only ones member states may adduce. Any member state can suggest another form of operation over which it wishes to exercise a particular oversight. It is then up to the Commission to decide whether it should be recognised. To date, none have been put forward.[20]

We have already glanced at Article 9 of the merger regulation, better known as the German clause. This enables the Commission to refer cases to national competition authorities if it sees fit, and if the threat to competition posed by the concentration is confined within a single member state. The Commission must decide whether to make a referral within six weeks of notification, if it has not by then begun an in-depth investigation. If proceedings have been started, the Commission has three months in which to make a referral. If the Commission has taken no action and made no referral within three months, the matter is referred back to the member state by default.

Article 9 is fittingly known as the German clause because Germany is the country that has requested cases be referred back to its national competition authorities more than any other member state. None of these requests has been granted (as of December 1993.) The only time the Commission has referred a case back to a member state was the Steetley/Tarmac case, which was referred to Britain on the grounds that the markets affected (brick and clay tiles) were confined to the UK. Moreover, one of the parties was subject to a takeover bid that was already being investigated by the UK Monopolies and Mergers Commission. It was therefore thought appropriate that the MMC should investigate both matters.

On a number of occasions the markets affected by a proposed concentration would appear to be confined to one country, but the case has still been dealt with by the Commission. For example, in early 1991 the German government applied to investigate the planned merger of two German battery makers, Robert Bosch and Varta, but the Commission insisted on looking into the case itself. The reluctance shown by the Commission to refer cases back to member states suggests that, for all its talk of subsidiarity, the Commission is eager to hold on to as much control as possible in vetting mergers and takeovers.

A third clause, known as the Dutch clause, works in the opposite direction to the English and German clauses. It extends rather than dilutes the Commission's powers, enabling it to investigate concentrations that do not have a Community dimension, at the request of a member state. The clause was designed to safeguard competition in those member states that have no effective competition authorities or legislation of their own.

Any request to the Commission to investigate must be made within a month of the date on which the member state was notified of the concentration. The Commission would then have one month in which to decide whether to take action.

The provision, contained within Article 22 of the merger regulation, has only once been used. That was on 30 November 1992 when the Belgian authorities requested that the Commission investigate a merger between British Airways and Dan Air that was expected to have a major impact on competition in Belgium.

The Commission agreed to take on the investigation, but Article 22(3) of the merger regulation gives it very limited powers. It cannot suspend the merger (the Commission had earlier found that the merger did not qualify for examination under the merger regulation because the acquisition fell below the necessary threshold). All it can do is take measures 'strictly necessary to maintain or restore effective competition within ...

the Member State at the request of which it intervenes'. In the case of Dan Air and British Airways, it found no action necessary.

The limited popularity of Article 22 led to widespread speculation that it might be deleted when the merger regulation came to be reviewed in 1993. In the event, the conservatism of member states ensured it was preserved, as was the rest of the regulation, warts and all.

BUT DOES IT WORK?

Cynics say the merger task force is popular with business because it is a watchdog without teeth – or rather, that it may have teeth, but it refuses to use them. Between 21 September 1990, when the merger regulation came into force, and 1 November 1992, the merger task force investigated 123 multi-billion ECU transactions involving EU companies. No fewer than 94 of them were approved unconditionally within a month. A further 14 were found to be outside the scope of the regulation. Only 8 were subject to conditions, like Nestlé–Perrier.[21] And only 1 – Alenia and Aerospaciale's proposed purchase of the Canadian plane-maker, de Havilland – was banned outright.

An impressive record? Philip Lowe, the man who took over as head of the merger task force in January 1993, says it is. He says the task force's work stands comparison with that of the strictest anti-trust agency in Europe, Germany's Bundeskartellamt. Maybe so, but it looks decidedly supine alongside Britain's Monopolies and Mergers Commission.

Of course the Monopolies and Mergers Commission (MMC) fulfils only part of the Commission's role in vetting mergers. Mergers investigated by the MMC have already been scrutinised by the Office of Fair Trading and an in-depth investigation recommended by the Secretary of State for Trade and Industry. MMC investigations therefore equate to 'stage two' investigations undertaken by the Commission, when it is seriously concerned that competition might be imperilled.

On the face of it, the MMC operates to less stringent standards than the mergers task force. The MMC can approve a concentration that is harmful to competition if countervailing advantages show the concentration to be in the public interest. The merger regulation confers no such freedom: it can take account of factors such as the 'the development of economic or technical progress' (Article 2.1[b]) but they cannot be used to justify practices found damaging to competition within the EU.

The fact remains, though, that the MMC has proved tougher to win round than the Commission. In the twenty-two months up to the end of October 1992, the MMC received seventeen notifications. Five of these were found to be against the public interest and prohibited. Another five were laid aside when the applicants abandoned their proposals. This looks pretty tough alongside the merger task force's record, in which only nine out of more than a hundred notifications submitted during the first two years provoked 'serious doubts' and only one was prohibited outright.

Officials at the MMC argue that the mergers task force perhaps sets too high a test before determining that a merger raises serious doubts and must be investigated further.

In addition, whereas the MMC has always been free to investigate oligopolistic market structures, the Commission's power to do this remains debatable, as we have seen.

Does this, then, explain the love-in between European business and the merger task force? Is the merger task force like the local policeman in an Irish country town who is universally popular because he fails to notice that the entire population is distilling illegal hooch from potatoes in their back gardens?

We need not be that cynical. The merger task force is popular for two other reasons: it acts, as we have seen, as a one-stop shop, and it acts swiftly. In an institution that often appears to operate with the urgency of a snail on Mogadon, the dispatch shown by the task force is highly valued. Given the necessary information, it delivers most of its decisions within a month and all of them within five months.

It achieves this because it is well staffed with highly able officials. Some lawyers in Brussels argue this was achieved by poaching the best talent available from elsewhere in DGIV. Colin Overbury, the task force's first director, denies this. 'I was accused of plundering everybody to set up the task force. That's not true – I only took four officials from DGIV.' True or not, there is no doubt that Mr Overbury created a widely respected unit. He ascribes this partly to the fact that he was '100 per cent supported by a very strong commissioner [Sir Leon Brittan]', and partly to what he calls a 'bureaucratic revolution in the task force that pushed responsibility down'.

As a result, there have been few complaints about the way in which the task force has arrived at decisions. Only four Commission decisions under the merger regulation were challenged in the European Court of Justice in the period up to March 1993. One of these was a complaint by three minority shareholders in Italian insurer Assicurazioni Generali that the Commission underestimated the influence the Mediobanca bank had acquired through its 12.84 per cent shareholding in the insurer. Mr Overbury calls this 'pure Florentine farce – we were not supposed to have seen a document which in fact we had seen'.

Two of the other challenges were launched by the then Air France chairman Bernard Attali over allegedly preferential treatment accorded to British Airways in the takeovers of Dan Air and TAT. The fourth came from trade unionists at Perrier over the Commission's alleged disregard for workers' rights as recognised by EU law.

At the time of writing, the European Court of Justice had not handed down judgement on any of the four cases, but Mr Overbury was surely entitled to express satisfaction that so few of the task force's decisions should have been subject to judicial challenges in the first place.

LOWERING THE THRESHOLDS

'The logic of the single market', said merger task force director Philip Lowe in April 1993, 'is that we should go for a reduction in [the merger regulation] thresholds.'[22] His argument was that, as economic integration in Europe proceeds, increasing numbers of cross-border mergers would take place below the original Ecu 5 billion combined global turnover threshold. They would unquestionably possess a Community dimension and should therefore logically be subject to EU scrutiny.

Sadly, logic is not always the Commission's lodestone. The political sensitivities of member states are far more important. Much as it may suit British politicians to lambast the European Commission as an unelected and overweening bureaucracy, real power in Brussels continues to reside with the Council of Ministers: and in the spring of 1993, it was by no means clear that most EU member states wanted to see the merger regulation thresholds lowered.

The thresholds have always been politically sensitive. As we have seen, the Commission originally proposed that mergers should be scrutinised where the combined global turnover of the companies concerned exceeded Ecu 1 billion. The EU turnover threshold per participant was originally going to be set at Ecu 100 million. Then, as Colin Overbury puts it, the thresholds 'got bid up'. After much political horsetrading in the Council of Ministers, the thresholds were finally set at Ecu 5 billion and Ecu 250 million respectively.

The Commission's consolation was the knowledge that the thresholds were due to be reviewed by the end of 1993. The procedure was laid down in the regulation itself: the Commission would make a proposal to the Council of Ministers, which would then decide whether or not to lower the thresholds. The merger regulation itself had required a unanimous Council vote: lowering the thresholds would only need a qualified majority. (For an explanation of how a qualified majority is obtained, see chapter 1.) In the spring of 1993, the merger task force was working full out to supply the information Mr Van Miert required to make up his mind.

It was a major operation. The Commission consulted nearly three hundred companies and trade bodies, as well as competition authorities in the EU member states. It soon became clear that there was little enthusiasm for lowering the Ecu 250 million Community turnover threshold. The Commission's investigations indicated that this was a convenient device to weed out the purely national transactions that should be dealt with by the member states.

However, the feedback from European business seemed to support the view of Commission officials that the Ecu 5 billion combined worldwide turnover threshold should be lowered, at least towards Ecu 2 billion, and ideally straight to Ecu 2 billion, as quickly as possible. UNICE, the European employers' federation, favoured lowering the Ecu 5 billion threshold, but neither of the other two. It wanted to offer the advantages of the one-stop shop system of merger review to more than the very biggest companies.

DGIV officials could readily identify a number of major mergers that had recently escaped Commission scrutiny on account of the very high thresholds imposed by the merger regulation. These included:

1. The Reed/Elsevier merger in 1992 had created the biggest publishing group in the European Union, second only to the US group Dun & Bradstreet at a global level. However, it fell outside the merger regulation because the two companies' combined worldwide turnover was only Ecu 3.1 billion.

2. ICI's proposed exchange of its polypropylene business for BASF's acrylic glass business, unveiled in January 1993, would have increased ICI's share of certain European markets to over 40 per cent. In the event, the deal fell through; but the European Commission would never in any case have had a say in what was unquestionably a major transaction because the EU turnover of BASF's acrylic business was only Ecu 165 million.

3. The 1992 takeover by German steelmaker Fried Krupp of Hoesch, another German steel firm, created a giant with EU turnover of Ecu 10 billion. The merger was scrutinised by competition authorities in four countries: Germany, Italy, France and Spain. It failed to reach the Commission's one-stop shop because both participants had over two-thirds of their EU turnover in Germany.

The Commission also investigated how many extra mergers per year it would trawl into its nets if the Ecu 5 billion threshold was lowered straight away to Ecu 2 billion. The answer appeared to be between fifty and sixty, roughly doubling the merger task force's existing workload. 'Clearly there would be an increased workload for the taskforce', Philip Lowe acknowledged in May 1993, when the Commission's research was beginning to yield results. 'The Commission would have to measure that in relation to any proposal.'

In the event, it was not the extra workload that determined the Commission's attitude, it was the prospect of implacable hostility from EU member state governments. Not all member states were happy with the merger regulation and the merger task force. The French, in particular, had never forgiven the Commission under Sir Leon Brittan for forbidding Aerospaciale and Alenia's takeover of the Canadian plane-maker de Havilland in October 1991 – the one time that the task force not only showed its teeth, but bit savagely.

The French government counselled caution. The argument it put was a favourite of Sir Humphrey Appleby, the smooth-talking English civil servant in the *Yes Prime Minister* television series. It asked: have we had enough experience of the application of the existing regulation? Are we in a position to assess adequately the impact of the current thresholds without more experience?

If this sounds a little thin (the mergers task force had after all reviewed 136 transactions by the spring of 1993), the French had a better argument. The European Union is likely to grow in a few years' time, through the admission of countries such as Austria, Sweden and Finland. Why not wait till then before lowering the thresholds?

The Germans, while more enthusiastic about rapid threshold reduction, urged that it should be accompanied by greater independence of the merger task force. This threatened to resuscitate the long-running debate over whether DGIV should be hived off and set up as an independent agency, a sort of Euro-Bundeskartellamt, free from political influence. The Commission was not eager to stir up such a debate.[23]

Finally, the British also raised difficulties. Britain has, with Germany, the longest established anti-trust operation in Europe. It takes merger policy seriously: indeed, as we have seen, Britain's Monopolies and Mergers Commission has outlawed many more mergers in the past few years than the European Commission has.

Thus there was a certain ambivalence in the British attitude towards EU merger control. On the one hand, the British goverment strongly approved of the tough line Sir Leon Brittan had taken in such matters. British Aerospace, one of Britain's biggest exporters, had argued strongly against the de Havilland takeover being allowed to proceed. The British government, unlike the French, had no quarrel with the way the merger regulation had been interpreted. Its objection to lowering the thresholds was that such a move conflicted – or appeared to conflict – with the principle of subsidiarity.

John Major's government had been beating the subsidiarity drum so long and so loudly that, by the spring of 1993, it could not afford to change tempo. Commission officials argued passionately that reduction of the Ecu 5 billion global turnover threshold would not offend against subsidiarity because the regulation would still be aimed at major cross-border mergers that could best be policed from Brussels. The Confederation of British Industry agreed, but this cut little ice in Whitehall and the British government sided with the French.

At the end of July 1993, Karel Van Miert decided not to recommend a lowering of the thresholds to the Council of Ministers. He was probably bowing to the inevitable: Britain, France and Germany could together have denied him the qualified majority he needed to change the thresholds. The alliance between the three governments was loose knit, but attempts by the Commission to unravel it might have led to the unravelling of the merger regulation itself. The Germans might have insisted on a more independent merger control authority as a *quid pro quo* for wider powers. The British might have insisted that more cases be referred back to member states under Article 9. Officials at DGIV remembered well the difficulties the Commission had encountered in winning agreement to the original merger regulation. The Commission was anxious, as Philip Lowe put it, 'not to open up a debate on principles without a certainty as to the result on the proposal'.

Mr Van Miert's decision was characteristically pragmatic, but it revealed, once again, the Commission's weakness. The 1989 merger regulation may, in retrospect, be seen as marking the high tide of centralisation in EU competition policy.

NOTES

1. *Financial Times*, Europe's top 500 companies ranked by market capitalisation, 10 February 1993.
2. Interview with author, 10 January 1991.
3. ECJ judgement of 21 February 1973, Case 6/72 *Europeemballage Corp. & Continental Can Company* v. *Commission* [1973] ECR 215.
4. See Christopher Jones and Enrique Gonzalez-Diaz, *The EEC Merger Regulation*, Colin Overbury (ed.). Sweet & Maxwell, 1992, page 80.
5. Interview with author, 4 May 1993.
6. UNICE position paper on Regulation 4064/89, 21 April 1993.
7. Raymond Calamaro, Chuca Meyer and Helen Lawson, attorneys at Winthrop, Stimson, Putnam & Roberts, *Financial Times*, 22 November 1990.
8. Speech at CBI/Nabarro Nathanson conference, London, 29 October 1992.
9. *The EC Merger Control Regulation* (2nd edn). Allen & Overy, November 1992.
10. European Court of Justice ruling, 16 July 1992, C-67/91.

11. Aerospaciale–Alenia/de Havilland, in *XXIst Report on Competition Policy*, April 1992.
12. Lucas/Eaton, OJC 328/15.
13. Article 9.7, merger control regulation.
14. *XXIst Report on Competition Policy*, April 1992, page 384.
15. Jones and Gonzalez–Diaz, *op. cit.* at n.5.
16. DOJ and FTC Merger Guidelines, 1992.
17. *The EEC Merger Control Regulation*, *op. cit.* at n. 10, page 17.
18. Interview with author, 4 May 1993.
19. Martin Bangemann, *Meeting the Global Challenge*. Kogan Page, 1992, page 33.
20. Interview with Philip Lowe, Director, Merger Task Force, 22 April 1993.
21. It should perhaps be noted that the Commission applied many more conditions to transactions in the third year of the merger task force's life. By 9 July 1993, fifteen mergers had been subjected to conditions – almost doubling the tally of eight months' earlier. See article by Claus-Dieter Ehlermann, Director-General for Competition, in the *Financial Times*, 9 July 1993.
22. Interview with author, April 1993.
23. See, for example, article by Claus-Dieter Ehlermann, Director-General for Competition, in the *Financial Times*, 9 July 1993.

CHAPTER 4

THE GREAT STATE AIDS DEBATE

STATE AIDS AND THE SINGLE MARKET

'A very touchy issue' is how Karel Van Miert described the European Union's policy on state aids in June 1993.[1] In the space of six months the new competition commissioner had found himself embroiled in conflict not only with member state governments over the aid they could give their industry as recession deepened but also with his own colleagues in the commission. 'From all points of view, a very touchy issue'.

The way Mr Van Miert and his successors handle this issue is important to British businesses in three ways:

1. Unchecked, state aids threaten to derail the whole single market project, which the British business community warmly supports. Furthermore, state aids must be brought under control if economic and monetary union, as envisaged in the Maastricht Treaty, is ever to be achieved. A subsidy race among member states would scupper European monetary union for certain.
2. In more practical terms, a slackly enforced state aids policy by Brussels threatens to cost British companies orders and British workers their jobs. Poorly controlled state aids can generate employment in the country where the subsidies are in force at the expense of neighbouring countries where subsidies are not available. Put

Table 4.1 *Overall state aids in the member states 1988–1990 and 1986–1988 (in brackets) in percentage of GDP, per person employed and relative to government expenditure*

	In percentage of GDP		In ECU per person employed		In percentage of total government expenditure	
	(1986–1988)	1988–1990	(1986–1988)	1988–1900	(1986–1988)	1988–1990
Belgium	(3.2)	2.8	(1153)	1040	(6.0)	5.4
Denmark	(1.0)	1.1	(385)	409	(1.8)	1.9
Germany	(2.5)	2.4	(964)	971	(5.3)	5.2
Greece	(4.5)	3.1	(640)	387	(9.2)	6.0
Spain	(2.7)	1.8	(668)	480	(6.5)	4.2
France	(2.0)	1.8	(779)	735	(4.0)	3.7
Ireland	(2.7)	2.0	(703)	564	(5.2)	4.5
Italy	(3.1)	2.9	(1016)	982	(6.2)	5.6
Luxembourg	(4.0)	4.0	(1390)	1389	(7.4)	7.6
Netherlands	(1.3)	1.3	(513)	528	(2.1)	2.2
Portugal	(1.5)	2.2	(167)	245	(3.4)	5.0
United Kingdom	(1.1)	1.1	(300)	312	(2.6)	2.9
EUR 12	(2.2)	2.0	(728)	687	(4.6)	4.3

Source: European Commission

another way, state aids can 'export' unemployment by undermining otherwise viable industries in other countries that enjoy no aid. This is particularly worrying for Britain, where state aids are by far the lowest in the Community, running at just over half the EC member state average as a percentage of gross domestic product between 1988 and 1990 (see Table 4.1).

3. Notwithstanding the low level of state aid in Britain, opportunities to break or bend the EC rules do arise and the government does not always resist them. Companies that receive state aid, in whatever form, need to know that the aid is being offered lawfully. If the aid is outlawed and has to be repaid, it is the companies, not their governments, that will suffer. British Aerospace, which was forced to repay £44.4 million, plus interest, in early 1993, is not the only British company to have discovered this to its cost.

In 1990 the European Court of Justice (ECJ) introduced the concept of the 'diligent recipient' of state aid. It was the duty of recipients to be sure that the donor of the aid had carried out the correct procedures, the court ruled.[2]

State aids are an emotive subject, both in Brussels and in member state capitals. The Commission insists that aid disbursed by member state governments must be rigorously controlled if an EU-wide subsidy race is not to destroy the Community's prospects of economic convergence. This means cracking down especially hard on aids spent by the governments of richer member states.

For member states, the right to grant state aid is bound up with delicate issues of national sovereignty. The closure of a major industrial plant in an area of high unemployment is something few governments can regard with equanimity. Even the traditionally non-interventionist Dutch preferred to pour money into lorry manufacturer Daf in early 1993, rather than weather the electoral consequences of letting the company close down. The European Commission interferes in such matters at its peril.

Opinions as to when state aids are justified vary with the political allegiance, national outlook and personal prejudices of politicians across the European Union. British Conservatives were horrified that FFr 6.68 billion worth of state aid to Compagnie des Machines Bull, the chronically ailing French state-owned computer manufacturer, was approved in July 1992. French socialists were equally aghast that the money the government invested in Bull should ever have been branded as state aid, and not classed as a normal commercial investment.

In the middle stands the Commission, caught in an ideological crossfire. Its task is made all the more difficult by the ambiguity of the rules on state aids laid down in the Treaty of Rome. When it comes to controlling state aids, the officials of DGIV are like Edward Lear's Jumblies, at sea in a sieve.

THE TREATY OF ROME: A LEAKY VESSEL

Article 92 of the treaty, which purports to outlaw state aids that threaten cross-border competition, is fraught with exceptions and qualifications. In Article 92.1, the six founder members of the European Union devoted 56 words to expressing their abhorrence of state aids. Then, presumably holding pomanders to their nostrils, the treaty's signatories devoted 252 words to listing circumstances in which the Article's opening statement could be ignored.

Article 92.1 forbids 'any aid granted by a Member State or through State resources . . . which distorts or threatens to distort competition by favouring certain undertakings or the production of certain goods . . . , in so far as it affects trade between Member States'.

Sections 2 and 3 of the same article list seven exceptions to the basic rule on state aids. These relate to:

1. Aids that have a 'social character' and are granted to individual consumers (Article 92.2(a)). Such aids may not discriminate between different producers. Thus, any member state could subsidise the purchase of wheelchairs by its disabled citizens; but the British government could not subsidise the purchase of British wheelchairs and not German ones.

2. Aids to repair damage arising from natural disasters 'or exceptional occurrences' (Article 92.2(b)). This could include, for instance, a chemical plant explosion. As the Italian 'emergency' relief aid described in the case study on pages 52–53 shows, there is no time limit on the disbursal of such aid.

3. Aid granted to certain parts of the Federal Republic of Germany affected by the division of Germany (Article 92.2(c)). The reunification of Germany has rendered this clause obsolete.

4. Aid for areas 'where the standard of living is abnormally low', or where there is

'serious underemployment' (Article 92.3(a)). The Edinburgh summit of EU leaders in December 1992 identified such aid as a priority in order to speed the pace of European integration. In February 1993, the Commission proposed that the Belgian province of Hainault together with Merseyside and the Highlands and Islands of Scotland should be added to the list of regions qualifying for the highest level of EU aid. In the process they were also sheltered from the full force of the state aid rules. The whole of Portugal, Greece and Ireland, and the bulk of Spain, already qualified for special treatment under this clause.

5. Aid towards 'an important project of common European interest' or to remedy a 'serious disturbance' in the economy of a member state (Article 92.3(b)). An obvious example of one such important project is the EU subsidised high definition television initiative.

6. Aid for certain economic activities, or certain economic areas, 'where such aid does not adversely affect trading conditions to an extent contrary to the common interest' (Article 92.3(c)). This has been a major category of aid in recent years: the Commission has defined it as 'aid ... to encourage activities that are in the interests of the Community as a whole, but which market forces alone might generate too slowly or in sufficient amounts'.[3] Into this category falls aid to cover the high costs of the EU's environmental policy, based on the principle that the polluter pays. The costs of installing anti-pollution safeguards can be prohibitively high for some companies and the Commission will often approve state aids designed to help in this process.

7. 'Such other categories of aid as may be specified by decision of the Council [of Ministers] acting by a qualified majority on a proposal by the Commission' (Article 92.3(d)). This all-embracing escape clause has been invoked to justify the exemption of aids to shipbuilding and the production of some agricultural products. Otherwise, it has been little used.[4]

As if all this were not enough, the Maastricht Treaty, which came into force on 1 November 1993, contains an eighth class of permissible state aid. The new clause 92.3(d) inserted into the Treaty of Rome at Maastricht permits 'aid to promote culture and heritage conservation where such aid does not affect trading conditions and competition in the Community to an extent that is contrary to the common interest'.

Most of the eight exceptions do not conflict head on with Article 92.1. For instance, it can be argued that 'aid to make good the damage caused by natural disasters' (Article 92.2(b)) is intended merely to indemnify local businesses – to return them to the condition they were in before disaster struck – rather than confer competitive advantage over businesses elsewhere in the Community.

Clearly it would be unreasonable, and politically impossible, to deny national governments the right to assist in the reconstruction of areas devastated by floods or earthquakes, but drawing a line between legitimate disaster relief and aid that could boost local businesses is a difficult task (see case study on Italian earthquake aid, below).

Case study
ITALIAN EARTHQUAKE AID ... TEN YEARS LATE

On a wintry Brussels day in early 1993, officials from Directorate General XVI, the division of the European Commission charged with regional policy, met to discuss a rather curious request from the Italian government. Between 1980 and 1982, the southernmost provinces of the Italian peninsula had been rocked by a series of damaging earthquakes. Now, over a decade later, the Italians were seeking leave to spend Lit 880 billion in state aid on the regions affected.

The first overtures had been made in 1992 and the Commission's response had been discouraging. The Commission considered that the aid threatened to distort competition between EU member states and was therefore inadmissible under Article 92 of the Treaty of Rome. The money the Italians wished to spend was supposed to be emergency relief. How, the Commission asked, could events that occurred ten or more years earlier be classed as emergencies?

On 24 February 1993 the Commission relented. The Italian authorities had convinced Brussels that the Lit 880 billion was in fact compatible with Article 92.2(b) of the Treaty of Rome, which permits 'aid to make good the damage caused by natural disasters or exceptional circumstances'. The Italians promised that the state aid would not subsidise southern Italian companies to compete unfairly with companies elsewhere in the European Union. Instead, it would be spent on infrastructure projects and on refinancing aids already approved by the Commission but not distributed because the Italian government had run out of money.[5]

The story suggests that George Hall, public affairs director of UK computer manufacturer ICL, is right when he argues that 'basic economics, basic housekeeping will have a greater effect [on state aids] than a strong competition authority in Brussels'.[6]

There is something Humpty-Dumptyish about the logic deployed in this section of treaty. (' "When I use a word," Humpty Dumpty said in rather a scornful tone, "it means just what I choose it to mean – neither more nor less." ')[7] State aids are defined in Article 92.1 as incompatible with the common market; but state aids that have been exempted in Article 92, sections 2 and 3 become, all of a sudden, 'compatible with the common market', even though an impartial observer might point out that they could both distort competition and affect trade between member states.

It might have been more honest if the officials who drafted the treaty had admitted that many of the exceptions were not compatible with the common market, but possessed other advantages. As it is, the concept of the 'common market' emerges from Article 92 looking rather woolly.

Unfortunately, Article 92 is the only weapon the Commission possesses. As with other articles in the Treaty of Rome, its meaning has been ceaselessly debated over the years by generations of lawyers. Through the gradual accretion of case law, the meaning of certain key words and phrases has developed. These need to be understood.

1. *State.* This refers to all public bodies or agencies acting on their behalf. It applies at both national and regional level. In a case concerning aid granted by one of the German Länder, the European Court of Justice ruled that Article 92(1) 'is directed at all aid financed from public resources', including aid granted by regional or local bodies 'whatever their status and description'.[8]

The Commission's scrutiny extends to aid granted to the subsidiaries of state-owned companies by their parents. It is no good these holding companies claiming that they are required to operate according to commercial criteria, and *ipso facto* any money they give their subsidiaries must be commercially justified. The Italians have tried this argument at the European Court of Justice: it failed.[9]

It is also worth remembering that aid which is raised by means of a levy on a particular industry or commercial activity is also classed as state aid for the purposes of the Treaty of Rome.[10]

2. *Effect on trade.* To be classed as state aid subject to Article 92(1) of the Treaty of Rome, money pumped into a particular industry must be shown to have an effect on 'trade between member states'. This is not such a limitation as it might appear. Firms which do not export any of their wares may be in receipt of illicit state aid, if the firm is in competition in its home market with producers from other member states.[11]

Even more alarming (from the beneficiaries' point of view), aids granted to EU companies for the sole purpose of encouraging exports to non-EU member states may not be exempt from Article 92(1). The European Court of Justice has ruled that, given the interdependency of markets, such aid may end up having an effect on intra-Community trade.

3. *Certain undertakings . . . certain goods.* Article 92(1) does not ban member states from taking actions designed to benefit their entire economies. Decisions relating to general economic, fiscal and social policy are classed as 'general measures' by the Commission and fall under different, far less toughly worded, articles of the Treaty of Rome (Articles 101 and 102). There can be no doubt that varying tax regimes, for instance, distort competition within the single market, but they are not normally covered under Article 92(1).

However, tax breaks may sometimes be used to benefit a particular sector of a member state economy or particular companies within that economy. Thus in 1992 the Commission opened an investigation into tax breaks offered by the Italian government for financial services companies setting up in the north-eastern city of Trieste.[12] The Commission argued that the privileged status for Trieste (which is not in a seriously disadvantaged region) risked enticing investment from around the Community at the expense of other regions.

Likewise on July 1990 the Commission objected to certain tax concessions proposed in a bill put before the Italian parliament in October 1989. The Commission found that the bill gave wide discretion to the government to determine exactly who should benefit from the tax breaks on offer. In particular, it concluded that the intended beneficiary was Montedison, a leading chemicals and fertilisers producer, which would have been spared Lit 774 billion in tax. The Commission stressed that only tax concessions that 'were available automatically and without any exercise of discretion in the economy as a whole constituted general measures' not covered by the state aid rules.[13]

The Commission points out that the competitive distortions caused by sectoral or industry-specific state aids are generally far more clear-cut than those created by fiscal differences. Tax breaks are, after all, not state aids in the classic sense: they represent relief from a burden, rather than a boost. This is not a semantic issue. A low tax burden on firms may not confer a competitive advantage. Low taxes may go hand in hand with poor infrastructure or public services which will damage companies' competitiveness.

There are, however, circumstances in which tax concessions may benefit particular participants in a market at the expense of others. This is the charge that was laid at the French government's door by the French insurers' association, the Fédération Française des Sociétés d'Assurances (FFSA), in early 1993. The FFSA claimed that the French post office, a state-owned company, benefited from tax breaks that helped it sell life assurance more cheaply than the French insurance companies. La Poste's savings on tax have been estimated at between FFr 600 and FFr 700 million a year.[14]

The French government countered these criticisms with the claim that La Poste must serve the whole of France and its overseas dominions and is thus at a commercial disadvantage to private companies that can pick and choose their locations. The tax breaks merely redress the balance, the government claimed.

As this book was going to press, it was far from clear how Brussels would react to the case. Earlier statements from DGIV suggested that the Commission would seek to draw a clear line between those activities of La Poste that were undertaken as part of its public service responsibilities and those where it competed in the commercial market. This would not bode well for La Poste and its political masters. Brussels wishes to highlight subsidies, not allow them to be obscured.

4. *The market economy investor principle.* State aid, to be so defined, must offer the recipient advantages not available on the private market. For instance, if a government pumps money into a state-owned enterprise, and can show that a private sector investor might have done exactly the same thing, the money will not be classified as state aid.

This is exactly what the French government attempted to prove over the FFr 4 billion in capital it injected into the ailing state-owned computer company, Compagnie des Machines Bull, in 1991 and 1992. Jacques Lovergne, the man in charge of state aids policy at the competition division of the French economy ministry, likens the capital contributions to the money the German private sector electronics company Siemens spent to acquire the computer firm Nixdorf in 1988/89. (The price that Siemens paid for control of Nixdorf was never disclosed, but sums of up to DM 1 billion have been quoted in the German press.) The European Commission was unimpressed by such arguments. Bull had not paid a dividend since 1983, it noted. The company's debt levels were well above industry averages. The Commission was adamant that the capital injections be classed as state aid; but it permitted the aid to be paid on the grounds that it accompanied a major restructuring at Bull which would ensure the company would not flood the market with artificially subsidised products.

The French government took umbrage at the Commission's decision, arguing that the FFr 4 billion should never have been classed as state aid in the first place. In December 1993, the case was still dragging on in the European Court of Justice and Bull was pressing the French government for FFr 9.2 billion more money.

The market economy investor principle is notoriously difficult to apply. The behaviour of commercial investors varies hugely. Deutsche Bank might be willing to

Figure 4.1 *Do the state aid rules apply?*

Measure of a public body in a member state?	→NO	*Rules do not apply (e.g. Community measures)*
↓		
YES		
↓		
Cost to the public purse? (including com- *pulsory levy)*	→NO	*Rules do not apply*
↓		
YES		
↓		
Benefit to enterprises?	→NO	*Rules do not apply (e.g. social welfare payments)*
↓		
YES		
↓		
Do normal market conditions apply	→YES	*Not an aid (e.g. loans on normal commercial terms)*
↓		
NO		
Special advantages for special sectors or *regions? Ad hoc aid for specific firms or groups* *of firms?*	→NO	*'General measure': rules do not apply*
↓		
YES		
↓		
Competition with firms in other member *states?*	→NO	*Rules do not apply*
↓		
YES		
↓		
Subject to state aid rules		

(*Source*: European Commission)

wait far longer to see a return on an investment than Lord Hanson. The Commission tends towards the Deutsche Bank approach. The market economy investor it has in mind takes a 'long term view of profitability'.[15] Clearly, though, a 0 per cent return on capital over ten years, such as Bull provided, would be enough to try the patience of the most long-suffering private investor.

Figure 4.1, drafted by the Commission, provides an easy to follow checklist of the preconditions for state aid, taking the above definitions into account.

THE COMMISSIONER'S BATTALIONS: RHETORIC AND REALITY

So much for the rules: but how conscientiously does the Commission enforce them? One way of measuring this is to compare the weight given to the state aids threat by competition commissioners in their speeches with the resources they allocate to counter it.

In recent years, the rhetorical geiger count has been very high. Peter Sutherland, competition commissioner from 1 January 1986 to 31 December 1988, argued that 'without Community control exercised by the Commission, one would very quickly see a chain reaction developing', leading to an 'infernal spiral' of competing subsidies. This would be 'disastrous' for all the countries involved, he maintained.[16]

Mr Sutherland's successor, Sir Leon Brittan, was every bit as outspoken about the need to control state aids. In the course of 1992 he stoutly defended the Commission's competence in this field against the advocates of subsidiarity, who were seeking to roll back the frontiers of the Commission's empire. 'A government cannot police itself', he pointed out.[17] And he took part of the credit for a 'policy which has been much tougher on state aids than in the past'.[18]

Under Karel Van Miert, who took over from Sir Leon Brittan as competition commissioner in January 1993, the message remained much the same. 'A single market will only make sense if customs barriers and other trade restrictions are not replaced by increased state aid', argued the Commission's twenty-second report on competition, published in May 1993. A few days later Mr Van Miert acknowledged that recessionary pressures were making the Commission's task harder. 'Each region pretends that its neighbouring region is allowed more', he complained. 'There is an extra workload.'[19]

The Commission had just over eighty people handling this workload at the end of 1992 – 21 per cent of the available manpower at DGIV. Two successive Commission reports on competition policy, published in early 1992 and early 1993, suggested that, in spite of Van Miert's claim, the job of monitoring state aids was in some respects becoming easier. To be sure, state aid notifications were up sharply in 1991 and continued at a high level in 1992, but in both years the number of proceedings opened by the Commission and the number of orders for repayment of state aids fell.

Table 4.2 gives some idea of the actions taken by the Commission in controlling state aid over the period 1981–1992.

The Commission has taken this as encouraging evidence that member states are paying increasing attention to the EU rules on state aids. They are much more willing than in the past to clear state aid schemes with the Commission before implementing them, and they are taking care to frame such schemes so as not to fall foul of the European Union's rules.

State aid investigations, or 'proceedings' as the Commission calls them, are more labour-intensive than routine monitoring of notifications. Yet Karel Van Miert continues to devote around a fifth of his staff to state aid cases. This suggests that, when he talks about the need to control state aids, he means it.

In only one area have the Commission's resources fallen lamentably far short of the competition commissioner's rhetoric. This is in the supervision of state aid to state-owned manufacturing companies. In July 1991 the Commission issued a communication to member state governments requiring them to supply detailed annual statistics on state aids to such companies. The Commission's twenty-first report on competition policy published in April 1992 hailed the communication as 'an important step towards the fair treatment of state aids'.[20] Ninety companies were affected. Yet Sir Leon Brittan allocated only two members of his staff to sifting through the large volumes of data supplied.

We shall return to the sad fate of the Commission's communication on state aids to

Table 4.2 *Activity in the control of state aid (excluding aid to agriculture, fisheries and transport)*

Year	Number of proposals notified	No objections raised	Action taken by the Commission			
			Initiation of proceedings under Article 93(2) EEC or Article 8(3) of Decision 2320/81/ESCS	Termination of proceedings under Article 93(2) EEC or Article 8(3) of Decision 2320/81/ECSC	Final decision under Article 93(2) EEC or Article 8(3) of Decision 2320/81/ECSC	Proposals notified and later withdrawn by member states
1981	92 (of which steel = 16)	79 (of which steel = 11)	30 (of which steel = 9)	19 (of which steel = 4)	14	–
1982	200 (of which steel = 81)	104 (of which steel = 25)	86 (of which steel = 56)	30 (of which steel = 13)	13 (of which steel = 1)	–
1983	174 (of which steel = 4)	101 (of which steel = 18)	55	18	21 (of which steel = 9)	9
1984	162 (of which steel = 10)	201 (of which steel = 66)	58 (of which steel = 1)	34	21	6
1985	133 (of which steel = 7)	102 (of which steel = 21)	38 (of which steel = 1)	31	7	11
1986	124	98	47	26	10	5
1987	326	205	27	32	10	1
1988	375	311	31	32	13	–
1989	296	254	37	27	16	7
1990	429	352	33	24	12	2
1991	472	383	53	25	9	21
1992	459	393 (N aid) 468 (all E/N/NN aid)	26 + 2 under Article 6(2) of Decision 322/89/ECSC	33	8	25

Note: The figures in the first column do not match those of the next four columns on account of carry-overs from one year to the next and because, if proceeding under Article 93(2) EEC or Article 8(3) of Decision 2320/81/ECSC are initiated, the Commission has to take two decisions, one to initiate proceedings and then a final decision terminating them

Source: European Commission

state-owned companies shortly. Despite the bullish tone of recent Commission competition reports on state aids, there are good reasons to fear for the future success of the policy.

THE ENEMY WITHIN: THE SUBVERSION OF EU STATE AIDS POLICY

One of the biggest problems that competition commissioners face is the seemingly limitless scope for conflicts between state aids policy and other European Union policies. EU industrial policy used to be the bane of the competition commissioner's existence, but in recent years regional policy has taken over this role. No longer is DGIII, the industrial affairs division of the Commission, the natural antagonist to DGIV, the competition division. It remains powerful, but today the regional policy division, DGXVI, with its vastly extended budget, looks a more formidable adversary.

The conflict has sharpened as the Union has struggled to achieve economic convergence between poorer and richer member states. Economic convergence is a precondition for monetary union as envisaged in the Maastricht Treaty. The idea is that the Commission should clamp down ever harder on state aids disbursed by richer member states, while allowing far more latitude to poorer member states. If the budget deficits of the poorer member states still inhibit their ability to offer aid, then the Union itself will lend a hand through its cohesion funds.

The Commission is alarmed at an apparent growing concentration of aid in the four central EC member states – Britain, France, Germany and Italy – relative to the poorer peripheral states.[21] Public support to industry in the four main EU economies accounted for 75 per cent of all industry aid in the Community during 1986–1988. This rose to 79 per cent between 1988 and 1990.

It is perhaps unfair to lump Britain in with France and Italy in this context, although the Commission did. State aids in Britain, both as a percentage of value added in the manufacturing sector and per person employed, were the lowest in the Community between 1988 and 1990.

Nevertheless, budgetary constraints on the Union's poorer countries were undoubtedly cramping their ability to deploy state aids to boost deprived regions and maintain or create jobs. A comparison between France and Spain shows the trend at its most alarming (see Table 4.3). Spain found herself with less to spend than her richer neighbour, even though her unemployment rate was one of the highest in the Union.

Table 4.3 *'Unto every one that hath shall be given . . . but from him that hath not shall be taken away even that which he hath' (St Matthew 26: 29)*

State aids to manufacturing per person employed, France and Spain, 1986–1990

	1986–1988	1988–1990	% change
France	Ecu 1,437	Ecu 1,380	−4%
Spain	Ecu 1,749	Ecu 936	−46.5%

Source: European Commission

Sir Leon Brittan expressed the problem crisply in a speech delivered in late 1992. 'Although the Commission authorises countries like Portugal and Greece to pay up to 75 per cent investment aid, in practice they can only afford to pay around 25–30 per cent on average. This may be compared to maxima of 18 per cent in West Germany and 25 per cent in France.'[22]

There are some who doubt whether the Commission's response to this problem – tightening state aid controls in the richer states, slackening them in the poorer states – is sensible. In a thoughtful discussion paper published in December 1992, Sean Shepley and Jonathan Wilmot of bankers Crédit Suisse First Boston in London argued that the best hope for the peripheral regions of the Union was tightly focused state aid to enable them to develop specialist manufacturing and service skills.[23] On this reading, money poured into, say, the Spanish steel industry is money down the drain because the future of the steel industry lies at the core of Europe, close to the regions of highest demand.

To take this into account would require a pan-European aid policy, which appears a remote prospect. Meanwhile, the power of the regional affairs directorate general, DGXVI, grows in line with its swelling budget. Commission staff say that Bruce Millan, Britain's second commissioner who was reappointed for two years at the end of 1992, argues his corner very effectively. There was, by all accounts, no love lost between him and Sir Leon Brittan when Sir Leon was in charge of competition policy.

Problems arise more often in certain industries than in others. Take textiles. Martin Taylor, the former chief executive of Courtaulds Textiles who took over as chief executive of Barclays Bank in August 1993, says the textile industry suffers from 'industrial snobbery' on the part of the Commission.[24] By this he means that complaints about distortions of competition caused by misconceived regional aid are not pursued with the vigour he would wish.

Evidence for such a view emerged in early 1993, when the European Court of Justice ruled that the Commission had erred in failing to investigate at least FFr 160 million granted by the French government to the US synthetic textiles manufacturer, Allied Signal. The regional aid was given to the company to assist it in setting up a high tenacity yarn factory in Lorraine, an old coalmining region of France.

There is no doubt that Lorraine is a depressed region: the decline of coalmining has left high unemployment. The court recognised Lorraine's right to claim regional aid from the French government, but not for the benefit of a synthetic textiles manufac-turer. Synthetic textiles are regulated under a longstanding EU agreement, renewed in January 1993, which restricts state aid even in deprived parts of the Community.

The case against the Commission was brought by the Comité International de la Rayonne et des Fibres Synthétiques (CIRFS), an association of European synthetic textiles manufacturers. The case turned on whether the high tenacity yarns produced by Allied Signal were covered by the sixteen-year-old EU agreement designed to control production in the sythetic fibre industry – a sector dogged by overcapacity.

Jean-Louis Juvet, the Swiss director-general of CIRFS, insisted that high tenacity yarns were covered by the agreement. The Commission disagreed and refused to open proceedings against Allied Signal under Article 92 of the Treaty of Rome. It took Juvet two and half years to win his case at the European Court of Justice. The Commission acted swiftly on the court's judgement and opened state aid proceedings against Allied Signal.

Mr Juvet bears no grudge against DGIV, but he fears that the EU's new aggressive regional policy may be pulling the rug from under the feet of the directorate general's officials, creating new opportunities for state aids that distort competition. There is, he says, an unwritten rule at the Commission that regional policy considerations should take precedence over competition policy issues.[25]

For British businesses, the problem with EU regional policy is that it does not always take account of capacity utilisation in the industries affected by regional aid. 'Overcapacity is not the only test', Sir Leon Brittan admitted in April 1992.[26] In other words, regional aid can be granted to businesses which are producing goods for markets that are already glutted. 'Stealing jobs' was how Martin Taylor described the effects of such aid while he was at Courtaulds Textiles.

In 1992, the UK textile industry employed around four hundred thousand people in Britain, according to the British Apparel and Textile Confederation (BATC). The industry's sales reached £15 billion and exports stood at £4.8 billion. 'It would be hard to find an activity in any member state that could be subsidised without it having a knock-on effect on some part of the British [textile] industry', says Colin Purvis, spokesman for the Apparel, Knitting and Textiles Alliance, the BATC's representative arm. Mr Purvis deals with what he describes as a 'steady stream of state aid cases'. They are almost always defended on regional policy grounds, he says.

BLOWING THE WHISTLE

What is to be done? Must British companies suffer in silence while subsidised Continental European competitors walk away with the business?

No. The odds against obtaining redress in individual cases are often long. At best, the aid is likely to be repaid only after a long delay, well after the damage has been done. The effort must be made, though, either by companies acting individually or in concert. In spite of setbacks, the European Union's rules on state aids are more widely respected today than in the past. If no business ever complained, the European Commission would end up functioning like a shoddy restaurant, with no incentive to raise standards.

Fortunately, British businesses are not like British restaurant-goers: they do complain. ICL, the biggest British computer manufacturer, complained vociferously to the Commission over the state aid granted by the French government to Compagnie des Machines Bull in 1991 and 1992. It lost because the French managed to panic the Commission into agreeing that Europe might not have a computer industry worth the name if companies such as Bull were allowed to go under.

Nevertheless, in the longer term, ICL's effort may pay off. Consider the following:

1. Within a few months of being appointed industry minister by France's new right wing government in March 1993, Gerard Longuet warned Bull not to expect any more handouts from the state. The company was on the list of twenty-one firms the new French government committed itself to privatising.

2. Increasingly, influential business figures in France have been asking whether the subsidy game is worth the candle. 'We offer rods for our own backs', says Jean Peyrelevade, formerly chairman of France's biggest insurance company, Union des Assurances de Paris (UAP) and now chairman of the Crédit Lyonnais bank. 'Illicit subsidies, abusive support for our state-owned companies, unjustified aid to such and such an industrial sector ... many are the motives for permanent sanctions.'[27] Mr Peyrelevade favours the more subtle form of protection adopted by the Germans – protection, not of markets, but of the ownership of capital. At least Brussels would then leave the French alone, he suggests.

3. The argument that companies like Bull must be helped because theirs is a vital strategic industry for Europe is falling out of favour across the European Union, and particularly in Brussels. 'The magic words "key industry" must not lead automatically to a claim for subsidy', says Martin Bangemann, the industrial affairs commissioner.[28] Under Dr Bangemann's guidance, EU industrial policy is evolving in favour of promoting co-operation among European companies, rather than propping them up when they stumble.

For all these reasons, ICL need not consider the time it devoted to lobbying against state aid to Bull as time wasted. The row sent a shot across the then French government's bows: future administrations are likely to act more cautiously.

When it comes to complaining about state aids, British companies have various options.

1. They can go straight to the Commission as ICL did: the company's public affairs director George Hall describes using a trade association as a 'waste of time'.

2. They can protest through their trade association (*pace* Mr Hall), as long as the body in question is well organised with good contacts in Brussels. For smaller companies, this will often be the best strategy because a major lobbying effort can be very costly.

3. They can complain to the Department of Trade and Industry (Competition Policy Division, DTI, Ashdown House, 123 Victoria Street, London SW1E 6RB) in the hope that the British government will take up their case with the Commission. ICL did this too. Jonathan Rees, a member of Britain's permanent representation in Brussels, wrote a stiffly worded letter to the Commission's general secretary David Williamson on 2 September 1991 protesting over the French government's planned support for Bull. Trade and industry secretary Michael Heseltine also took the matter up with Sir Leon Brittan.

   The DTI says it receives complaints on state aids 'fairly regularly', but keeps no figures on the number it refers to Brussels. Apparently, many of the complaints are directed not at foreign governments for offering state aid to their industry but at the British government for not doing the same.

4. They can write to their MEP, who may be able to extract a rapid response from the Commission. The Commission has described MEPs' role in alerting it to unnotified state aids as 'most useful'.[29]

5. They can retain the services of a professional firm of political lobbyists. This is only

likely to be cost-effective if the aid in question threatens to have a major impact on the business of the recipient's competitors. Political lobbyists do not come cheap, but if the beneficiary of the aid has professional lobbying support (as, for example, Bull did), then perhaps its competitors should too.

6. They can air their grievances in the press. The Commission is sensitive to its public image and does not like to be portrayed as dragging its feet.

Whichever avenues complainants choose, they should stress certain points. First, they must be confident that the aid offends, *prima facie*, against Article 92, as explained above. They do not need to establish whether the aid is likely to be exempt under the same article: that is the Commission's job.

Second, they should describe the effect of the aid. Overcapacity, as Sir Leon Brittan has admitted, is not the only test the Commission applies to industries in receipt of state aid: but it is an important test. If the supply of a particular product already exceeds demand, the Commission is unlikely to welcome plans to boost supply still further.

Third, the purpose of the aid should be clearly explained. The Commission is not so bothered about the form of the aid, whether it be via grants, soft loans, tax concessions or other means, but its purpose is crucial. The Commission is likely to take a more critical view of rescue or restructuring aid, for instance, than of aid for research and development or employment and training.

ENFORCEMENT OF STATE AID DECISIONS: WAITING FOR GODOT?

We now come to the third major problem of EU state aids policy. Let us suppose the aid is in flagrant breach of the Treaty of Rome. Let us further suppose that its damaging effect on competition is not outweighed by any other benefits. The Commission directs the member state government involved to reclaim the aid. End of story?

Sadly not. Member state governments quite often simply ignore the Commission. Worse still, governments have been known to ignore the European Court of Justice when it backs Commission decisions. In the state aids field, the Commission's powers of enforcement leave much to be desired.

The Commission did not even begin trying to enforce the repayment of state aids until 1985. This was twelve years after the European Court of Justice confirmed that the Commission had the right to order the repayment of state aids, and two years after the Commission announced its intention to exercise this right.[30]

One of the first cases the Commission tackled concerned aid granted by the Belgian government to Beaulieu, a carpet manufacturer, in the early 1980s. The Commission ordered the Belgian government to recover the aid. Nothing happened, so the Commission took its case to the European Court of Justice. Armed with a court judgement, it once again tried to make the Belgian government recover the aid. Again, it failed. A decade after the aid, worth around £15 million, was granted, the European Commission has still failed to make Beaulieu repay a centime.

This is far from being an isolated case. In 1989, the European Commission ordered the Italian government to reclaim Lit 615 billion paid by the state-owned holding company IRI to its engineering and high technology subsidiary Finmeccanica to shore up Finmeccanica's car-making operation, Alfa Romeo. The European car market was suffering from excess capacity and the Commission found that the aid would offer Alfa Romeo a competitive advantage.

Alfa has since been sold to Fiat and the aid has been repaid by Finmeccanica to its parent, IRI. But in the summer of 1993 IRI had still not repaid the aid to the Italian state, despite a European Court of Justice ruling in early 1991 upholding the Commission's original decision.[31]

These and other cases make life trying for the officials at DGIV charged with monitoring state aids. However, they have recently acquired some extra leverage. They can now add interest to the aid that must be repaid, dating from the time at which repayment was first ordered. British Aerospace was the first company in the EU to suffer from this: in May 1993 BAe paid the British government £57.6 million, representing the original £44.4 million plus interest it had received from the government as an incentive to buy Rover Group in 1988.[32]

Better still from the Commission's point of view, the Maastricht Treaty empowers the European Court of Justice to fine member state governments for failing to comply with EU law, including refusing to enforce repayment of illegal state aids. The procedure is lengthy. First, the ECJ must uphold the Commission's decision that state aid should be repaid. Then, if the aid is not repaid, the Commission must issue a 'reasoned opinion' giving the member state a deadline to implement the court's judgement. If this is ignored, the Commission can return to the court to claim a 'lump sum or penalty payment' from the member state.[33]

Clearly, the whole process will take years, but at least member states will have something to lose if they ignore Commission decisions backed by the court's judgements.

UNNOTIFIED AIDS: GETTING BETTER

The unco-operative response of many member state governments in recovering state aids must be galling to officials at DGIV. Many of the cases date back years. Usually, abuse of the state aid rules has been detected long after the event and enforcing repayment is a task akin to unscrambling eggs.

The good news for the Commission is that similar problems are less likely to arise in the future. State aids schemes are now far more commonly submitted for Commission approval before they come into force than was formerly the case.

There was certainly scope for improvement. Between 1985 and 1990 unnotified state aids to state-owned enterprises were running at around Ecu 1 billion a year, according to the Commission.[34] In all, the Commission discovered thirty-six instances of such aid during this period, most of it taking the form of capital injections into loss-making companies. The aid often came to light many years after it was granted.

State-owned companies are not the only beneficiaries of unnotified aid. Capital injections into lame-duck state-owned companies are rather a blatant form of state aid.

It does not reflect well on the Commission's scrutiny that so many such injections seem to have been made undetected.

Unnotified aid to private sector companies commonly takes more subtle forms. The state can waive an employer's social security contributions for a while, or it can sell or rent land to a company at a subsidised price, as when Derbyshire County Council sold land for a car plant to Toyota at £4.2 million below its market value. In July 1991, the Commission requested the aid be refunded to Derbyshire County Council and by October that year it had been.[35]

Aid of these kinds can be fiendishly difficult to detect, but there is evidence that the Commission is making some headway. One of the biggest stumbling blocks was removed in 1990 when the ECJ endorsed the Commission's right to order member state governments to suspend unnotified aid payments, pending the receipt of full details from the member state.[36] Previously, the member state could carry on doling out money while the Commission sought to unravel its purpose.

The Commission now has the ECJ's authority to request full details of unnotified aid schemes from member states, to be supplied within thirty days. (If it appears that the aid is doing serious damage to the recipients' competitors, the time limit may be even shorter.) In the absence of such information, the Commission can order the member state to suspend the aid immediately.[37]

The Commission's first opportunity to flex its muscles came on 11 June 1991. Various tax breaks granted by the French government to Pari Mutuel Urbain (PMU), a horse race betting agency, had formed the subject of a complaint to the Commission from one of PMU's competitors. On 11 June the Commission ordered the French government to suspend these aids immediately and to confirm their suspension within fifteen days.

The case shows that, on occasion, the Commission can act swiftly to curb potentially anti-competitive behaviour. The Commission argues that the sharp increase in state aid notifications in 1991 and 1992 was due in part to the growing realisation among member states that the Commission meant business in clamping down on state aids. Between 1985, when the Commission first tried to enforce the payment of state aids, and 1990, state aid notifications (excepting steel) were running at an average of 279 per annum. In 1991 the figure hit 472 and in 1992 it remained high at 459. The Commission brandishes these figures as evidence of a healthier respect for its authority. 'Member states pay increased attention ... to avoid ... [state aid] measures previously sanctioned as ... incompatible with the common market', it asserts.[38]

The Commission receives information on unnotified aids from a wide range of sources. Quite a number of cases come to the Commission's attention through press reports. For example, the Italian press knew about plans to create an 'off-shore' financial services and insurance centre in Trieste before the Commission. In 1992 the Commission opened an investigation into the tax breaks offered to Trieste which, it feared, might have 'a particularly distorting effect' on competition.

STATE AIDS TO STATE-OWNED COMPANIES: A COMMISSION DEFEAT

The sixteenth of June 1993 was a black day for the European Commission. Its efforts to clamp down on state aids, so widely advertised by Sir Leon Brittan during his time as competition commissioner, had met with some success, as we have seen, but on 16 June 1993, the European Court of Justice declared one of Sir Leon's most valuable weapons – a 1991 Commission communication on state aids to state-owned industries – invalid.

The Commission saw the communication, which had been adopted in July 1991, as 'an important step towards the fair treatment of state aid, whatever the system of ownership of the recipient undertakings'.[39] It required member states to report annually on their financial dealings with state-controlled manufacturing companies with a turnover of more than Ecu 250 million a year.

Communications from the European Commission are not universally popular with EU member states. They set out the Commission's interpretation of existing EU law and require the member states to take swift action to comply with that interpretation. Communications can thus take effect far more quickly than EU directives, which must pass through a series of legislative hoops before they are adopted.

In the case of the communication on state aid to state-owned industries, it was the French who objected most strenuously. The French government argued that the communication went well beyond the scope of a 1980 directive on the transparency of financial relations between member states and state-owned enterprises.[40] It imposed, the French argued, 'new obligations' and 'disproportionate demands' on member state governments.[41] On 14 December 1991, the French government took its case to the European Court of Justice in Luxembourg.

A year and a half later, the court upheld the French government's complaint and ordered that the communication be annulled. For Karel Van Miert and his toiling officials at DGIV it was back to the drawing board.

The contents of the Commission's 1991 communication remain of interest, despite its sorry fate at the hands of the EU judiciary. Thirteen days before the court handed down its judgement, Mr Van Miert reaffirmed the Commission's determination to maintain the pressure on member state governments. If the communication were to be annulled, the Commission would seek to maintain its scrutiny by other means, he said. 'We need to be able to make up our minds.'[42]

The 1991 communication itemised the transactions that the Commission wished (and still wishes) to monitor. These were:

1. The provision of capital/equity to state-owned companies and the forms it took (e.g. ordinary or preference shares).
2. Non-refundable grants, or grants refundable only in certain circumstances. (In the private sector, investors do not give something for nothing.)
3. Details of any loans to the enterprise, specifying the rates and terms of such loans, and the nature of any security pledged in return.

4. Guarantees given to the enterprise in support of any loan finance, specifying terms and charges paid, if any.
5. Dividends paid out and profits retained.
6. Changes in any previous form of state intervention. In particular, the Commission was interested to learn whether the state had waived repayment of debts – whether for loans or grants, or for corporate or social taxes – due from the enterprise.

Between 1985 and 1990, member state governments paid over Ecu 5 billion to state-owned companies through one or other of the above means. The Commission was not notified of any of the thirty-six separate transactions involved.[43]

State-owned companies have long posed a problem for the Commission. Private sector companies are quick to cry foul if they believe that state-owned companies are enjoying favoured treatment from member state governments: but the Commission must be sure it does not tip the balance in the opposite direction, making life harder for state-owned companies than for private sector firms. The Treaty of Rome is categorical: 'This Treaty shall in no way prejudice the rules in Member States governing the system of property ownership', it states (Article 222). In other words, public ownership of the means of production, distribution and exchange (to quote Clause IV of the British Labour Party's constitution) is quite compatible with the Treaty of Rome.

Article 222 has given officials at DGIV frequent headaches. Sir Leon Brittan, an impeccably dry Thatcherite who never allowed himself to go native in Brussels, professed to find state ownership of industry 'mysterious and mystical'.[44] However, his attempts to ensure that state ownership was not exploited to distort competition within the common market met with powerful resistance.

Detecting state aid to state-owned industries is notoriously difficult. When is a capital transfusion commercially justified? What is a reasonable rate of return that the state should expect from its investments? Will it ever be possible truly to ensure that state-owned companies play the game by the same rules as private companies? If they did, what would be the point of their being state-owned?

Fortunately, governments across Europe are pondering the last of these questions ever more deeply. They are increasingly coming to the conclusion that there is little point in their owning companies that should be perfectly well able to compete in the private sector. In France, Spain, Germany and Italy, governments are planning to sell off billions of dollars worth of commercial and industrial assets. In Britain there is very little left in the public domain to sell. The Commission's task in these circumstances is to ensure that sweeteners are not paid to encourage private sector buyers to take weak state-owned companies off governments' hands.

Meanwhile the Commission is also trying to ensure that those companies that remain in the state sector are not unfairly assisted. In the long term, the Commission may even thank the European Court of Justice for annulling its communication. UNICE, the European employers' federation, has urged the Commission to beef up the original 1980 directive on state aid to state-owned companies as a replacement for the 1991 communication. Whereas the communication only referred to aid for industry,

UNICE argues that aid to service companies – a growing preoccupation of the Commission – should be covered by an amended directive.[45]

On 16 June 1993, the Commission lost a battle: it may yet win the war.

Case study
SUBSIDISED SPROCKETS – ONE MAN'S BATTLE AGAINST BRUSSELS

The European Commission's task in controlling state aids is far from easy. The Treaty of Rome's prohibition on such subsidies is fraught with qualifications. The growing importance of EU regional policy threatens to sap the Commission's resolve in reducing state aid across the Union. Even when the rules have clearly been broken and the European Court of Justice agrees they have been broken, member states can simply refuse to reclaim the aid.

Imagine, then, the irritation among officials at DGIV when, in addition to their daily frustrations, a British businessman stands up and castigates them for not really trying to control state aids.

The businessman is Andrew Cook, chairman of William Cook plc, Britain's biggest steel foundry company, based in Sheffield. Since 1990, Mr Cook has been sniping at the Commission from every vantage point he can find. He has complained to the press and before the European Court of Justice about the Commission's handling of his grievances. He has even produced a video, entitled 'Who pays the price? . . . for the unlevel playing field', giving vent to his own frustrations and those of other British businesspeople.

Mr Cook is a barrister by training and his dogged pursuit of disputes with Brussels has won him no friends at the Commission. When, in the spring of 1992, I attempted to obtain an interview with senior officials in DGIV to discuss Mr Cook's complaints, the normally co-operative attitude of Sir Leon Brittan's then spokesman evaporated. Nobody was available to talk on that subject, I was told.

However, Andrew Cook's case is not without merit. On 19 May 1993 the ECJ ruled in Mr Cook's favour that the Commission had acted unlawfully in approving Ptas 673.3 million in subsidies and guarantees granted to the Spanish steel foundry company Piezas y Rodajes (Pyrsa) by a range of local authorities in the province of Teruel in northern Spain. The ECJ ordered the Commission to reopen investigations into the aid, which it had cleared in May 1991.

Pyrsa makes sprockets (toothed wheels that engage with chains, used mainly in the mining industry) and GET parts (used in the construction of earth-moving and excavation equipment). Mr Cook's firm makes GET parts too. Mr Cook contended that aid to Pyrsa, granted both by the Spanish government and by local government in Teruel, threatened to harm competitors in a market that was already suffering from overcapacity.

Before the European Court of Justice, counsel for the European Commission argued that the market for GET parts was not glutted, as Mr Cook contended; but the court found the Commission's evidence for this assertion to be inconclusive. To make such an assertion with confidence, the Commission would have had to undertake a 'complex analysis of the sub-sector in question', the court found. No such analysis had been attempted. Companies that might have been able to contribute to such an analysis, such as William Cook plc, were never consulted. The court insisted the Commission should look again at Pyrsa.[46] Andrew Cook argues that officials at the European Commission have never had their heart in the task of clamping down on state aids. He is pleased with his legal victory, but worries that the most damaging state aids are those that are approved, entirely legally, by the Commission under the Treaty of Rome. The motives of national self-interest that have driven the recent growth of the Community make state aids even harder to control, he argues. 'The more recent joiners ... , such as Spain and Portugal and Greece, have joined specifically for what they can get out of it – i.e. money grants, regional aid.'[47]

He is upset that the ECJ should direct the Commission to reinvestigate aid granted to Pyrsa by local government in Spain, but should raise no doubts over a further Ptas 975.9 million granted by the national government. The aid from Madrid was approved by the Commission under Article 92(3)(a) of the Treaty of Rome because Teruel is deemed to have an 'abnormally low standard of living' and 'serious underemployment'. Nothing obliged the Commission to investigate levels of capacity utilisation in the market to which this aid related.

'The question of capacity *is* relevant', argued Sir Leon Brittan, the then competition commissioner, when I eventually succeeded in raising Mr Cook's case with him in April 1992. 'This is one case out of thousands. You are building rather a lot on one case.' He proceeded to list a string of cases in which the Commission had only approved state aids in return for undertakings from the recipients that capacity would be reduced.

EU STATE AIDS POLICY: SUCCESS OR FAILURE?

Are the European Commission's putative efforts to rein back state aids a farce, as Andrew Cook contends? Or is real progress being made towards smoothing out competitive inequalities caused by subsidies?

The case for the prosecution looks pretty strong. Its witnesses even include some senior Commission officials. Take Joseph Gilchrist and David Deacon, two high-ranking DGIV officials who have argued that 'in practically all cases of rescue of major ailing companies, whatever the industrial sector, the Commission has approved all, or the major part of the aid'.[48] That was in 1990: the Commission's subsequent approval of generous restructuring aid to Bull suggests little has changed since.

The essential problem confronting the European Commission is that the disbursal of aid is one of the most jealously guarded prerogatives of government. To put it crudely, every democratic government knows – or soon learns – the value of bribing the electorate with its own money. This is why Article 92 of the Treaty of Rome contains such a long list of exceptions to the basic prohibition on state aids. The medicine needed to be well watered before it would be palatable.

Over the past decade the European Commission has preached the need to limit state aids with increasing vehemence. Its exhortations have often fallen on deaf ears.

Governments have preferred to risk the ire of Sir Leon Brittan or Karel Van Miert than that of their electors.

To judge EU state aids policy a failure on the basis of the cases described in this chapter would, however, be a mistake. Press coverage of state aid issues tends to polarise the debate: newspaper articles refer to the latest 'showdown' between the tough-talking competition commissioner of the day and a recalcitrant member state government. The irresistible force against the immovable object. In the event, the force of the commissioner's rhetoric frequently proves far from irresistible, as we have seen.

This polarisation is misleading. EU member state governments have their own reasons for wishing to reduce state aid. During the course of 1993, the onset of recession in Continental Europe sent national budget deficits soaring. In Italy, one of the most generous providers of state aid to industry, a former central banker, Carlo Azeglio Ciampi, was appointed prime minister. Politically his task was to carry on the business of government with Italy's corruption purge in full spate. His economic task was scarcely easier: to reduce the massive state handouts that had kept former governments in power.

In Belgium, home country to competition commissioner Karel Van Miert, the budget deficit was spiralling out of control. Salomon Brothers International in London predicted in 1993 that Belgium's national debt would hit 147 per cent of GDP the following year. In 1993, the cost of servicing the national debt was already costing the Belgian government around 40 per cent of its budget.[49] To be sure, the main culprit was a cradle-to-grave welfare state that had grown far faster than the Belgian economy, but generous state aids to Belgian industry also took their toll. At Ecu 1,655 per person employed, Belgian state aid to manufacturing industry ranked as the third highest in Europe between 1988 and 1990, after Italy and Ireland.

In such circumstances, the success of the European Union's state aids policy depended on the relative strengths of two opposing forces. As unemployment rose, member state governments came under increasing pressure to help troubled companies preserve jobs. At the same time, lower tax revenues and mounting social security costs were pushing up budget deficits, forcing governments to review public expenditure.

In late 1993, it looked as if the advocates of budgetary prudence were gaining the upper hand. At the end of November, British chancellor Kenneth Clarke unveiled a budget of notable austerity, raising taxes and slashing public spending in an attempt to trim a public sector borrowing requirement then running at a billion pounds a week. A few days later, France's National Assembly debated a five year plan designed to reduce the state's budget deficit from 4.5 per cent of GDP in 1993 to 2.5 per cent in 1997.

It looked, then, as if the European Commission might be pushing at an open door in seeking to persuade EU member state governments to reduce state aids. Of course, the bill for propping up the odd steel company or textile manufacturer did not compare with the cost of the huge social security or national health programmes that had proved the real drain on member state finances, but as successive British Conservative governments had shown, determination to reduce subsidies to industry tends to accompany a resolve to push back the frontiers of the welfare state.

Most importantly of all, ambitious privatisation programmes unveiled by governments across Europe promised to reduce state aid to industry in the long term. State aids were never going to be easy to control in those countries where the state was the main shareholder in many of the biggest industrial groups. Despite the politicians' protests, the manipulation of these state holdings for political ends was really the *raison d'être* of state ownership. Sir Leon Brittan described state ownership as mysterious and mystical because he was working on the Commission's assumption that state-owned firms should always act on the same commercial principles as privately-owned firms. Member state governments did not always share that assumption.

The privatisation of companies such as the Italian steelmaker Ilva or the French computer manufacturer Bull was clearly going to pose short-term problems for the Commission. Who would buy these loss-making dinosaurs? In the long term the disposal of such holdings will make it easier for the Commission to enforce a strict and impartial policy on state aids across the European Union.

The pressures on EU member states to reduce state aids come less from without than from within. Competition commissioners have kept up the rhetoric and their officials have worked hard to expose infringements of Article 92 of the Treaty of Rome. However, the Commission's best chance of success lies in the dawning realisation among EU member state governments that generous state aids to industry are not in their best economic interests. If the European Commission eventually wins the great state aids debate, it will be because its opponents have thrown in the sponge.

NOTES

1. Interview with author, 3 June 1993.
2. ECJ Case C-5/89, *Commission* v. *Germany*.
3. *XXIst Report on Competition Policy*, April 1992.
4. *European Economy*, September 1991, page 53.
5. Commission press release IP(93) 128, 24 February 1993.
6. Interview with author, 12 August 1993.
7. Lewis Carroll, *Alice Through the Looking Glass*.
8. ECJ Case 248/84.
9. ECJ Case C-305/89 Alfa Romeo.
10. ECJ Cases 47/69, 78/76 and 259/85.
11. ECJ Case 102/87.
12. *XXIInd Report on Competition Policy*, May 1993, chapter 3.1.A, section 8.8.
13. *XXth Report on Competition Policy*, page 180, item 305.
14. *Les Echos*, 15 April 1993, page 20.
15. Commission press release IP(92)539, 2 July 1993, page 2.
16. Peter Sutherland, *Ier janvier* 1993 : *ce qui va changer en Europe*. Presses Universitaires de France, November 1988, page 59.
17. Speech to the Centre of European Policy Studies, Brussels, 7 December 1992.
18. Interview with author, 15 April 1992.
19. Interview with author, 3 June 1993.
20. *XXIst Report on Competition Policy*, April 1992, chapter 1.I., section 3.2, page 15.
21. European Commission, *Third Survey on State Aids*, 3 July 1992.
22. Speech given at Centre of European Policy Studies, Brussels, 7 December 1992.
23. Credit Suisse First Boston, *Europe: Core versus periphery*, December 1992.
24. Interview with author, 25 August 1992.
25. Interview with author, 17 June 1993.

26. Interview with author, 15 April 1992.

27. Jean Peyrelevade, *Pour un capitalisme intelligent*. Editions Grasset et Fasquelle, 1993, page 85.

28. Martin Bangemann, *Meeting the Global Challenge*. Kogan Page, 1992, page 124.

29. *XXIst Report on Competition Policy*, April 1992, chapter 3.I.A, section 8.10, page 286.

30. ECJ Case 70/72, judgement of 12 July 1973, *Commission of the EC* v. *Federal Republic of Germany*.

31. ECJ Case C-305/89 Alfa Romeo.

32. Commission press release WE/21/93.

33. Article 171, Treaty on European Union ('the Maastricht Treaty').

34. *XXIst Report on Competition Policy*, April 1992, chapter 3.I.A, section 2.2, page 179.

35. *Ibid.*, chapter 3.I.A, section 4.e.5, page 224.

36. ECJ Case 301/87 *France* v. *Commission* ('the Boussac case').

37. Letter from European Commission secretary general David Williamson to member states, 4 March 1991, in annex II of *XXIst Report on Competition Policy*, page 302.

38. *XXIst Report on Competition Policy*, April 1992, chapter 1.V, section 3.4, page 77.

39. *Ibid.*, chapter 1.I, section 3.2, page 15.

40. Directive 80/723/EEC.

41. ECJ judgement, 16 June 1993, C-325/91.

42. Interview with author, 3 June 1993.

43. *XXIst Report on Competition Policy*, April 1992, chapter 3.I.A, section 2.2, page 179.

44. Interview with author, 15 April 1992.

45. UNICE information bulletin, no. 4, 1993, page 12.

46. ECJ Case C-198/91, court judgement 19 May 1993.

47. Interview with author, 13 February 1992.

48. Joseph Gilchrist and David Deacon, 'Curbing Subsidies', in P. Montagnon (ed.), *European Competition Policy*. Royal Institute of International Affairs/Pinter Publishers, 1990.

49. *Wall Street Journal Europe*, 30 November 1993.

CHAPTER 5

PURSUING A GRIEVANCE: FIRST CHOOSE YOUR BATTLEFIELD

SUBSIDIARITY AND EU COMPETITION POLICY

The authority of the European Commission in questions of EU competition policy has been hard won. New battles are fought to maintain and develop this authority every year. It might therefore be thought that the first port of call for the aggrieved victim of anti-competitive practices should be the Commission.

Not so. The Commission is, in this respect, the victim of its own success. The empire surveyed by the satraps of DGIV is now so huge, so sprawling, that the satraps feel obliged to limit the number of complaints addressed to them. In conversation they regularly lament being bombarded with what they regard as frivolous complaints. These are conscientiously filed, and soon forgotten.

So unless you feel your case is a really interesting or important one, you would be well advised not to complain to the Commission, at least not at first. The Commission, by its own admission, is only interested in complaints that have 'particular political, economic or legal significance for the Community'.[1] The Commission's right to ignore complaints that it finds uninteresting was upheld by the Court of First Instance in September 1992.[2]

Of course, a complaint is never frivolous to the complainant, nor uninteresting. Nevertheless, complainants should be able to stand back and ask themselves: does my grievance possess political, economic or legal significance for the Community?

If in doubt, you would probably be better off suing your competitor in your own national courts. This has not been a very popular course in the past because national courts have been ill-equipped to handle such complex cases; nevertheless the Commission has become keen of late that competition cases should be heard, whenever possible, at national level. The Commission has two reasons for this new-found enthusiasm. The first is that national courts stand to relieve it of part of its workload, leaving officials free to concentrate on what they regard as the more important cases. The second is that it enables the Commission to profess its faith in subsidiarity, the idea that decisions should be taken 'as closely as possible to the citizen', to quote one of the few ringing phrases in the Maastricht Treaty. There are reasons to suppose this profession of faith is less than sincere, as we shall see.

FOUR ADVANTAGES OF NATIONAL COURTS

There are four good reasons why national courts will often be able to give fuller redress to the victims of anti-competitive behaviour than the Commission can do. These are supplied in a notice published by the Commission in February 1993 and later cited in the *XXIInd Report on Competition Policy* as proof of the Commission's enthusiasm for subsidiarity. They are as follows:

1. *Compensation.* Only national courts can award compensation for losses suffered as a result of behaviour that is in breach of Articles 85 or 86. The Commission cannot do this. (The Commission suggests, a little tendentiously, that this makes national courts more fearsome adversaries of wrongdoing than the Commission itself. 'Companies are more likely to avoid infringements of the Community competition rules if they risk having to pay damages or interest in such an event', the Commission argues. This overlooks the fact that the Commission can fine malefactors pretty heavily – up to 10 per cent of their previous year's turnover.)
2. *Speed.* National courts can impose injunctions on defendants that will end any infringement of the competition rules far faster than the Commission could manage.
3. *Combined actions.* A national court may hear claims under EU law and claims under national law together. The Commission is only empowered to investigate claims under EU law.
4. *Costs.* In many member states the courts are able to award legal costs against defendants if wrongdoing is proved. The Commission cannot do this.

ONE BIG DRAWBACK OF NATIONAL COURTS

In hearing cases brought under Article 85 of the Treaty of Rome, national courts have one big drawback: they can judge the merits of the plaintiff's allegations, but they cannot judge the merits of the defendant's most likely defense. Only the Commission can do that.

The defence is enshrined in Article 85(3) of the Treaty, which enables the Commission to overlook infringements of Article 85(1) in certain cases (see chapter 1). Brussels still has exclusive authority to grant exemptions to Article 85(1) under the terms of Article 85(3). In other words, a national court can rule that a market association or distribution agreement distorts competition and is therefore illegal, but it cannot waive this judgement on the grounds that the association or agreement has countervailing economic or technical advantages that will benefit consumers.

This two-tier arrangement creates many problems. Under EU law the only defence against proceedings under Article 85(1) of the Treaty of Rome is contained in Article 85(3). Any putative cartel would be highly likely to deploy this defence. Yet national courts are not empowered to assess its merits. In his last major speech as competition commissioner, Sir Leon Brittan admitted that this remains a 'major obstacle ... to enforcement of Community rules at a national level'.[3]

The Commission appears in no hurry to remove this obstacle. Sir Leon Brittan was content to applaud the progress that member states had made in developing their own national competition rules. Furthermore, he suggested that, as soon as these national regimes had had a chance to mature, the Commission might be willing to hand over to national courts the right to interpret Article 85(3) of the Treaty of Rome. Since that speech, though, senior officials at DGIV have played down the likelihood of this happening soon: the Commission's enthusiasm for subsidiarity has its limits.

The reason commonly given for this backtracking is that different EU member states have widely differing experiences of enforcing competition policy. Sir Leon Brittan did not want the playing field that has been rolled smooth by the Commission over thirty years to be disfigured by differing standards of national anti-trust enforcement. He foresaw companies indulging in forum shopping around the European Union. There is no evidence to suggest that his successor, Karel Van Miert, disagrees.

In fact, there are ways around this problem as it affects national courts, although the Commission itself admits that the procedure can be complex.[4] The solutions are spelled out in the Commission's notice of February 1993. First, national courts must establish whether the Commission has already exempted the agreement or concerted practice that is the subject of the complaint. An exemption may have been granted individually to the defendant(s), or the agreement may be the subject of a block exemption, in which latter case no individual exemption is required (individual and block exemptions are discussed in chapter 1).

An individual exemption may take one of two forms. It may be an official Commission decision or a comfort letter sent to the defendant. Although the European Court of Justice (ECJ) has ruled that a comfort letter does not bind national courts, it has also said that national courts are free to take such a letter into account.[5] If the defendant possesses such a letter, the national court is unlikely to pursue the matter further.

If the agreement or concerted practice has not been exempted, the national court must establish whether exemption has even been sought. Council Regulation 17 of 6 February 1962 obliges companies to notify the Commission of agreements that might be covered by Article 85(3) of the Treaty of Rome. If exemption has not been sought, it cannot be claimed. The national court can proceed to a judgement on the plaintiff's case.

THE COMMISSION'S OFFER TO NATIONAL COURTS

The Commission has pledged to give national courts as much help as it can in making decisions in cases of EU competition law. It has offered courts the chance to consult it on points of law.[6] British courts are not used to seeking advice on points of law from administrative bodies (although the practice is known on the Continent) and the legal status of the Commission's advice could be open to challenge in a British court.

In the last resort, a national court always has the right to appeal to the European Court of Justice for clarification of a point of law. This right, enshrined in Article 177 of the Treaty of Rome, is proving more and more popular as national courts broach delicate issues of EU competition policy. In 1992, the Court of Justice issued over one hundred judgements on references for preliminary rulings, as they are called. Indeed, some officials at DGIV suggest that the ECJ is the real motor for progress in some fields of competition policy, offering interpretations of the Treaty of Rome that go well beyond what the Commission itself would dare to propose (see chapter 8).

However, harnessing the power of this motor can be a laborious task. Referrals to the ECJ take a long time to be heard – commonly adding about eighteen months to the length of cases heard in national courts. Preliminary rulings on points of law from the ECJ may push back the frontiers of EU competition law, but for the plaintiff in a case brought before a national court, the wait could prove very tedious.

THE RISKS OF SUBSIDIARITY

Subsidiarity, like democracy, is an attractive idea that is often untidy and irksome in practice. Even that may be overstating its charms: many representatives of European business regard subsidiarity as a potentially disastrous idea when applied to EU competition policy. Thus Hans Kroeger, director responsible for company affairs (including competition policy) at the European employers' federation, UNICE, professes enthusiasm for subsidiarity in most aspects of EU policy but doubts it has much value in competition policy.[7] UNICE has been a strong defender of the 'one-stop shop' principle enshrined in the 1989 merger regulation, which takes large-scale merger cases out of the jurisdiction of national competition authorities.

Likewise, Peter Morgan, former director-general of Britain's Institute of Directors, endorses the need for a supranational authority in competition policy. 'In the whole area of competition policy . . . the IOD does not support subsidiarity. We want the law of the Commission to run right through the Community, without exception. In this context, application of Article 92 concerning the use of state aids and subsidies is particularly important.'[8]

Certainly it is hard to see how the power to approve or reject state aids could be devolved. Member states can hardly be expected to police themselves in this matter. More broadly, though, many European businesses fear that too much subsidiarity in competition policy could weaken its effect and create nasty bumps in the playing field that has been so painstakingly levelled.

As far as Articles 85 and 86 are concerned, Sir Leon Brittan stoutly defended the 'effect on trade' test as the 'logically correct limitation of Community competence'. His argument was that 'if an anti-competitive agreement or practice appreciably affects trade within the Community, the Commission is the authority best placed, in terms of linguistic resources and fact-finding powers, to examine the case'.[9]

For all these reasons, it was not surprising that Sir Leon reacted so strongly when, in early 1992, Commission president Jacques Delors raised the possibility that some of DGIV's powers might be stripped away to placate critics of the 'Brussels bureaucracy' around the European Union. Sir Leon wanted to tackle the sensitive issue of subsidiarity in his own way and at his own pace.

SUBSIDIARITY HERE TO STAY

One thing is certain: the issue will not go away. During 1992, Article 3b of the Maastricht Treaty, enshrining the concept of subsidiarity, became a rallying point for those defenders of the Union who wished to rebut accusations that excessive powers were being transferred to Brussels. Article 3b stipulates that 'in areas which do not fall within its exclusive competence, the Community shall take action, in accordance with the principle of subsidiarity, only if and in so far as the objectives of the proposed action cannot be sufficiently achieved by the member states'. The article goes on to suggest that EU action, rather than member state action, might be appropriate where the 'scale or effects of the proposed action [can] be better achieved by the Community'.

The application of Article 3b to EU competition policy arouses strong and conflicting passions among member states. Britain, one of the strongest advocates of subsidiarity in most areas, was broadly happy with the approach adopted by Sir Leon Brittan. France – which advocates the exercise from Brussels of a range of powers to regulate working conditions – was not. Thus in alluding to competition policy as a candidate for the more rigorous application of subsidiarity, Jacques Delors was putting his British critics in a tight corner.

Narrow political considerations aside, subsidiarity clearly has a major role to play in improving the effectiveness of EU competition policy. The Commission is determined to keep the initiative in deciding awkward and contentious cases, and rightly so. Its ability to do that, however, will depend on the number of routine cases it can palm off on to national courts. Resources at the Commission are limited and new tasks are being discovered every year.

Subsidiarity, for Sir Leon Brittan, was a means of developing 'a flexible and efficient system of resource management' between the Commission and member states. The prize for DGIV remains alluring. Instead of becoming bogged down in the minutiae of hundreds of national cases with limited European Union repercussions, the Commission could concentrate instead on what Sir Leon called the 'detection and prohibition of really important cartels, abuses of dominant positions, and the opening of previously monopolised sectors to free competition'.[10]

Subsidiarity need not be a stick with which member states can beat the Commission.

Effectively applied, it can be a means to achieve ever more ambitious competition policy goals within the single market. This idea has been espoused enthusiastically by Karel Van Miert. The *XXIInd Report on Competition Policy*, published five months into Van Miert's term of office in May 1993, refers to the enthusiasm for subsidiarity as one of two new developments that had influenced the Commission's work in the competition field in 1992. The other, more ominously, was the slowdown in Europe's economies.

NOTES

1. *Notice on co-operation between national courts and the Commission in applying Articles 85 and 86 of the EEC Treaty*, OJ No. C 39, 13 February 1993.
2. ECJ Case T-24/90 *Automec* v. *Commission*, judgement of 18 September 1992.
3. Speech to Centre of European Policy Studies, Brussels, 7 December 1992.
4. Article 32 of the Commission's February 1993 notice on co-operation between national courts and the Commission, *op. cit.* at n. 1.
5. ECJ Case 99/79 *Lancome* v. *Etos* (1980) ECR 2511, paragraph 11.
6. Article 38 of the notice, *op. cit.* at n. 1.
7. Comments made at Club de Bruxelles conference on EC competition policy, Brussels, 6–7 May 1993.
8. Speech delivered at European Policy Forum, London, 3 November 1992.
9. Speech to Centre of European Policy Studies, 7 December 1992. See also chapter 2.
10. *Ibid.*

CHAPTER 6

SECTORAL ANALYSES: CARS, STEEL, INSURANCE, BANKING

CARS

The motor industry is western Europe's largest employer and one of its most troubled. Pressures on car-makers to stifle competition wherever possible grew in the course of 1993. European sales were already plummeting by April of that year and Peugeot chairman Jacques Calvet claimed not to have seen such a shock to the market since 1973–1975.[1]

Broadly speaking, conflicts between car-makers and the EU competition authorities have taken two forms. Either the Commission has demanded the repayment of state aid, as in cases involving Rover, Renault and Alfa Romeo (see chapter 4), or it has pounced on anti-competitive clauses contained in car-makers' standard dealership contracts.

Sections of this book might suggest that, in competition policy terms, the British are always on the side of the angels – or at least on the same side as the European Commission. State aids in Britain run at lower levels than in any other state in the European Union, and Britain has needed no encouragement from Brussels to liberalise her telecommunications and airline markets. However, the recent history of Britain's biggest car-maker, Rover, shows that UK companies can just as easily fall foul of DGIV as Continental European companies. On two occasions, Rover's then parent company, British Aerospace (BAe), suffered bruising encounters with the EU competition authorities over its car-making subsidiary.

BAe's first contretemps with the Commission related to sweeteners it received from the British government in 1988 as an inducement to buy Rover. In May 1993, BAe repaid the money, with interest – £57.6 million altogether. (The case is described in chapter 4.)

The second contretemps occurred in November 1993. Although far less costly than the previous problem, it was nonetheless embarrassing for BAe. The Commission found Rover had committed a serious breach of Article 85 of the Treaty of Rome in limiting its dealers' ability to offer discounts on cars sold between May 1986 and October 1990. Such is the glacial speed of DGIV's deliberation on such issues that the Commission only condemned the company's restrictive practices three years after they had been abandoned.[2]

Like a tolerant judge sentencing a felon whose felony has cost him his job and his position in society, the Commission concluded that Rover had been punished enough for its misconduct. The company was potentially exposed to lawsuits in the UK courts from car-buyers who believed they had lost out as a result of the restrictions on discounts applied to the Rover 200, 400 and 800 ranges – although it appeared unlikely that customers would be able to quantify their losses. Rover had also agreed to donate £1 million to fund two independent projects: one offering consumers information on dealer margins, car prices across the EU and insurance and other running costs; and the other providing new car assessments for people with special needs, such as the elderly and disabled.

The first of these projects may mean that, in future, car manufacturers trying to coerce their UK dealers into withholding discounts or special offers will be shooting themselves in the foot. Through the new Association for Consumer Research database, consumers will be able to quantify dealer margins and thus work out the potential for obtaining discounts.

Rover is not the only European car manufacturer that has found itself in trouble with the Commission over the terms of its dealership contracts. Indeed, few issues have given the Commission more trouble. Consumer groups have held the current EU rules on motor dealerships to blame for massive variations in the price of the same model of car across the European Union.

The subject of motor dealerships is covered by a controversial block exemption to Article 85(1) of the Treaty of Rome, which came into force on 1 July 1985 and will expire on 30 June 1995. The purpose of the block exemption regulation is to allow car-makers to enter into exclusive distribution agreements with dealers in defined areas. In the years up to 1985, the Commission had been inundated with individual applications for exemption from Article 85(1), on the grounds that exclusive dealerships satisfied Article 85(3), namely they contribute 'to improving the ... distribution of goods ... while allowing consumers a fair share of the resulting benefit'.

The Commission spelt out its reasoning for granting a block exemption in clause 4 of the regulation. Exclusive and selective distribution clauses were, it claimed, 'indispensable measures of rationalization in the motor vehicle industry' because motor vehicles require expert maintenance and repair, not always in the same place. The Commission argued that this necessitated specialist servicing contracts, which 'on grounds of capacity and efficiency alone ... cannot be extended to an unlimited number of dealers and repairers'.[3]

Reasonable enough, it might seem. However, seven years later, Sir Leon Brittan grew concerned that the motor industry's exclusive distribution contracts were permitting the survival of major car price differences across the Community. A Commission investigation, published in May 1992, revealed that certain models produced by Ford, Honda, Mazda, Peugeot and Volkswagen were at least 40 per cent more expensive in some parts of the European Union than in others. The UK and Spain were the countries with the highest prices; yet a notice annexed to the 1985 block exemption regulation stipulated that the price variation of a single model across the Union should never exceed 12 per cent.[4] Sir Leon Brittan acted fast. He wrote to all car producers in the EU, warning them that the 1985 block exemption was in danger of falling into disrepute and asking them to take immediate action. In particular, they should:

1. Write to all their dealers in the Community, informing them that they were free to sell cars to other approved distributors throughout the single market, as well as to end-users in other member states. In other words, they were to make it clear that parallel exports were permitted.
2. Ensure that cars were available to meet demand ensuing from 1 above. In particular, this meant supplying, where requested, model specifications and options not normally demanded in the dealer's home state. Thus if a German dealer requested Volkswagen to supply it with right-hand-drive VW Golfs, the company could not refuse.
3. Publish price lists every three months to enable consumers to compare prices in different member states for models with the same specification.
4. Work to ensure that price differentials on the same model across the Community should never exceed 18 per cent at any one time, and not exceed 12 per cent over a period of time.

Despite Sir Leon's assurance in his letter that the measures listed above were 'in everybody's interest', car manufacturers were not happy. Their trade association, ACEA, argued that the disclosure requirements were unnecessarily burdensome,[5] and Jacques Calvet, the outspoken chairman of Peugeot, suggested that the price reporting requirement amounted to price control.[6]

Sir Leon's response was characteristically robust. 'The allegation is absurd', he told the French financial daily *Les Echos* in October 1992. 'There is no question of price control. If Mr Calvet is incapable of telling the difference between price transparency and price control, he is not the man of great intelligence that I have always believed him to be.'

A few months later, the car manufacturers had been won round. Through their trade association they agreed to compile, every six months, comparable pricing data for one widely sold car model in each car line. A standard form would show prices before and after tax and provide details of the extra cost of major options, such as air conditioning, automatic gearboxes, power steering and automated braking systems. Prices for right-hand-drive versions – a major cause of complaint among British consumers seeking to purchase cars abroad – were also to be included.

The Commission's report on car price variations around the Community, published in May 1992, was already yielding results a year later. The Commission's *XXIInd Report on Competition Policy*, published in May 1993, noted a fall in the number of complaints from consumers wishing to buy cars in other member states. In particular, would-be purchasers of right-hand-drive models seemed far less irate.[7]

Meanwhile, disputes over distribution contracts between the Commission and individual car-makers rumbled on. One of the more acrimonious concerned Mr Calvet's company, Peugeot. In early 1992 the Commission found Peugeot had acted illegally in instructing its dealers in Belgium, France and Luxembourg to withhold supplies from Eco System, a company based in Rouen in France which helped French consumers buy cars in Belgium and Luxembourg.

Peugeot argued that it was entitled to withhold supplies from Eco System under the 1985 block exemption regulation. The regulation permits car manufacturers to ban their distributors from selling cars to resellers outside the manufacturer's approved distribution network. The Commission pointed out, that, under the regulation, distributors are free to sell cars on to intermediaries acting on specific instructions from end-users. Eco System worked to written mandates from named clients. In April 1993 the Court of First Instance found Peugeot had acted illegally in refusing to supply cars, through its dealers, to Eco System. The court rejected Peugeot's claim that Eco System was acting as a reseller.[8]

The European Union's rules on motor distribution contracts have caused Europe's car-makers a number of problems. Could they have been avoided? In Peugeot's case the answer is probably no. The company was sure enough of its ground to take its case right through to the European Court of First Instance. It did not accept the Commission's argument that it had misinterpreted the block exemption regulation.

In the case of Rover, however, the Commission's displeasure might well have been avoided. There was never any question of the company's action being covered under the 1985 block exemption. Rover was clearly in breach of Article 85 (1) and it did not pretend otherwise. In late 1992 Rover announced that it was implementing a wide-ranging anti-trust compliance programme. If it had done this in 1986, the anti-competitive clauses would probably never have found their way into the company's distribution contracts.

Europe's car-makers face a broader challenge from the EU competition authorities. The block exemption regulation for motor dealerships expires on 30 June 1995. The task of renewing it, or of deciding what should replace it, will fall to newly appointed as competition commissioner Karel Van Miert. Europe's car manufacturers know they will need to tread carefully if they are not to lose their right to choose their own exclusive distributors. The 1985 block exemption regulation defends exclusive distribution clauses as 'indispensable measures of rationalization in the motor vehicle industry'. The evidence suggests this defence has been much abused.

STEEL

The recent history of the European steel industry can scarcely be considered a triumph for EU competition policy regulators. In few industries has free competition been so notable for its absence. Indulgent governments have pumped money into inefficient state-owned steel producers for political ends – usually the maintenance of employment in backward regions, such as southern Italy. The laws of supply and demand have ceased to function and overcapacity has become endemic. The management at many of Europe's biggest steel companies has become adept at lobbying, but inept at producing steel economically.

Seasoned observers of the industry have likened Europe's steel producers to the restored Bourbon monarchs after the French Revolution: they seem to have experienced everything but learned nothing. In 1993 there was talk of a return to the 'manifest crisis' measures undertaken in the late 1970s and early 1980s when Brussels practically took over the running of Europe's steel industry, imposing production quotas and price and import controls.[9]

A glance at newspaper coverage of the earlier crisis reveals an industry where time appears to have stood still. On 1 November 1980 the *Financial Times* reported that the German government would be 'demanding at Council of Ministers meetings ... that the whole issue of State subsidies to steelmakers and restructuring measures to reduce levels of unused capacity should be tackled immediately'.

Twelve years later, state aids and high levels of unused capacity were still plaguing the European steel industry. In November 1992, industrial affairs commissioner Martin Bangemann appointed a special advisor, Fernand Braun, to negotiate capacity cuts with European steelmakers. The scale of the closures sought by the Commission was frightening. In 1992, EU steelmakers produced 114 million tonnes of hot rolled steel and 132 million tonnes of crude steel: the Commission sought plant closures that would reduce hot rolled steel capacity by between 19 and 26 million tonnes, and crude steel capacity by over 30 million tonnes.

In reality, the European steel industry had changed much during the 1980s, but not fast enough. Under the Commission's so-called Davignon Plan (named after industrial affairs commissioner Viscount Etienne Davignon) hot rolled steel production capacity fell from 194.5 million tonnes in 1980 to 165 million tonnes in 1988. Employment also fell, from 672,000 to 409,000.[10] However, demand for steel in Europe was on a downward path which was steeper than the industry recognised. During the brief boom period of the late 1980s it looked as if the earlier cuts would prove sufficient, but from 1991 recession returned with a vengeance.

Throughout 1993, Mr Braun and his colleagues from the Commission negotiated a series of deals with Europe's steelmakers. Heavy cuts in capacity were traded for generous state aid packages. No-one seemed happy. The less efficient steel producers, such as Italy's Ilva and Spain's Corporacion de la Siderurgica Integral (CSI), complained that the Commission was being too tough, forcing redundancies in areas of high unemployment during a recession. The more efficient steel producers, such as British Steel and Usinor Sacilor of France, complained that the Commission was too generous, approving state aids to lame duck steel companies without enforcing adequate production cuts. 'Virtue does not pay', lamented Usinor Sacilor chairman Francis Mer in December 1993.[11]

It appeared the Commission could not win. Competition commissioner Karel Van Miert took office in January 1993 protesting that he would not sacrifice the European steel industry on an altar of neo-Thatcherite free market dogma,[12] but within six months he was admitting he had been dubbed 'Sir Leon Van Miert' by steelmakers in Spain and Italy who could see no change of policy from his predecessor, the former Thatcher cabinet member, Sir Leon Brittan.[13]

The apparently endless crises of the European steel industry reveal the weakness of the European Commission in enforcing free competition when confronted by powerful vested interests in member states. Cheap imports into the European Union from Eastern Europe have added to the strains on EU steel producers, but the Commission's main problems are home-grown. Three problems in particular have dogged its progress:

1. The rules of the game are lax. The steel industry is not governed by the Treaty of Rome, but by the earlier European Coal and Steel Community Treaty (also known as the Paris Treaty) signed in 1951. In Article 4(c), the Paris Treaty appears to lay down strict rules on state aid, but later articles undermine its effect.
2. Many of the leading companies are state-owned and have been kept afloat by indulgent governments for years. Not all state-owned companies are inefficient: France's Usinor Sacilor is widely respected in the industry; but companies like Ilva in Italy or CSI in Spain would never have survived in one piece in the private sector without subsidies.
3. Chronic overcapacity has meant that subsidies lavished on one producer deny business to another producer. Hence Mr Mer's comment about virtue not paying. The danger in such a situation is that EU member states could abandon the free market altogether and join a subsidy race.

To understand how Europe's steel producers have repeatedly found themselves in crisis, it is worth examining the Commission's problems in a little more detail.

The Paris Treaty – a protectionist's charter?

At first glance, the 1951 ECSC Treaty appears as clear as the tablets of stone brought down by Moses from Mount Sinai. State aids and subsidies are condemned with almost Old Testament fervour. Article 4(c) declares 'subsidies or aids granted by States, or special charges imposed by States . . . incompatible with the common market'. They are accordingly to be 'abolished and prohibited' within the six-nation European Coal and Steel Community.

Sadly, the ban on state aids contained in the Paris Treaty has fared even worse than the biblical Ten Commandments. European governments have continued to subsidise their steel and coal industries massively. In September 1991, the European Commission admitted what European steelmakers and their governments had known for years: the ban on state aids contained in Article 4(c) of the Paris Treaty 'now has little practical relevance'.[14]

The rot started with the treaty itself. Member states have latched onto Article 95 of the Paris Treaty as a means of sidestepping Article 4(c) and justifying state aids to their steelmakers. On the face of it, Article 95 does not read like a get-out clause at all. Indeed, it is very hard to know, on first reading, what to make of it. Article 95 would doubtless qualify for a golden bull award from the Campaign for Plain English. It runs for three hundred words and begins:

> In all cases not provided for in this Treaty where it becomes apparent that a decision or recommendation of the High Authority is necessary to attain, within the common market in coal and steel and in accordance with Article 5, one of the objectives of the Community set out in Articles 2, 3 and 4, the decision may be taken or the recommendation made with the unanimous assent of the Council and after the Consultative Committee has been consulted.

The most curious feature of Article 95 is the way it undermines Article 4(c) while claiming to buttress it. It refers to measures 'necessary to attain ... objectives ... set out in Articles 2,3 and 4'; and later on it stipulates that any new rules created to deal with 'unforeseen difficulties' in the common markets for coal and steel 'must not conflict with the provisions of Articles 2, 3 and 4'.

Yet for more than forty years Article 95 has served member state governments as a key with which to unlock Article 4(c). As the Commission admitted in early 1992, 'Article 95 has been used to derogate from the prohibition [against state aids], in particular in order to introduce aid codes laying down Community rules for aid to the steel industry.'[15]

The ECSC Treaty is due to expire in 2002. From then on the Commission will be able to treat steel like any other industry. Until then, member state governments will continue to be tempted to protect inefficient steel producers by calling upon the Commission to approve state aid schemes sanctioned by the treaty.

State ownership – the root of the problem?

In the early 1980s, British Steel was widely regarded as an industrial basket case. Its products were uncompetitive on world markets; much of its plant was obsolete; its losses were borne by the British taxpayer and those losses were very large.

British Steel did not become lean and fit overnight. Tough decisions were taken long before the company's privatisation in 1988; and although the closure of the Ravenscraig plant in Scotland in July 1992 would have been well nigh impossible if the company had remained under state ownership, the political outcry was still deafening. Far less efficient steel mills than Ravenscraig remain in operation under state control in Italy and Spain.

In 1993 the Italian and French governments committed themselves to following British Steel's lead and privatising their biggest steel producers, Ilva and Usinor Sacilor. The two companies presented two very different faces of state ownership. Usinor Sacilor had succeeded in convincing the Commission that capital injections made, directly or indirectly, by the French state were not state aid because a private sector investor might have done exactly the same.[16] Ilva's case for massive capital injections and debt write-offs was far weaker and was repeatedly rejected by the Commission (see case study).

The privatisation of these major steel companies, along with other state-owned firms in Spain, Germany and Portugal, holds out the prospect that commercial logic will finally replace politics as the guiding star of the European steel industry. The process is likely to be messy, with accusations that governments are offering buyers sweeteners as inducements to take on inefficient plant. In the end, though, privatisation should make life easier for the Commission and for those companies which, like British Steel, have enhanced productivity but failed to reap the full rewards.

Ongoing problems

Meanwhile, Karel Van Miert must continue to monitor very carefully the agreements he has reached with EU member state governments. If steel companies do not make the capacity cuts the Commission requires, the whole industry will suffer.

The Commission sees private capital as the key to putting the European steel industry on a sound commercial footing. However, private investors will not be tempted to put money into the European steel industry if state-owned companies can continue to produce steel at uneconomic prices without feeling the normal commercial consequences.

The problems of Europe's steel industry seem to have engaged competition commissioner Karel Van Miert emotionally as well as intellectually. Asked in June 1993 how he would like his stint as competition commissioner to be remembered, he stressed his commitment to resolving the 'steel problem'.[17] He was determined that the European Union should not resurrect the Davignon Plan in any form. In the Commission's view the market-wide production quotas imposed under the Davignon Plan had the effect of sheltering inefficient plant from the full effects of competition. 'We learned from that,' said Mr Van Miert. He vowed too that the Commission would not allow itself to be 'dragged into a policy that might ease the pain for some time and not solve the problem'.

On Friday, 18 December 1993 the European Council of Ministers approved state aids worth Ecu 6.791 billion to state-owned steel producers in Italy, Germany, Spain and Portugal, in return for capacity cuts of over 5 million tonnes. Private steel company chiefs reacted angrily: Ruprecht Vondran of the German steel federation described 18 December as 'a black Friday for the private steel industry in Europe'. Capacity cuts 'will be made on paper only', he claimed.[18]

This did not augur well for the Commission's plans to persuade Europe's private steel producers to cut their production by 25 million tonnes. Clearly Mr Van Miert still had much work to do before he could claim that the European steel industry's long-term problems had been solved once and for all.

Case study
ILVA

'A totally over indebted enterprise which is adding new losses month by month.' The speaker was Ruprecht Vondran, president of the German steel industry federation; the date February 1993. The subject of his diatribe was Ilva, Italy's biggest steel producer and *bête noir* of steel producers throughout northern Europe.

'Nobody knows what its debt position is,' Mr Vondran went on, 'but we believe it is somewhere between DM11 billion and DM14 billion [£4.6 billion to £5.9 billion]. There is no suggestion of bankruptcy: they just go on producing.'[19]

Ilva was a child of strife, born of a stormy relationship between the Italian government and the European Commission in 1989. The company's predecessor, Finsider, had not made a profit in fourteen years. In one of his last acts as competition commissioner, Peter Sutherland approved the liquidation of Finsider on 23 December 1988. Massive debts were written off and Finsider's better-performing business was transferred to Ilva.[20]

The whole of the Commission's six-page decision is eloquent of distrust for the Italian government's bona fides over Ilva. It even went so far as to insist that all plant closures should be rendered irreversible 'by the demolition of the installation concerned or by their disposal outside Europe'. In all, the new company would employ 28 per cent fewer people than Finsider had done, reducing staff from 70,340 to 50,425.

For a couple of years all appeared to go well. Ilva even managed to make a profit in 1989 and 1990. Then the sharp downturn in demand for steel hit the company, along with its competitors around Europe. Ilva plunged to a Lit 500 billion loss in 1991 and a Lit 2,309 billion loss in 1992. The company's debts began to soar. In a gesture that infuriated the Commission, Ilva blamed Brussels for some of its problems, claiming that annual debt financing costs of 5.5 per cent of turnover imposed under the Sutherland plan were too onerous.

In early 1993, Ilva's parent company, Istituto per la Ricostruzione Industriale (IRI), took the remarkable step of appointing a Japanese manager, Hayao Nakamura, to run Ilva. Ilva bruited the fact that Mr Nakamura had previously worked for Nippon Steel, 'the biggest steel group in Japan and the "number one" at the international level'.[21] It omitted to point out that Mr Nakamura had never run a steel-making company: his previous job was selling steel-making equipment for Nippon Steel in Italy.

More ominously, Ilva described Mr Nakamura as having a 'profound awareness of Italy's industrial reality, having lived and worked for more than thirty years in our country'. At least as far as Ilva and its predecessor Finsider were concerned, Italy's industrial reality consisted of chronic losses and state subsidies, and eternal wrangling with the European Commission.

In no time, Mr Nakamura had thrown himself into the fray. Throughout 1993 the battle raged between the new competition commissioner, Karel Van Miert, and the man Ilva had dubbed 'the Italian with almond eyes'. The debate was a familiar one: the Commission sought to enforce sweeping capacity cuts as a precondition for state aid, while the Italians sought to keep plant open wherever possible.

Throughout the summer and autumn of 1993, Mr Van Miert kept up the pressure. In October, Ilva announced that 11,600 more jobs would be shed between 1994 and 1996, taking the total workforce down to around 30,000. However, a compromise deal agreed between Mr Van Miert and Italian industry minister Paolo Savona on 10 December showed a marked softening of the Commission's position. Mr Van Miert had previously been pushing for capacity cuts of 1.7 million tonnes at Ilva's steel plant in Taranto, southern Italy – the largest in Europe. He was now prepared to settle for cuts of 1.2 million tonnes in the plant's nine million tonne a year output.

Ilva's troubles were still far from over, however. The Italian government had ambitious plans to break up and sell off the component businesses of IRI, including those parts of Ilva that could find buyers. It was not clear how much could be sold without sweeteners, and the Commission was on the alert for any financial inducements which might give a private sector buyer an unfair advantage over other steel producers.

Throughout 1993, Italy was in political trauma as the police and judiciary attempted to root out corruption that had been endemic in Italian society for decades. Public sector industry was one of the main breeding grounds for this corruption. The best hope for the Italian steel industry in the future lies not in the negotiating talent of Hayao Nakamura and his colleagues, but in the painful rebirth of Italy's public sector industry into the private sector.

INSURANCE

Insurance is one of Europe's more successful exports. Nowhere else in the world are insurers so international in their outlook. In the United States, American International Group is considered unusual in the range of its interests outside its home country. The Japanese behemoths have, on the whole, preferred to stay at home. European insurers and reinsurers, however, have been laying down roots outside their domestic markets for decades. British and Dutch insurers have long enjoyed a strong presence in the United States: more recently AXA of France and Allianz of Germany have made major US purchases. Mapfre of Spain has subsidiaries throughout Latin America. The big British insurance brokers channel business to London from around the world.

The task of the EU competition authorities in this context has been clear: to ensure that protectionist barriers hindering the progress of foreign insurers in EU member states are dismantled as rapidly as possible. The biggest share of this task fell to Sir Leon Brittan, whose served both as competition commissioner and as financial services commissioner between January 1989 and December 1993.

The liberalisation of Europe's insurance markets ranks as one of Sir Leon's more impressive achievements. At the beginning of the 1980s protectionism was rife: a bewildering array of tariff and non-tariff barriers prevented insurers from selling life or non-life insurance across borders without first establishing themselves in their target markets. Insurance brokers, in theory the vectors of cross-border competition among insurers, were largely confined to national markets.

British insurance buyers, who have long been accustomed to think of insurance as a consumer product like any other, might be surprised by the barrage of regulations that constrained the operation of market forces in many Continental European countries throughout the 1980s. Until the European Court of Justice delivered a landmark judgement in January 1987 (described below), it was unclear how far the Treaty of Rome's basic competition rules, Articles 85 and 86, applied to insurers. Even in 1992, the European Commission still regarded insurance as a 'regulated industry', like telecommunications or energy, where competition had not historically been allowed free rein.[22]

This high degree of regulation in insurance continued to have its champions.

Prominent among them was Michel Albert, until recently the high profile chairman of Assurance Générales de France, a company which ranked in 1993 as the second biggest state-owned French insurer. In a book entitled *Capitalisme contre capitalisme*, published in September 1991, Mr Albert held up the German and Swiss models of insurance regulation as paradigms of a more efficient, more socially responsive form of capitalism.

Mr Albert contended that the quality of service provided by British and American insurers suffered as they competed ever more aggressively on price. He also argued that the security afforded by insurers was inevitably inferior where regulation was light. He identified advantages in what he termed the Alpine view of insurance as 'a quasi-public service operating through institutions that are submitted to rigorous regulation but limited competition'.[23] Central to this quasi-public service was the notion that risks should be mutualised through tariff structures that standardised premium rates. In the German motor insurance market, for instance, good drivers have long subsidised bad drivers.[24] At least, though, all policyholders enjoyed impeccable security and their premiums were not loaded with hefty commissions to brokers.

Mr Albert's plea for a compromise between the high regulation of the German insurance market and the free-for-all competition of the UK market fell on deaf ears in Brussels. 'I can see [how the Anglo-Saxon system of regulation] is less comfortable', said Sir Leon Brittan. 'I can see it's less cosy. But I can't see the argument for it being less efficient.'[25]

So, in the end, it was the Anglo-Saxon approach to insurance regulation that triumphed; but the process was long and hard. As late as November 1989, Sir Leon was complaining to insurers in Brussels that insurance liberalisation was lagging behind the 'more rapid progress being achieved in creating the single market for other financial services.'[26]

Sir Leon clearly felt a strong responsibility to chivvy insurers and their governments along. In this he was very successful. Three years after his Brussels speech, insurance was fast catching up with banking in the single market stakes, and had outstripped investment services. In July 1994, two new directives, known as the framework directives, abolished all remaining premium tariffs for life and non-life insurance. In both sectors of the European insurance market, insurers will be able to sell their products across borders via brokers. They will no longer have to submit to local regulation in the host state: Europe's governments have committed themselves to mutual recognition of one another's insurance regulation regimes.

A few problems remain. One of the most awkward is the European Union's failure to harmonise tax regimes for insurance across the Union. In November 1993, Britain's chancellor of the exchequer Kenneth Clarke announced plans to impose a 3 per cent premium tax on most forms of non-life insurance. Britain has since joined the other EU states where premium taxes have long been widespread. In France, insurers have long grumbled about premium taxes that often exceed 20 per cent.

The problem with such a fiscal patchwork is that it makes life very difficult for companies seeking to buy insurance for all their European subsidiaries from a single source. Different taxes have to be calculated and paid for risks in each different location. In April 1992, Sir Leon Brittan predicted that 'market pressures' would 'reduce [fiscal] differentials over time'. No attempt was made to harmonise these taxes in the way that had been done with value added taxes.

Sir Leon's optimism that the market would achieve what politicians feared to attempt proved only partly justified. The French government has reduced some of its premium taxes – for long the highest in Europe – because it feared they would become almost uncollectable in the single market. When Kenneth Clarke slapped premium taxes on most lines of UK non-life insurance, he exempted marine, aviation and transport insurance on the grounds that taxing such geographically mobile risks would drive away business from British insurers. Reinsurance was exempted on similar grounds.

Varying tax regimes can still cause competition problems, though. Consider the case of Mr Bachmann, a German citizen resident in Belgium who bought life and health insurance from a German insurer, together with a pension. Under Belgian law, the premiums payable for these products are tax deductible. But when Mr Bachmann sought to obtain tax relief on his outlay, he was denied it. The Belgian tax authorities argued that tax relief on premiums was a *quid pro quo* for taxable benefits, and how could the Belgian taxman obtain a cut of the benefits from Mr Bachmann's pension and insurance if Mr Bachmann had returned to Germany before a claim was made?[27]

The case went before the European Court of Justice in late 1991. The European Commission supported Mr Bachmann's contention that the attitude of the Belgian tax authorities was anti-competitive, as it discriminated between Belgian and non-Belgian insurers. Nevertheless, the European Court of Justice sided with the Belgian state.

Co-operation, not competition, the problem

Tax, then, remains a barrier to perfect competition among insurers within the European Union. However, a bigger concern for insurers has been how far the European Commission will let them co-operate, not compete.

Co-operation is essential to insurers because some risks are too big or too complicated for individual companies to underwrite on their own. Risks such as pollution – known rather cumbrously as environmental impairment liability (EIL) risks – require insurers to pool claims data before a premium rate that reflects the risk can be set. Major risks such as oil rigs, jet airliners or supertankers are commonly shared among dozens of insurers: this is the way the London insurance market has worked for decades.

Clearly there is plenty of scope here for anti-competitive cartels. On 27 January 1987 the ECJ upheld the Commission's decision to outlaw hefty premium rises for property insurance recommended by the German property insurers' association, Verband der Sachversicher.[28] The Commission had concluded that the co-ordination of premium rates in this way, with the support of German reinsurers, reduced competition and affected trade between member states. It was thus contrary to Article 85(1) of the Treaty of Rome.

Following the ECJ's ruling, the Commission was inundated with applications from insurers for their agreements and associations to be exempted from Article 85(1) under the terms of Article 85(3). In other words, the insurers were claiming their co-operation improved the production or distribution of insurance, or promoted technical or economic progress in some way, to the benefit of policyholders. Among the agreements approved by the Commission was a risk-sharing agreement among Protection and Indemnity Clubs, which insure third-party marine risks. Another exemption covered a French reinsurance pool for environmental risks: known as Assurpol, the pool increased the underwriting capacity for industrial pollution risks in Europe, always in short supply.

Altogether, over three hundred applications for individual exemptions were sent by insurers to the Commission in the years following the German property insurance judgement. It soon became apparent that a block insurance exemption to Article 85(1) would save time for both insurers and the Commission. After the usual protracted negotiations, the block exemption regulation was signed by Sir Leon Brittan on 21 December 1992 and came into force in 1 April 1993. It will run until 31 March 2003.[29]

The block exemption lists various forms of co-operation among insurers which it deems permissible under Article 85 of the Treaty of Rome. The main ones are:

1. *Standard policy conditions or wordings.* These are useful to insurance buyers because they enable buyers to compare like products with like. But the Commission insists they can only serve as models, not as binding requirements of an association.

2. *Co-insurance or co-reinsurance agreements.* These are acceptable where they increase the available cover for risks which might otherwise be difficult to cover 'because of their scale, rarity or novelty'. The idea of such pooling arrangements is to develop centres of underwriting expertise for difficult risks that a number of insurers or reinsurers can support.

3. *Collaboration among insurers on standards for security devices.* The idea here is that insurers can co-operate to insist on uniform standards among the suppliers of alarm systems, for instance. A system acceptable to one insurer would thus be acceptable to another.

4. *Calculation of 'pure premiums'.* These are premiums designed to cover a particular risk, without weighting for profits or the insurer's expenses. (The German property insurers' agreement was outlawed because it affected gross premiums, with the profit margin included.) The Commission accepts that insurers should be allowed to pool claims and other statistics in order to 'improve the knowledge of risks and facilitate the rating of risks for individual companies'.

In recent years Europe's insurers have come to recognise that the European Commission is no soft touch. Try asking the chairman of an association of marine or aviation insurers in London how he expects premium rates to move over the next year: he is likely to reply that he has no idea, because premium rates are a matter for individual companies, not their association. Sometimes it is difficult to work out exactly what these associations do deal with. Lawyers do brisk business ensuring that their charters do not infringe EU competition rules.

All the same, the demands of the European Commission are as nothing compared with the oversight of national regulators in the days before liberalisation. In Germany, the Federal Insurance Supervisory Office (BAV) insisted that every new insurance policy wording be carefully vetted before it could go on the market. In Spain, strict investment rules for insurers guaranteed the government a captive market for treasury bonds. AGF's Michel Albert may warn that liberalisation is proceeding too fast, but many insurers welcome their new freedoms; and so in time should their policyholders.

BANKING

Politicians are wont to treat banks as sensitive organisms, to be handled with care. They have good reasons to do so: as J.K. Galbraith puts it: 'A banking failure is not an ordinary business misadventure . . . It has not one but two adverse effects on economic activity: owners lose their capital and depositors their deposits, and both therewith lose their ability to purchase things'.[30]

The sensitivity of banking supervisors was demonstrated in Britain in May 1993 when the Bank of England admitted that it had spent over £100 million propping up some of Britain's smaller banks that looked especially vulnerable to recession.

The problem for the European Commission is to determine when the security of the banking system is being used as a cloak to conceal anti-competitive practices that protect established banks and erect barriers to entry around their markets. In other words, how to strip away the 'priestly incantation' identified by Galbraith and get at the truth.

The Commission's view was succinctly expressed in the *XXIst Report on Competition Policy*, published in April 1992. The Commission acknowledged the monetary authorities' desire to supervise money supply and interest rates and the need to protect investors and lenders, but it argued that 'less restrictive arrangements' than those currently in force could achieve the desired ends.

At the same time the Commission declared itself 'open to legitimate forms of co-operation which, in the light of the peculiar features of the [financial services] industry, contribute to the introduction of efficient arrangements that benefit consumers'. Such arrangements must not, of course, jeopardise competition.

As with insurance, there are two main planks to EU competition policy affecting banks. The first is to break down the wide range of non-tariff barriers that have impeded banks' access to one another's markets. This was Sir Leon Brittan's responsibility as financial services commissioner from January 1989 to December 1992. It was Sir Leon who pushed through the notion of a single banking licence or passport enshrined in the second banking directive: this enables a bank based anywhere in the European Union to obtain a certificate from its home state authorities entitling it to trade in any other member state. The same principle of home state control was adopted, with rather more opposition, in Europe's insurance markets.

The second plank of EU competition policy in the banking field is ongoing supervision of banks' behaviour to ensure that competition is not being restricted. There are many ways in which banks can co-operate with one another and most of them are susceptible to abuse.

One of the worst of these abuses used to be the creation of interest rate cartels orchestrated by national banking associations. Such agreements were widespread during the 1980s and the Commission fought shy of outlawing them. In the jargon of

EU officialdom, it 'reserved its position'. Central banks would routinely defend such agreements on the grounds that they helped implement national monetary policy. The Commission accepted this line until 1989, but in November of that year it concluded that interest rate agreements between banks restricted competition every bit as much as price agreements between manufacturers.

As for the monetary policy argument, the Commission concluded that national banking authorities could pursue monetary policy objectives without encouraging what amounted to price cartels. The Commission undertook to root out such cartels and break them up. In June 1991 it started sending letters to national banking associations seeking information on their current practices.

The feedback was encouraging. Only two countries, Italy and Belgium, retained any formal agreements on co-ordinating interest rates, and both these countries insisted that the agreements were no longer enforced. Following the Commission's letter, both agreements were formally abandoned. The Luxembourg banking association also scrapped a system of recommended debtor and creditor interest rates.

The exercise also revealed a *de facto* price agreement among Belgian banks over the charge to be imposed for Eurocheques drawn abroad. The Belgian banking association had sent its members standardised lists of banking services with a blank space beside each service where the individual banks could write their charges. The charge for Eurocheques drawn abroad, however, was printed on the forms: the Commission concluded this 'could be regarded as a recommendation amounting to a price agreement'. The Belgians protested that the Eurocheque charge was included by mistake and agreed to delete it.

The Commission later took a less indulgent view of another abuse of the Eurocheque system, this time perpetrated by French banks. On 25 March 1992 the Commission fined the French banks that were members of the Eurocheque system Ecu 5 million for price-fixing as prohibited under Article 85(1)(a) of the Treaty of Rome.[31] This was the first occasion that banks had ever been fined for anti-competitive behaviour under the Treaty of Rome.

Under the so-called Helsinki Agreement, which ran from 1983 to 1991, French banks charged French retailers the same commission for cashing foreign Eurocheques as they charged for payment by bank card. The Commission concluded that this amounted to price fixing. It also found the practice in breach of undertakings made by Eurocheque members in 1980 not to charge retailers for cashing Eurocheques.

Co-operative agreements among savings banks have also received close scrutiny from the Commission. These have mushroomed as savings banks seek to track the increasing mobility of their customers around the Union – a development the Commission naturally welcomes. However, there are four types of clause inserted into such agreements which have been deemed anti-competitive.[32] These are:

1. Mutually exclusive clauses, prohibiting signatories from establishing branches in the geographical market of the other parties.
2. Clauses prohibiting the conclusion of agreements with other credit institutions in such regions.

3. Clauses granting exclusive rights to each party to market and distribute common products in its home country.
4. Clauses making bilateral agreements concluded by national banking association members subject to prior approval by those associations.

On occasions, forms of co-operation championed by the European Commission can be warped to restrict competition. Thus in 1990 two Belgian savings banks and a Dutch savings bank joined together to form a European Economic Interest Group (EEIG).[33] EEIGs are a form of cross-border co-operation devised by the European Commission and approved by the European Council in 1985. They enable companies or partnerships to pool resources without forming capitalised joint ventures. Any debts incurred by an EEIG fall to their member companies. The Belgian–Dutch savings bank grouping, named the European Group of Financial Institutions (EGFI), was set up to develop new investment products that could be sold by member companies in their own countries. Several other banks have since joined EGFI from other countries.

The Commission was unhappy about one clause in EGFI's charter. This provided that the existing members need give no grounds for refusing admission to another bank. The Commission considered this smacked of a cartel. EGFI agreed to amend the clause.

Case study
BARCLAYS BANK

The decision to report an EU member state government to the European Commission for anti-competitive behaviour is one that should never be taken lightly. Governments have ways of making life difficult for businesses that seek to embarrass them so publicly. Fortunately, such drastic action is not always the only solution to anti-competitive laws. Barclays Bank has shown how some nifty legal footwork can save time, money and the bad blood that a complaint to Brussels would produce.

In the autumn of 1992 Barclays launched an interest-bearing current account in France. The bank has never had a major high street presence in that country, nor did it wish to develop one. It saw itself as providing, instead, a private banking service to high net worth individuals: the aim of the new *compte cheque dynamique* was to woo these mainly professional people with a product that was not generally available from domestic banks. Barclays was hoping to carve itself a niche.

The local banks reacted with fury. They argued that Barclays was circumventing a key feature of the French banking system: French banks do not share the returns on current account balances with their account holders, but nor do they charge for current account transactions. Interest-bearing current accounts are formally banned under French law.

Barclays evaded this ban by switching funds invested in each *compte cheque dynamique* between two accounts: one a standard non-interest-bearing current account and the other a money market fund paying interest at half a percentage point below fluctuating money market rates. Deposits in excess of FFr 10,000 could thereby earn an attractive investment return.

The French banks cried foul, arguing that Barclays' new product complied with the letter but not the spirit of the law. They enjoyed some leverage: the Banque de France had been leaning on French commercial banks to keep base lending rates down so as not to deepen the recession, even though short-term money market interest rates were being kept high to support the franc. French finance minister Michel Sapin owed the banks a favour: on 14 October 1992, he announced that the ploy adopted by Barclays would be outlawed.

Some commentators now suggested that Barclays should think about taking its case to Brussels,[34] but the bank had a better idea. Just as it had found a loophole in the earlier law, so it managed to find a loophole in Mr Sapin's new law. Previously, it had automatically switched current account funds into the money markets: that was now banned; but Barclays found it could continue the practice as long as it first obtained the account-holder's permission.

Why did the French government not close this loophole as well? Officials at the French finance ministry are loathe to comment, but it seems likely that the risk of being found in breach of EU competition rules weighed heavily on their minds. Barclays had recently launched interest-bearing current accounts in both Spain and Portugal. How would the government have justified denying French citizens the right to authorise their banks to take action that was permitted to British, Spanish and Portuguese citizens?

Just over a year after Mr Sapin attempted to quash Barclays' *compte cheque dynamique*, the bank was reporting booming business. A spokeswoman for Barclays in London said that the interest-bearing current account was the bank's most popular product in France, and forty new branches had been opened in the Paris region in 1993 to take advantage of its success.

NOTES

1. *Wall Street Journal Europe*, 4 March 1993.
2. *Financial Times*, 17 November 1993.
3. Commission Regulation (EEC) No. 123/85, Official Journal No. L 15/16, 18 January 1985.
4. See *XXIst Report on Competition Policy*, chapter 2.I.D, section 1.7, page 118.
5. *Il Sole 24 Ore*, 22 September 1992.
6. *Les Echos*, 7 October 1992.
7. *XXIInd Report on Competition Policy*, May 1993, chapter 2.I.D, section 1.11, page 176.
8. Case T-9/92, *Automobiles Peugeot SA and Peugeot SA v. Commission*, CFI 2CH, 22 April 1993.
9. The phrase 'manifest crisis' is drawn from Article 58(1) of the European Coal and Steel Community treaty, which was invoked by industry commissioner Viscount Etienne Davignon in 1980 to justify production quotas.
10. *Financial Times*, 16 October 1992.
11. *Les Echos*, 7 December 1993.
12. *Les Echos*, 22 February 1993.
13. Interview with author, 3 June 1993.
14. European Commission DGII (economic and social affairs), *European Economy*, no. 48, September 1991, page 49.
15. *XXIst Report on Competition Policy*, April 1992, chapter 3.I.A, section 4.b.1, page 201.
16. See, for example, *XXIst Report on Competition Policy*, chapter 3.I.A, section 4.b.8, page 208.
17. Interview with author, 3 June 1993.
18. *Financial Times*, 18 December 1993.
19. Quoted in the *Financial Times*, 22 February 1993.

20. Commission decision 89/218/ECSC, OJ no. L 86/76 of 31 March 1989.
21. Company press release.
22. *XXIst Report on Competition Policy*, April 1992, chapter 1.II.1, page 20.
23. Michel Albert, *Capitalisme contre capitalisme*. Editions Seuil, 1991, page 109.
24. This is likely to change after the third non-life insurance directive abolishes premium tariffs for third party motor risks in Germany from 1 July 1994.
25. Interview with author, 15 April 1992.
26. Speech to the Comité Européen des Assurances, Brussels, 27 November 1993.
27. Barlow Lyde & Gilbert, *Insurance Law Quarterly*, no. 9, spring 1992, page 20.
28. ECJ Case 45/85. The case is described in detail in the Sigma, Swiss Re report, *Competition Law – increasing significance for the insurance sector*, May 1992, page 12.
29. Commission Regulation (EEC) No. 3932/92, Official Journal no. L 398/7, 31 December 1992.
30. J.K. Galbraith, *Money: Whence it came, where it went*. Bantam Books, 1976, page 137.
31. *XXIInd Report on Competition Policy*, May 1993, chapter 2.I.A, section 1.f.11, page 94.
32. *XXIst Report on Competition Policy*, April 1992, chapter 1.II, section 3.3, page 35.
33. *XXIInd Report on Competition Policy*, May 1993, chapter 1.II, section 3.4, page 36.
34. *The Economist*, 17 October 1992.

CHAPTER 7

EUROPE'S LIFEBLOOD: EU COMPETITION POLICY AND SMALL BUSINESSES

SMALL AND PERFECTLY UNINFORMED?

Ignorance of EU competition policy among small and medium-sized enterprises (SMEs) has long dogged the Commission. Small businesses cannot afford direct representation in Brussels; they cannot afford expensive lobbyists or consultants to advise them on how their interests might be affected by a Commission decision or a European Court judgement; and, very often, they cannot afford to sue.

The result is that small businesses frequently lose out twice over. They fail to take full advantage of the national and EU aid schemes that are available to help them counterbalance the competitive advantages enjoyed by bigger firms. Even more frustratingly, they are unsure how to identify breaches of the competition rules perpetrated by bigger companies and how to blow the whistle on them.

This book cannot hope fully to bridge an information gap as broad as this, nor is it really the job of a guide on EU competition policy to describe the range of aid schemes available to small businesses across the Union. Instead, this chapter will explain how the competition rules in the Treaty of Rome have been tailored to suit the Commission's oft-declared objective of encouraging the growth of SMEs. It will also suggest ways in which SMEs can use the competition rules offensively, to open up markets and obtain redress for grievances.

THE IMPORTANCE OF SMALL AND MEDIUM-SIZED BUSINESSES

The European Commission, in common with member state governments, makes all the right noises about small businesses. 'The lifeblood of any economy' it calls them, with sad lack of originality.[1] It can produce impressive research too in support of this claim. In 1992, the Commission had several reasons to encourage a flourishing small business sector in the European Union. One of the most important, at a time when much of Europe appeared to be heading into recession, was what the Commission termed the 'disproportionate role [of SMEs] in employment creation, especially at times when large firms are shedding labour'.[2] The Commission's research indicated that firms employing fewer than two hundred people, including sole proprietors, accounted for 62.7 per cent of EU employment in 1989.

Another attraction was the fact that small businesses, being 'more flexible and adaptable than large firms' are often 'in the forefront of innovation'. This meant that SMEs are a strong force in favour of competition in markets: in the Commission's words 'they keep markets "contestable" – and act as the main motor of structural change and regeneration in the economy as a whole'.

SMEs also have a growing role in certain sectors of national economies. The industrial giants of Europe have been slimming down, sourcing larger quantities of their components from external suppliers. This trend has been particularly evident in the motor industry, but it has been happening elsewhere as well. 'Many large manufacturers are relying on subcontractors for a growing proportion of the value added in their products', notes the Commission. The SMEs that provide this added value are taking on heavier R&D responsibilities.[3]

SMES AND THE TILTED PLAYING FIELD

The case for assisting SMEs is the familiar one of levelling the playing field. In the Commission's view, small businesses face a number of handicaps in competing with large firms. These are:

1. Problems raising finance.
2. Greater weight of burdens imposed by government. For example, health and safety compliance costs may well be higher. Tax rates may also be higher, with fewer opportunities to offset taxes.
3. Higher research and development costs. Such costs are spread across a far narrower range of products than would be the case for a big company.

The Commission has concluded that these relative disadvantages call for 'positive action by government to level the playing field and perhaps tip it slightly in their [SMEs'] favour'. The European Commission's first problem was to define what a small or medium-sized business was. The twelve EU countries presented a wide range of definitions. In France, *petites et moyennes entreprises* are companies employing up to five hundred people. By contrast, the Confederation of British Industry identifies medium-sized firms as employing between twenty-one and fifty people.[4]

Even within the Commission, there is disagreement over what constitutes a small or medium-sized enterprise. Directorate General XXIII, the multipurpose division of the Commission handling *inter alia* SMEs, does not have a hard-and-fast definition.[5] However, companies with up to five hundred employees tend to qualify.

By contrast, DGIV has selected a tighter definition. This is spelled out in *Community Guidelines on State Aids for Small and Medium-Sized Enterprises*, adopted by the Commission in May 1992. The Commission defines SMEs as companies meeting at least two out of three possible criteria. These are:

1. That no SME may employ more than 250 people; and
2. That every SME must possess one of the following:
   (a) a turnover of not more than Ecu 20 million;
   (b) total assets net of depreciation ('balance sheet total') not exceeding Ecu 10 million.

Where it is necessary to distinguish between small and medium-sized companies, the ceilings are lowered to less than a quarter of their former level. A small business, in the Commission's view, is one that has no more than fifty employees and meets one of two further criteria: annual turnover no higher than Ecu 5 million, or a balance sheet total no higher than Ecu 2 million.

Both medium and small businesses must meet one further condition. They may not be more than 25 per cent owned by one or more companies that do not meet the above criteria. This is designed to ensure that the subsidiaries of big companies do not seek the advantages that are supposed to be reserved for independent small businesses. There are exceptions, though: venture capital companies, public investment corporations or institutional investors (provided no control is exercised) may hold more than 25 per cent of an SME without disqualifying it from the more lenient state aid rules.

LIMITED RISK TO COMPETITION IN AID TO SMES

The Commission has indicated that it will be far more willing to take a charitable view of more generous state aids to small business than to big ones. In its May 1992 guidelines, the Commission spells out its reasons for adopting this view.

The Commission concludes that state aid is less likely to 'adversely affect trading conditions [between member states] to an extent contrary to the common interest' when given to small companies than when given to large ones. The Commission bases this conclusion on the fact that small firms preponderate in the non-tradable good and services sectors (areas like construction, certain food manufacturing and retailing). Both sales and turnover per employee tend to be lower at small firms.

SMES AND THE POORER EU REGIONS

DGIV has also indicated it will take an especially generous view of state aids to SMEs located in the poorer parts of the European Union. The Commission is keen to dovetail its policy of aid to SMEs with its policy on regional and economic cohesion – bringing the level of the poorer parts of the Union up to the level of the richer parts. Indeed, the Maastricht Treaty on European Union commits the Commission to pursuing policies that will 'reduce the backwardness of the least favoured regions' of the Union (Articles 130a and 130b).

For this reason, state aids to SMEs in backward parts of the Union such as Portugal and Greece are highly likely to qualify for generous treatment. Such a policy used to be of little interest to British businesses. No longer. In March 1993, the Commission announced proposals to add two new UK regions to the list of areas entitled to the highest level of EU aid. These were Merseyside and the Highlands and Islands of Scotland. Previously, only Northern Ireland had been a recipient of the highest level of EU aid, destined for what are known as Objective 1 regions.

The British government had applied for Objective 1 status for a host of other allegedly impoverished British regions, including rural Wales, Devon and Cornwall and south Yorkshire. 'It is a moot point whether the UK was serious', observed one official at DGXVI, the regional policy division of the Commission, in the spring of 1993. 'None of these regions met the criteria.'

Nevertheless, the trend is evident – although the prophets of doom who claim that Britain is rapidly becoming an honorary southern European country, desperate for handouts from Brussels, may be jumping the gun. Between 1994 and 1999, Ecu 96.3 billion in regional aid will be disbursed by Brussels to the poorest parts of the European Union. Merseyside, Northern Ireland and the Highlands and Islands of Scotland will be among them. Astute businesspeople in these regions will not look a gift horse in the mouth: they will know how that money is being spent and how to apply for it. This knowledge starts with an understanding of the May 1992 guidelines on state aids to SMEs.

AIDS THAT NEED NOT BE NOTIFIED

The key provision of the May 1992 guidelines for SMEs – small and medium-sized companies alike – is the setting of a *de minimis* threshold for state aids that can be granted without the bother of notifying the Commission. This is set at Ecu 50,000 in any three year period. Aid of Ecu 50,000 or less over three years is deemed imperceptible in its impact on competition. The only precondition is that the aid be for a specified form of expenditure.

It should be noted that the *de minimis* rule does not apply only to small and medium-sized businesses: ICI or Shell could exploit it if they wished. Its benefits, though, are likely to be more valued by small businesses.

As with other forms of state aid, money given by EU member states to SMEs is usually measured not by its absolute value, but by its 'intensity' – the percentage of the money required for a particular task that is contributed by the state. Thus aid of Ecu 100,000 paid to company A might be disallowed because its represented, say, 70 per cent of the company's retraining budget, whereas aid of Ecu 120,000 paid to company B might be cleared because it represented only 40 per cent of the company's retraining budget. Aid to SMEs is supposed to offer a leg-up, not a crutch.

The Commission distinguishes two broad categories of state aid. The most sensitive covers what are called 'near-market activities' such as investment aid. Less controversial forms of aid provide money for consultancy help, training or R&D expenses. The distinction was made because investment aid is deemed to have a bigger impact on competition than other forms of aid. The Commission concluded that ploughing investment aid into medium-sized companies might have a 'significant trade-distorting effect'.

The guidelines lay down generally acceptable intensities of aid for SMEs. The lowest intensity is reserved for investment aid to medium-sized firms trading in relatively prosperous parts of the European Union. Recipients will be allowed to receive up to 7.5 per cent of their investment costs in the form of grants and interest subsidies (before tax).

Alternatively, if the aid is for job-creation purposes at medium-sized firms, a maximum of Ecu 3,000 per job created can be made available. If the aid is for neither job creation nor investment, the aid ceiling for such companies in monetary terms is Ecu 200,000. Small businesses as defined above will be entitled to twice this intensity of investment aid, in other words 15 per cent of the investment costs incurred by the firm.

However, the aid levels permitted increase sharply when the SME is based in a disadvantaged part of the European Union. These regions are defined as areas where unemployment is above the EU average. (These areas are known technically as Objective 2 and Objective 5b regions: they change frequently and small businesses in the UK should consult either the European Commission or the Department of Trade and Industry to find out which UK regions are covered.) In these regions, further aid worth between an extra 10 per cent and 15 per cent of the recipients' investment costs is permitted.

The Commission also sets some absolute ceilings for levels of aid intensity to small businesses. In regions that benefit from national aid schemes but which are not among the poorest in the European Union, the mix of regional and SME aid cannot exceed 30 per cent of the total investment costs. However, in the most backward areas suffering from 'serious underemployment' or 'abnormally low' living standards, the much more generous level of 70 per cent aid intensity is set as the maximum. This is sanctioned under Article 92(3)(a) of the Treaty of Rome.

As far as research and development expenses are concerned, SMEs can accept up to 10 percentage points more aid as a proportion of their total R&D expenditure than larger firms can. As a general rule, the Commission will not permit aid for basic industrial research to exceed 50 per cent of the gross cost of the project or programme. For SMEs the aid intensity ceiling is therefore 60 per cent.[6]

The bulk of the aid offered by EU member states to SMEs takes the form of grants to obtain consultancy help or training for various purposes. Under the new Commission rules issued in mid-1992, this aid can still be authorised throughout the Union up to 50 per cent. Thus a small business could hire software consultants to upgrade its computer systems, and cover half the cost through a government grant – without it falling foul of the EU state aid rules.

Another advantage posed by the new guidelines for SMEs is the accelerated approval procedure for 'low intensity aid', in other words the basic SME aid that does not exceed 7.5 per cent of the company's total gross investment expenditure or Ecu 3,000 per job created. The Commission has undertaken to give its decision on aid schemes of this kind proposed by member states within twenty working days. The Commission's decision will 'in principle' be favourable.[7]

The guidelines will remain in force until May 1995 and will be the subject of a review by the Commission shortly before their expiry.

THE RISKS OF IGNORANCE

It may appear unnecessary for small businesses to be conversant with the full details of the Commission's guidelines on state aid schemes for SMEs: after all, it is up to member state governments to clear aid schemes with the Commission. However, it is certainly in the interests of small businesses to have a clear idea of their rights under EU law: if a particular scheme is retrospectively outlawed by the Commission, it will be the businesses involved, rather than the government, that will have to repay the aid. The European Court of Justice has ruled that companies have a duty to ensure they are not in receipt of illicit state aids (see chapter 4).

Having said that, the opprobrium of retrospectively disallowing an aid scheme to small businesses might make the Commission think twice. Demands for the repayment of state aid are almost always addressed to big companies that can readily afford it. The Commission has repeatedly made it clear that it is after the biggest fish, not the small fry.

Nevertheless, the Commission cannot afford to turn a blind eye to blatant breaches of the state aid rules contained in the Treaty of Rome: such insouciance could land it with a legal challenge in the European Court of Justice. Therefore the rule for SMEs, as well as for multinationals, should be *caveat emptor*.

Small and medium-sized companies should also be aware that the aid rules apply equally to money disbursed from Brussels as to money spent by member states.

SMES AND ARTICLE 85: `AGREEMENTS OF MINOR IMPORTANCE´

In addition to state aids, SMEs also enjoy certain exemptions from the Treaty of Rome's basic cartel rule enshrined in Article 85(1). Again, the theory is that the economic advantages of allowing SMEs to co-operate with one another will outweigh the impact on competition that such co-operation will entail.

The rules on SMEs and Article 85 are laid down in the Commission's notice of 3 September 1986, relating to agreements of minor importance. This notice updates an earlier version from December 1977, and significantly broadens its scope. Its objective is expressly to facilitate co-operation between small and medium-sized undertakings.

Under the terms of the notice, the Commission will not concern itself with agreements between undertakings which meet two *de minimis* criteria:

1. The agreement affects goods or services representing less than 5 per cent of the

total market for such products 'in the area of the common market affected by the agreement'.

2. The aggregate annual turnover of the participating undertakings does not exceed Ecu 200 million.

The notice gives guidance over how to calculate market share for the purposes of rule 1 above. Two kinds of market exist: the product market and the geographical market. The Commission's methodology for calculating market share is set out more fully in chapter 3, dealing with the merger regulation.

The aggregate turnover rule requires some elaboration. It covers the largest possible number of independent businesses that are party to the agreement. For the purpose of the notice, independence exists when a company is less than 50 per cent owned or controlled by another. In other words, if one of the signatories to the agreement is more than 50 per cent owned by another company, or if another company has more than half the voting rights or more than half the boardroom seats, then the turnover of that other company will also be included in the aggregate turnover figure.

Straightforward enough; but suppose your agreement is a borderline case. What happens if a major competitor bows out of your market, suddenly boosting your combined market share under the agreement to, say, 6 per cent? What happens if your aggregate turnover rises above Ecu 200 million? Does your agreement automatically become subject to scrutiny under Article 85(1)?

No. The notice has some flexibility built in. If the market share or turnover criteria mentioned above are exceeded by 'not more than one-tenth during two successive financial years', then the agreement will still qualify for exemption from Article 85(1).

The 1986 notice marks a major advance on its predecessor. Previously, only businesses with aggregate turnover of Ecu 50 million were exempted from Article 85(1), and services were not included in the scope of the exemption.

GETTING EVEN WITH GOLIATH

None of the foregoing will be of much use if the markets you wish to break into as a small or medium-sized business are already sewn up or rigged in some way to the advantage of your bigger competitors. For this you need the leverage provided by the competition rules of the Treaty of Rome. In particular you are likely to need Article 86 to tackle whichever of your competitors is abusing a 'dominant position within the common market or ... a substantial part of it' to your disadvantage. On a number of occasions, timely recourse to Article 86 has saved small or medium-sized businesses from being driven into bankruptcy.[8]

The most common abuses involve large companies that refuse to supply essential products to smaller ones, or which try to squeeze smaller companies out of a particular market by selling products as loss-leaders at uneconomical prices. If you believe this is happening to you, you have a range of (relatively cheap) options you can pursue:

1. Contact the European Commission immediately. Point out that as a small business

you are not equipped to mount a legal challenge to the behaviour in question but that you feel the abuse is serious and should be brought to the Commission's attention.

2. Contact your MEP. He or she may well have received similar complaints from other companies. Armed with a clutch of such complaints, your MEP may well be able to exert greater pressure on the Commission. In 1992, MEPs submitted 141 written questions on competition to the Commission.[9]

3. Contact your local and/or trade press. Most big companies will take steps to avoid the opprobrium that negative press coverage will bring. (If your trade publication fails to run with the story, do not worry — it probably reflects less on the merits of your case than on the advertising buying power of your competitor.)

4. Your own trade association may also be of value, providing it represents only your interests and not those of the company you are attacking as well. Pitting one member against another is not really a trade association's task, unless the anti-competitive behaviour of one member is bringing the whole trade into disrepute.

Why not try all four of the above steps (if applicable) together? Draft one concise, clearly worded statement of your grievance and send it to everyone who might possibly be of assistance. There is no point in waiting weeks or months for one possible source of help to respond before contacting another.

NOTES

1. From *Community Guidelines on State Aids for Small and Medium-Sized Enterprises*, adopted by the Commission in May 1992.
2. *Ibid.*
3. *Ibid.*
4. Peter Danton de Roufignac, *Europe's New Business Culture*. Pitman Publishing, 1991, chapter 7.
5. Heinrich von Moltke, Director-General DGXXIII, in response to a question raised at Club de Bruxelles conference on EC competition policy, 5–6 May 1993.
6. *R&D Guidelines*, OJ no. C 83/2, 11 April 1986, page 2.
7. *Communication* (92/C 213/03) to the Member States on the Accelerated Clearance of Aid Schemes for SMEs and of Amendments to Existing Schemes, adopted by the Commission on 2 July 1992, OJ no. C 213/10, 19 August 1992.
8. Comments by Martine Frager-Berlet, Manager, Europe Point, Euro Info Centre, Paris, at Club de Bruxelles conference on EC Competition policy, Brussels, 6–7 May 1993.
9. *XXIInd Report on Competition Policy*, May 1993, chapter 4.I, section 1.2, page 317.

CHAPTER 8

ARTICLE 90: THE COMMISSION'S NUCLEAR OPTION

THE MONOPOLIST'S NIGHTMARE

In the competition commissioner's arsenal, one weapon might appropriately be labelled 'handle with care'. This is Article 90. It gives the Commission the right to apply the competition rules contained elsewhere in the treaty to traditionally protected state monopolies like energy supply, postal services and telecommunications.

Paragraph 2 of Article 90 reads:

> Undertakings entrusted with the operation of services of general economic interest or having the character of a revenue-producing monopoly shall be subject to the rules contained in this Treaty, in particular to the rules on competition, in so far as the application of such rules does not obstruct the performance, in law or in fact, of the particular tasks assigned to them.

For over thirty years following the signing of the Treaty of Rome in 1957 competition commissioners found it politic to ignore Article 90. They had plenty of work to do applying Articles 85 and 86 to private sector companies and to those state-owned companies that were engaged in entirely free market activities. Why antagonise member state governments by interfering in the workings of cherished national institutions like France Telecom or Britain's Royal Mail?

In the late 1980s, however, the political mood across Europe began to change. Businesses began to ask why the cost of international telephone calls within and from Europe was so much higher than the cost of calls over comparable distances within and from the United States. Industry began to question the price it was paying for energy, and European policymakers began to notice that widely divergent energy prices across the European Union threatened economic convergence among poorer and richer member states. Businesspeople began to wax wrath at price rises for postal services that seemed to bear no relation to prevailing inflation rates.

The new mood was well expressed in comments on postal services contained in the Banking Federation of the European Community's 1992 annual report. 'As users, banks require faster, safer and cheaper services, within a more transparent framework', the report notes. 'It is for this reason that the Federation wishes to see greater liberalisation of postal services within a clear regulatory framework.'[1]

The justification for state-owned monopolies was and remains that they serve a social as well as an economic purpose. In 1983, the Italian state telecommunications company SIP incurred a loss on its business in the Mezzogiorno, the impoverished south of Italy, equivalent to 46 per cent of its operating profits in the rest of the country.[2] In a completely free market for telecoms, SIP would have faced stiff competition for its profitable northern Italian business and would have had no chance to cross-subsidise its operations in the Mezzogiorno. Indeed, a private sector company dedicated to the maximisation of profits would very likely have pulled out of the Mezzogiorno altogether.

The question, then, is how much more competition can we afford, while continuing to offer a universal service at reasonable cost. According to BT chairman Iain Vallance, the answer is a great deal more. In November 1993, Mr Vallance challenged the notion that telecommunications liberalisation in Europe will benefit business users while costing private users in outlying regions dear. 'Parts of Europe are in favour of blocking liberalisation on the grounds that it will somehow risk the provision of services to rural and disadvantaged customers', said Mr Vallance. 'They cite the UK as an alleged example. Yet the quality and range of services provided today in, say, rural Scotland or rural Wales is just the same as that offered anywhere else in the United Kingdom.'[3]

Article 90 does not deny the social obligations of state monopolies such as SIP or France Telecom. All it does is threaten to remove the figleaf whereby these social obligations are commonly employed to defend all kinds of anti-competitive behaviour. That threat has been enough to leave various member state governments distinctly uncomfortable about the Commission's new-found enthusiasm for Article 90.

The beauty of the article from a procrastinator's viewpoint is that for a long time it permitted governments to shelter behind the argument that increased competition would, as the article puts it, 'obstruct the performance' of the tasks assigned to industries like telecommunications and energy supply. However, as the single market programme developed, the protection enjoyed by these industries came to look increasingly anomalous. Privatisation encouraged the scepticism: with Britain's BT privatised and Deutsche Telekom going the same way, the argument that increased competition would unleash anarchy in telecommunications, for instance, became harder to sustain.

In addition, the EU objective of an 'ever closer union among the peoples of Europe', as stated in the Treaty of Rome and reiterated at Maastricht, seems incompatible with public service monopolies organised on purely national lines. As Jonathan Rickford, director of government relations at BT, points out: 'There is a very strong Community principle that you don't create inhibitions to commercial activities by reference to national frontiers.' As far as telecommunications is concerned, this principle has been more honoured in the breach than in the observance.

The range of businesses covered by Article 90 is, on the face of it, rather surprising. Telecommunications is there, to be sure. So is energy, both gas and electricity, and postal services. So too are audiovisual services, such as television and radio; and so, astonishingly, are both banking and insurance. These are not, as the Commission noted with considerable understatement in its *XXIst Report on Competition* in April 1992, minor industries. By early 1992 their importance (both actual and symbolic) had become such that the Commission contended that 'abolishing the remaining barriers to competition in these industries is one of the Community's main priorities'.

The evidence of the past five years suggests that abolishing these barriers is much easier said than done. In both banking and insurance, tremendous progress has been made; likewise in transport. In energy and telecommunications, though, certain member states are fighting a very effective rearguard action against the liberalising initiatives of the Commission. In this chapter we concentrate on the potential impact of EU competition policy on the three services that businesses use every day: energy, telecommunications and postal services.

ENERGY

The Commission began to show how it planned to use Article 90 to liberalise the energy market in 1991. In January of that year, the Commission ruled that the leading Dutch energy generating companies, grouped together under the rather unwieldy title of Samenwerkende Electriciteitsproductiebedrijven, or SEP, were distorting competition by monopolising electricity imports and exports.

The SEP argued that it had a public interest obligation to ensure the security of electricity supplies to the national grid, but the Commission, in a pioneering ruling, concluded that this did not 'justify the monopolisation of exports and imports'.[4] It refused to grant the SEP exemption from the competition rules. Three months later, in April 1991, the then competition commissioner, Sir Leon Brittan, declared that the Commission would use Article 90 to lever open EU energy markets.

In his first few months as competition commissioner Karel Van Miert chose to take a softly-softly approach to the use of Article 90. In June 1993 he denied that the Commission was shelving Article 90, but he insisted that 'it should be used with caution'.

This caution is evident in the way Mr Van Miert has approached the liberalisation of EU markets for telecommunications and postal services; but energy is a different story. Van Miert chose not to distance himself from the tough position Sir Leon Brittan had taken over the break-up of national monopolies on the export and import of gas and electricity. Sir Leon had threatened the eight offending countries (Britain, Belgium, Denmark, France, Greece, Ireland, the Netherlands and Spain) with proceedings in the European Court of Justice. In his first months as competition commissioner Mr Van

Miert kept the threat alive, claiming the import/export monopolies were 'dead contrary to our basic rules'.[5]

By that time, the number of countries in the Commission's firing line had reduced to six: Denmark and France for gas, and France, Italy, Spain, Ireland and the Netherlands for electricity. The Commission had decided only to confront those monopolies that were *de jure* (in other words, written into the countries' national law), rather than *de facto*, where no competitor happened to be around. All the countries with *de jure* monopolies were claiming stoutly that these statutes were essential to maintain security of supply for domestic users.

The Commission need not rely exclusively on Article 90 in its battle against these monopolies. Article 30 of the Treaty of Rome bans quantitative restrictions on imports between member states, together with 'all measures having equivalent effect'. Article 34 does the same for exports.

Claude Rakovsky, the DGIV official in charge of pursuing the Commission's competition policy relating to state monopolies, argues that the Commission's tough approach towards the energy sector is already beginning to yield dividends. In August 1992, Electricité de France (EdF), the French state-owned electricity company, came to terms with a small private sector French generating company called Société Hydro-éléctrique de Grangevieille in the French Alps that wished to sell its surplus electricity to the Italian state-owned company ENEL.[6] EdF tried but failed to persuade the company to sell the electricity to it first, in accordance with its monopoly export rights. When Grangevieille refused, EdF did not press the point.[7]

Sir Leon Brittan, EU competition commissioner at the time the compromise was struck, welcomed it as 'a step towards the opening up of national energy markets'. EdF preferred to play the case down, arguing that it had few broad implications. This was scarcely surprising. Despite the Grangevieille compromise, the French government was still arguing vociferously that the export/import monopoly enjoyed by EdF and the state-owned gas utility company, Gaz de France, were essential to guarantee the security of electricity and gas supplies to French consumers.[8]

The moral of the story is that it is sometimes possible to get away with flouting national laws where those laws have been described as anti-competitive by the European Commission, and where there is no reason to suppose the European Court of Justice will dissent from the Commission's view. Sadly, such occasions are rare.

Fortunately, however, Commission pressure does sometimes eventually produce less ambiguous gains. In 1992 a longstanding monopoly over the distribution of diesel fuel to farmers in Portugal, held by the state-owned Portuguese oil company Petrogal, was finally relaxed. A complaint to the Commission lodged back in 1991 finally bore fruit, ensuring that any distribution company may now enjoy access to this section of the Portuguese market.[9]

More importantly, in January 1993 the Spanish government finally yielded to pressure from Brussels to dissolve the sixty-six-year-old monopoly enjoyed by the Campsa distribution company over supplying Spanish petrol stations. For decades Campsa had given its three shareholders, the oil refinery companies Repsol, Cepsa and Petromed, a stranglehold over petrol sales in Spain.

The result was less apparent in the price of petrol, which was and remains carefully controlled by the Spanish government, as in the spread of service stations. At the end of 1992, Spain had one service station for every 10,724 inhabitants – less than one-third the proportion in France or Italy.[10] The abolition of Campsa's monopoly is likely to result in service stations mushrooming around the country, a boon to motorists who have driven for tens of miles along barren Spanish highways, suffering agonies watching the fuel gauge needle edging towards zero.

Nevertheless, these remain modest victories. A large number of member states have set their faces against the three-pronged energy liberalisation programme proposed by the Commission in January 1992. The goal was to allow energy consumers, starting with large industrial ones, a choice in their purchase of gas and electricity. The key elements to the Commission's programme were:

1. The opening up of investment in production and transport of gas and electricity to independent operators.
2. 'Unbundling' of the components of vertically integrated electricity companies, dividing the generation, supply and distribution of electricity under separate management with separate (and transparent) accounting for each function.
3. Permitting third party access (TPA). Transmission and distribution companies would be obliged to offer access to their networks to big energy consumers and rival distributors at a reasonable cost. From the beginning of 1996, the Commission planned to extend the principle of third party access to the benefit of smaller consumers.

It is the third element of this plan that has run into most opposition from member states. The British government had signalled its desire to press forward with the proposals just before it took over the presidency of the European Union in the second half of 1992. However, next to no progress was made. In May 1993 Karel Van Miert admitted that 'things are not moving' in the energy sector.[11] 'The policy suggested by the Commission has been held up and we will therefore have to find a different approach.'

By the early summer of 1993 it looked as if the hard-line positions previously adopted by both the Commission and member state governments over third party access were beginning to soften. On 25 June Gerard Longuet, the French minister responsible *inter alia* for energy policy, emerged from an EU Council of Ministers meeting saying that the stalemate had been resolved.[12] Instead of making third party access compulsory throughout the Community, the Commission's energy commissioner Abel Matutes had indicated that third party access could be negotiated on a case by case basis.

In return, the state-owned French utility companies, Electricité de France and Gaz de France, would abandon their dogmatic resistance to TPA. It seems unlikely that small industrial energy consumers will have a choice of energy suppliers come 1996, as the Commission originally planned, but their bigger counterparts may.

TELECOMMUNICATIONS

Better progress has been made in telecommunications, where security of supply is not a plausible rationale for doing nothing. In June 1993, EU telecommunications ministers agreed to accept the Commission's proposed deadline of 1 January 1998 as the date by which state monopolies in voice telephony should be abolished. Four member states – Spain, Portugal, Greece and Ireland – will enjoy derogations until January 2003 to enable them to adapt. Luxembourg and possibly Belgium will have until the year 2000.

It is unlikely that '1998' will ever resound in the public consciousness in the way '1992' once did. The deadline may well prove unnecessarily generous. Jonathan Rickford at BT predicts that most of the more developed EU member states will abolish their telecommunications monopolies far earlier, under pressure from business users.

The agreement bears many of the hallmarks of Mr Van Miert. It is cautious, offering new entrants to the market freedom of access to existing telecommunications networks, rather than freedom to create new ones (out of the EU's twelve national telecommunications operators, only Britain's BT favoured the latter freedom); it gives member states plenty of time in which to brace themselves for the rigours of competition, and it is the child of consensus rather than conflict.

It was, though, a consensus that took some time and trouble to reach. Only four months before the Council of Ministers April 1993 meeting it had looked likely that the Commission would have had to accept an even more conservative target. As it stands, Europe's telecommunications operators will have to make some major changes to the way they run their businesses.

For decades, telecommunications companies have used profits from the most lucrative parts of their monopolies – notably international services – to subsidise loss-making operations at home. The result, as the Commission noted in February 1993, is a patchwork of telecommunications tariffs across Europe that bear little relation to the costs of the services offered. The break-up of state monopolies over both domestic and international calls will make such arrangements unworkable.

This is especially good news for business users, who rely on international telephone links far more than private users. According to the Commission, calls across frontiers within the European Union tend to cost between two-and-a-half and three times as much as calls over a comparable distance within a single member state. At off-peak times the cost ratio of national to international calls can widen to $1:6$.[13] Worse still, from the Commission's pan-European perspective, is the huge disparity in the cost of telephone calls travelling in opposite directions along the same lines between member states.

Case study
INTERNATIONAL CALL CHARGES AND THE LEVEL PLAYING FIELD

'It is unreasonable', said Sir Leon Brittan in late December 1992, 'that a three minute telephone call between two member states should cost two to three times more than the most expensive call within a single country. Nor can we accept that a three minute call between Belgium and Denmark should be billed at Ecu 2.54, whereas the same call coming from Denmark should cost Ecu 1.36.'[14]

It is worth considering for a moment the impact of these widely varying call charges on European business. Take the example quoted by Sir Leon Brittan above. Let us imagine two companies, one Belgian, the other Danish, each with subsidiaries in one another's countries. Let us further imagine the head office of each company speaks for an hour a day, on average, to its subsidiary.

In the course of a year, the Danish company will notch up a bill of Ecu 9,928 on telephone calls to its Belgian subsidiary. Over the same period, the Belgian company will have pay Ecu 18,542 to keep in touch with its Danish subsidiary. All other costs being equal, a Belgian company will pay Ecu 8,614 per annum more for the privilege of doing business in Denmark than its Danish counterpart will pay for doing business in Belgium. By any standards, this constitutes a massive distortion of competition in the single market.

But what of the British? Are British businesses at a disadvantage *vis-à-vis* their Continental European competitors as a result of high international call charges?

In 1991, the answer appeared on the whole to be no. The European consumers' association, the Bureau Européen des Unions de Consommateurs (BEUC), found that intra-EU calls from Britain, whether through BT or Mercury, were among the cheapest in Europe. Only the Danes and the Germans undercut Mercury Communications' average peak-time international rate to thirteen other European countries, and only the Danes, the Germans and the Dutch undercut BT's international peak time rates to the same spread of countries.[15]

Nevertheless, even in this broadly creditable performance, there were some worrying discrepancies for British businesses. A peak-rate call from Stuttgart in Germany to Cambridge cost Ecu 2.79 for five minutes. A call in the reverse direction cost Ecu 3.12 using BT and Ecu 3.09 using Mercury. Using the same multiplier as we used on the Denmark–Belgium and Belgium–Denmark call charges earlier, the annual telephone bill for a Cambridge-based business with a subsidiary in Stuttgart would be either Ecu 1,314 or Ecu 1,445.5 more expensive than the annual telephone bill of a Stuttgart-based company with a subsidiary in Cambridge. (The smaller difference would apply with Mercury, the bigger one with BT.)

There is a major element of swings and roundabouts in such calculations. For instance, Mercury's off-peak rates to EU countries beat those offered by Deutsche Telekom, pushing the 'average' 5 minute intra-EU call on Mercury (peak and off-peak) below that of the German monopoly operator. However, Mercury's charges to Switzerland and Austria were higher, and if these countries were included in the calculations, Deutsche Telekom again emerged as cheaper.

Furthermore, tariffs are changing all the time. The Belgian state-owned monopoly operator Belgacom, obliquely criticised by Sir Leon Brittan in late 1992 for the high cost of its international services, emerged as one of the stars in a 1993 survey of telecommunications companies catering for high volume business users. The survey, conducted by London market research company Tarifica/Intelidata, found that telephone costs for a typical multinational in Belgium were 20 per cent below the European average.[16] Sir Leon's indignation may have been based on out-of-date information.

Ironing out these differences is more easily said than done. A report published in 1991 by the Bureau Européen des Unions de Consommateurs (BEUC)[15] identified an issue at the core of the debate on how – and how fast – Europe's telecommunications monopolies should be broken up. The BEUC found that in Britain – the only country where competition between telephone companies had already been introduced – the cost in international calls was falling, but the cost of fixed rate charges (such as connection charges and information services) was rising. 'From the consumers' point of view, this looks worrying', the BEUC concluded. Of course, that depends on what kind of consumer you have in mind. For the private individual making a small number of calls, it is indeed worrying. For the large or medium-sized company making large numbers of peak-time international calls, it is heartening.

The debate over telecommunications liberalisation since the publication of the BEUC report has centred on how to strike the right balance between the needs of the high volume business user and the low volume private user. The French state-owned telecommunications company France Telecom has presented itself as the champion of the small consumer and has argued that attempts to force harmonisation of EU telephone charges through competition will cost the small consumer dear. The Spanish government has expressed reluctance to lower its extremely high international call charges at the expense of raising higher domestic rates, which currently benefit from generous cross-subsidy.[17]

For the Commission, the first step was to harmonise the technical standards of Europe's diverse national telecommunications networks. This is indispensable if liberalisation – opening the networks to new users – is to proceed smoothly. Therefore technical harmonisation was the goal set by the open network framework directive adopted in 1990.

The Commission's second step was to establish that it had the right to force the break-up of Europe's powerful telecommunications monopolies, should it consider such action desirable. Four countries – Belgium, France, Italy and Spain – challenged that right in the European Court of Justice. On 17 November 1992 the European Commission got what it wanted: formal authority from the ECJ to use Article 90 of the Treaty of Rome to prise open anti-competitive national monopolies, including monopolies inhibiting the liberalisation of telecommunications services.

The case had concerned the Commission's plans to liberalise European markets for a range of non-voice telephone services, including facsimile and data transfer. The four EU member states had resisted this, claiming that Article 90 only enabled the Commission to monitor existing national rules under the Treaty of Rome, rather than take a proactive role in breaking up monopolies. The plaintiffs argued that existing monopolies were protected from direct intervention by the Commission without special authority from the Council of Ministers. According to this reading of the Treaty of Rome, the Commission was only empowered to act against extensions of monopoly power.

The ECJ disagreed. It found the Commission entirely within its rights in instructing member states to break up revenue-producing monopolies without consulting the Council of Ministers.

On the face of it, the ECJ's decision was a famous victory for the Commission. In theory, it cleared the path for enforced liberalisation of the vast European market for voice telephony, beside which services like fax and electronic data transmission were small beer (voice telephony revenues generated by Europe's telecommunications operators were valued at Ecu 110 billion in 1992).[18] The four member states that had brought the European Court action had hoped to send a warning shot across the Commission's bows, deterring it from venturing further into the hugely lucrative voice telephony market.

However, politics suggested the Commission should tread still warily. The case had shown the intensity of resistance among EU member states to the enforced break-up of major monopolies in fields such as telecommunications and energy production and distribution. Although Sir Leon Brittan welcomed the ECJ's decision, officials hinted that the Commission would proceed cautiously henceforth.

Hence the new approach adopted by Karel Van Miert, Sir Leon's successor. The first evidence for this came at the beginning of February 1993, when the Commission sent a consultative document on the telecommunications sector through to member states. The document contained four 'options for progress':[19]

1. Freezing the liberalisation process and maintaining the situation as it stood at the end of 1992. This would enable the existing reforms to bed down. However, it might be open to attack under the 1990 directive on telecommunications services, which stipulates that exclusive control over voice telephony services can only be justified on an exceptional basis.

2. Regulating extensively on tariffs and investments in order to remove the sur-charge on intra-EU tariffs. (The Commission had found that telephone calls between EU member states were far more expensive that within member states, regardless of the relative distances.)

3. Liberalising all voice telephony services internationally (within and outside the Union) and also national domestic services. This would involve other countries such as Japan and the United States, through the framework of the GATT negotiations. The Commission estimated that, if achieved, it could result in annual growth of 6–7 per cent in real terms in Europe's telecommunications markets.

4. Opening competition on voice telephony services between member states.

It might well be asked in what sense option 1, under which the Commission and member states would simply tread water, could be described as an option for progress. The Commission made it plain that its favoured course was option 4, which it saw as maintaining the 'balance between liberalisation and harmonisation' which the more far-reaching option 3 might disrupt.

However, between February and April 1993, the Commission had a change of heart. The Germans indicated they would favour more thorough-going liberalisation of voice telephony from 1998, when the company will have completed a massive DM 60 billion investment programme in eastern Germany. Across the Channel, British Telecom was pushing hard for rapid action from the Commission. Thus encouraged, Mr Van Miert switched his support to option 3 and total liberalisation of Europe's voice telephony services by 1 January 1998.

By April 1993 Mr Van Miert was waxing lyrical in support of option 3. In an interview with the French financial newspaper *Les Echos*, he promised it would yield a 'notable reduction in communication costs, [enabling] networks to be used more intensively and [allowing] their costs to be written off over a shorter period'.[20] To wait until the year 2000 'would not be a sensible option', he said.

BT's management was unimpressed. The company had lobbied for freedom of services by 1 January 1994 and freedom to build new networks by 1 January 1995. Jonathan Rickford, BT's government relations director, points out that networks account for between 70 per cent and 80 per cent of the costs against which telecommunications revenues must be set. 'If you don't liberalise this, the virtuous healthy effects of competition are all but lost', he says.

The cost of installing new telephone networks might be prohibitive, were it not for the fact that cable television lines can readily be converted to carry telecommunications signals. In Britain in late April 1993, thirty cable television franchisees had over 143,000 telephone exchange lines in service. This represented an increase of 363 per cent in the course of a year.[21] In Continental Europe, cable television operators were still not permitted to offer telephone services.

The European Commission commissioned a study into the liberalisation of telecommunications networks, published in 1993. Progress may be slow, but it looks unlikely that the right to build and operate telecommunications networks will remain a monopoly privilege for ever.

POSTAL SERVICES

The third major service sector that the Commission has had in its sights is the post. The debate is similar to the debate over telecommunications but clearer because the technology does not get in the way. Envelopes come in all shapes and sizes and the harmonisation of technical standards is not a *sine qua non* of progress (although some harmonisation is still needed, as we shall see).

The dilemma for the Commission is stark. How can Europe's postal monopolies be opened up to competition while ensuring that crofters in the Shetland Islands or villagers in the wilds of Tras-os-Montes in northern Portugal can still receive and send mail? How can private sector competitors be prevented from creaming off profits from the most lucrative parts of national post office monopolies to the detriment of post office customers in outlying areas?

In 1993 the awkwardness of this problem even gave pause to Europe's most enthusiastic advocates of privatisation, the British Conservative government of John Major: plans to privatise the Royal Mail were quietly put to one side. Little wonder, then, that enthusiasm for Thatcherite 'market solutions' elsewhere in Europe was lacking.

The upshot was that when, in June 1993, the European Commission listed the four

CHAPTER 9

KAREL VAN MIERT: 'UN SOCIALISTE PAS COMME LES AUTRES'

Karel Van Miert wears his allegiance to the European Union on his sleeve – literally. A rather garish wristwatch depicting the flags of the twelve EU member states commonly relieves the sobriety of his otherwise conservative attire.

Within a year of taking office as competition commissioner, Mr Van Miert had dispelled some, but not all, of the fears expressed by British business leaders when it was announced late in 1992 that Sir Leon Brittan, the dry-as-a-bone former Thatcher cabinet minister, was handing over the competition portfolio to a Flemish socialist.

A Flemish socialist . . . Few British businessmen knew exactly what that meant – but it sounded worrying. Their disquiet was put into words in March 1993 by Colin Overbury, former head of the Commission's merger task force and a close associate of Sir Leon Brittan. Writing in the bi-monthly *Competition and Trade Law Review* published by his new employers, the British law firm Allen & Overy, Mr Overbury identified three likely effects of Mr Van Miert's appointment:

1. The new commissioner would probably 'take a more liberal view of competition matters'. In practice this would mean that he would not 'impede the creation of large undertakings which may be better placed to compete on a worldwide market *even if this led to high EC market shares*' [my italics]. The principle is simple: the bigger your market, the less likely you are to distort competition within it.

2. On state aids, Mr Van Miert was likewise expected to take a more liberal view than his predecessor, emphasising not just the effects of aids on competition but their social impact as well. The word liberal in this context meant 'less vigorous' and 'accepting greater state intervention'.

3. The new commissioner would prove less determined than Sir Leon Brittan to prise open public monopolies using Article 90 of the Treaty of Rome. As we have seen, the Commission's use of Article 90 during Sir Leon's tenure as competition commissioner sparked fierce opposition from several member states.

We have the advantage of hindsight over Mr Overbury, whose tentative predictions were based on his knowledge of the new competition commissioner's previous career. Nevertheless, a knowledge of Karel Van Miert's background is still worth having. For a man likely to remain an important player on the European stage, the label 'Flemish socialist' will not suffice.[1]

Karel Van Miert is a self-made man. He was born into a farming family in the Flemish village of Oud-Turnhout on 17 January 1942, the eldest of nine children. He learned responsibility early when his father died and he had to help his mother bring up the rest of the family. Friends describe his salient virtues as personal loyalty and determination, both of which probably owe much to his upbringing.

Another childhood characteristic that has never left him is his love of the land. Mr Van Miert's favourite pastime – apart from wrestling with 'problems of European integration', as his official CV drily relates – is gardening. 'He wants to keep in contact with the ground', says a friend at the Commission.

Mr Van Miert's emotional attachment may be to the soil of his native Flanders, as well as to his wife and son, but his intellectual training is that of an academic. After postgraduate studies at the European University in Nancy in France (where his MA dealt, appropriately, with the supranational character of the European Commission), he became a lecturer in political science at the Brussels Free University. His academic work was supplemented by an internship at the Commission in the mid-1970s, where he worked closely with another Belgian socialist, Henri Simonet, the Commission vice-president responsible for tax, financial institutions and energy.

At the same time he was was making his way in the Belgian socialist party, becoming its chairman in 1978 – a position he was to hold for a decade. Colleagues remember him as being to the left of the party, leading the resistance to the siting of US nuclear warheads in Belgium.

His career since 1978 has alternated between national and European politics in a fashion common enough in Belgium but rare in Britain. 'His version of patriotism is loyalty to the EC', says a British lobbyist who has dealt with him on a number of occasions. Mr Van Miert was twice elected to the European Parliament, in 1979 and 1984 – the second time with a greatly increased majority. He served as a Belgian MP from 1985 to 1988.

In 1989 he landed his first job as a commissioner, acquiring responsibility for transport, credit and investments and consumer policy. His appetite for hard work is said to have impressed Commission president Jacques Delors. On several occasions he held the fort in Brussels for other commissioners during summer and Christmas holidays.

Mr Van Miert's background would appear to set him a world apart from the combative, sometimes acerbic, right-wing former barrister whom he succeeded as competition commissioner in January 1993, but some observers of Mr Van Miert's career have argued that the differences in outlook between him and Sir Leon Brittan are less pronounced than they at first appear. They point to Mr Van Miert's biggest achievement as transport commissioner, the 'open skies' airline liberalisation programme, which was achieved in the teeth of fierce opposition from some national airlines. The idea was to inject competition into a business that had long operated though a series of officially sanctioned cartels. The intended beneficiary was the consumer.

However, Mr Van Miert did not always see eye to eye with Sir Leon Brittan on competition matters, and on two occasions he crossed swords with the then competition commissioner. Their disagreements concerned product and geographical market definitions – the yardsticks against which distortions of competition are measured.

The first case was close to home, involving two Dutch coffee producers, Douwe Egberts and Van Nelle. In 1990, Sir Leon considered outlawing Douwe Egberts' takeover of Van Nelle on the grounds that the two companies would control 70 per cent of the Benelux market for coffee. Mr Van Miert teamed up with the Dutch commissioner Frans Andriessen to argue that the Benelux countries were not a relevant geographical market. Sir Leon eventually dropped his objections.[2]

The second case was more momentous. In October 1991 the European Commission outlawed a bid by two state-owned aerospace companies, Aerospaciale of France and Alenia of Italy, to purchase de Havilland, a Canadian turbo-prop aircraft manufacturer, from Boeing. It was the first (and, during Sir Leon Brittan's stewardship, the only) outright rejection of a transaction to occur under the 1989 merger control regulation. Mr Van Miert was one of a number of commissioners who thought the decision was a mistake. Martin Bangemann, the heavyweight industrial affairs commissioner, was another.

The Commission's decision sent shockwaves through French government and industry. Sir Leon was branded a 'malign and reckless meddler' and an 'economic criminal' in sections of the French press. He was accused of sacrificing Europe's economic interest on an altar of Thatcherite prejudice. The Commission had rejected the de Havilland takeover on the ground that it would leave Aerospaciale and Alenia dominant in both the world and EU markets for 40–59 seat and 60-plus seat turbo-prop commuter aircraft. French politicians, led by the then prime minister Edith Cresson, protested that the Commission had defined its product markets too narrowly.

Mr Van Miert agreed – but as competition commissioner he likes to claim that the de Havilland decision was 'exceptional' and to stress that 90 per cent of the merger cases referred to the Commission are approved within a month.[3] At every opportunity he emphasises the continuity of policy between Sir Leon Brittan and himself. That is not surprising. EU commissioners always stress continuity: once they start to claim innovation, member state governments begin to wonder whether they are overstepping their authority.

Naturally, it is exceptional rather than routine cases that determine the shape of EU competition policy. If Karel Van Miert had held the competition portfolio during the merger regulation's first two years of life, it seems unlikely that a single merger would have been rejected outright.

Did, then, Mr Van Miert's attitude towards the de Havilland case augur a major change in EU competition policy? He can point to evidence that, even before Sir Leon left, EU merger policy was moving away from the rigorous, letter of the law approach seen in the de Havilland judgement. Mr Overbury admits that during his time as director of the merger task force (in other words, up until Mr Van Miert's arrival in January 1993) the Commission's policy towards mergers became 'more liberal'. The relevant markets were defined ever more broadly. 'If anything, it was letting more [mergers] go through.'

However, Mr Overbury's judgement that Mr Van Miert's arrival would probably usher in a still more liberal policy towards mergers appears well-founded. Mr Van Miert complains that EU competition policy in the past has failed to take sufficient account of the globalisation of markets. Ask him how he would like his two-year stint as competition commissioner to be remembered, he replies that he would like to 'develop further the global dimension of competition policy'.

Early on, he was given the chance to put this preference into practice. In April 1993, the Commission cleared a co-operative joint venture to manufacture active matrix liquid crystal displays (AM-435 LCDs) involving Philips of the Netherlands and Thomson and Sagem of France. Together the three partners dominate the European Community market for AM-LCDs. Mr Van Miert admits as much, but says it does not bother him: 'That's not a real issue because it is a world market situation where Japanese companies are ahead. The only way to have real competition on a world level is to have strong European competitors.'[4]

Unfortunately, competition policy is more complicated than this, and Mr Van Miert knows it. Competition policy creates friends and enemies as surely as competition itself throws up winners and losers. France's Aerospaciale was aghast at the de Havilland decision, but British Aerospace, one of Britain's biggest exporters, was relieved: it had feared being squeezed out of the market for 64-seat turbo-prop commuter aircaft. Nine months later, the French were cock-a-hoop when the Commission approved FFr 6.68 billion in state aid to the chronically ailing state-owned French computer manufacturer, Compagnie des Machines Bull, but ICL, Britain's biggest computer manufacturer, was dismayed (see chapter 4).

This brings us the second of Mr Overbury's predictions – that Mr Van Miert would be softer on state aids than his predecessor. This has not proved to be the case. Mr Van Miert has amply demonstrated that he does not intend to relax the Commission's treatment of state aids. He jokes that government officials in Italy and Spain have taken to calling him Sir Leon Van Miert because they can see no change in state aids policy, particularly relating to the steel industry. He has rejected rescue plans for state-owned steel companies in Italy and Spain with every bit as much firmness as Sir Leon Brittan would have mustered.

Mr Van Miert's handling of state aid applications shows why crude labels such as Flemish socialist are inadequate as a basis on which to predict a commissioner's actions. State aid to industry runs at high levels in his native Belgium – but Belgium is not Europe. As EU competition commissioner, Mr Van Miert frequently alludes to the damage that a subsidy race among member states could inflict on the Union. On 19 February 1993 he told the European Parliament's economic and monetary committee that he would not tolerate 'beggar my neighbour' aid schemes that merely 'export unemployment and push problems onto other member states'.[5] Sir Leon Brittan could not have put it more clearly.

Yet such views do not necessarily conflict with Mr Van Miert's socialist beliefs. The problem with an uncontrolled subsidy race, as seen from the Commission, is that it would boost the richer member states of the Union at the expense of the poorer ones. Richer countries obviously have more money to spend on helping their industry

than poorer countries. The Commission's well-established poli
by tightly controlling state aid disbursed in the richer countries. ₁
Union's regional policy, with its swelling budgets, is designed to shift re₋
wealthy core of Europe to the impoverished periphery.

Mr Van Miert is a canny politician. He stresses continuity of policy, but he als₋
how to draw specious contrasts in order to put himself on the side of the angels.
conversation he often conjures up an ultra-liberal theory of competition of a kind the
European Commission has never espoused, only in order to knock it down. 'If all were
left to competition inside and outside the Community, what would be left of agricultural policy?' he asked a *Financial Times* journalist, rhetorically, in March 1993. 'What
would be left of shipbuilding? Nothing. What would be left of steel? Not very much. Of
textiles? Not very much.'[6]

He was too polite to tell the man from the *FT* where he believed such wilfully
destructive doctrines originated, but in conversation with Jacques Docquiert, a journalist on the *FT*'s French sister publication *Les Echos*, he was less inhibited. 'If one takes the
steel sector, from a strictly liberal point of view one can say: "The situation is bad but,
tough, the market wills it." And do nothing. That would be a neo-Thatcherite
approach.' Later in the same interview he referred to the 'ravages of hard-line liberalism'
that could be seen in the UK and the United States.[7]

Mr Van Miert's experience of Belgian politics has also moulded his outlook in a way
some British Conservatives may find surprising, and possibly reassuring. To be sure, he
will happily inveigh against Thatcherism, but he is hesitant about rolling forward the
frontiers of the state once again. 'We must not go back to the old state aid practices that
explain, for example, the phenomenal indebtedness of Belgium', he told *Les Echos*.

In search of his *via media*, Mr Van Miert is prepared to take some tough decisions. In
June 1993 he told the management of Ekostahl, an east German steelworks close to the
Polish border, that he was unable to accept a restructuring plan proposed by the
Treuhand, the German privatisation agency. The plan would have saved three thousand
jobs for the small town of Eisenhuttenstadt, already plagued by massive unemployment,
but at the price of adding to the glut in European steel markets. 'It was, politically
speaking, an extremely difficult decision', the commissioner recalls.[8] The Treuhand
was told to think again.

By the autumn of 1993 the pressure on Mr Van Miert to adopt a more accommodat-
ing policy on state aids was growing by the day. Continental Europe appeared mired in
recession. The steel market was in crisis. The car market was in crisis. The computer
market was in crisis. Most of Europe's airlines were in crisis. Unemployment was high
and climbing. Set against this background, it was questionable whether the commissioner's personal determination to keep a lid on state aids would be enough.

In such circumstances, a commissioner must chose his battles – and his allies – with
care. Even when times are good, no competition commissioner can wage a dozen
battles at once; and times were far from good in the summer of 1993. In July, Mr Van
Miert abandoned the idea of lowering the merger regulation thresholds, a cause dear to
the heart of many of his officials at DGIV: the political odds were stacked against him
(see chapter 3).

As his term as competition commissioner continues, the problem for Mr Van Miert is that the ground on which he has to fight is becoming more and more treacherous. Eurocrat bashing is gaining popularity as a political sport across the Community. Subsidiarity is a subtle concept, but it is often used as a blunt instrument with which to club the European Commission. British government ministers frequently argue for a tougher EU competition policy, but they regularly vote against giving the Commission extra resources. In the summer of 1993 Britain joined forces with France and Germany to resist lowering the merger regulation thresholds.

There is perhaps more value, then, in mapping out Karel Van Miert's constraints than in analysing his convictions. Who, for instance, are his political friends and who are his enemies? He has done much to repair bridges with the French, destroyed during the de Havilland row, but relations with the British government are, at best, lukewarm.

In an effort to display his Eurosceptic credentials, UK prime minister John Major has lost few opportunities to put the Commission in its place. Writing in *The Economist* on 25 September 1993, Mr Major stated bluntly that the role of the 'bureaucrats' at the Commission was to implement the agenda laid down by ministers, not to make policy themselves.

For his part, Mr Van Miert won himself no friends in Whitehall by sniping at what he saw as the obduracy and incompetence of the British government. In February 1993, he complained about Britain's opt-out from the social chapter of the Maastricht Treaty. 'You cannot play a game of football when one player is using his hands – and that is what is happening in Britain.'[9] A few months later he lamented the snail's pace of Britain's attempts to ratify the rest of the Maastricht Treaty.

Unlike Jacques Delors, Karel Van Miert enjoys a low profile in Britain. His is scarcely a household name and there is little political capital to be made in opposing him. Ironically, it is the French who gave him most trouble in his first six months as competition commissioner, despite welcoming his appointment. The French government brought a successful European Court of Justice action which, in June 1993, deprived the Commission of the means to scrutinise state aids to state-owned industry (see chapter 4). The ECJ ruled that a communication, addressed to the member states by Sir Leon Brittan in July 1991, overstepped the Commission's authority in demanding regular information on financial relations between states and their large industrial holdings.

Mr Van Miert had made it clear that he regarded the communication as very useful in monitoring potential state aids. Less than a fortnight before the court delivered its judgement, he confirmed that, if defeated, the Commission would still seek out this information. 'We will have to do it case by case, which is more cumbersome.'[10]

If Karel Van Miert survives his two years as competition commissioner with only a few cumbersome procedures to complain about, he may count himself lucky. Nineteen ninety-three will not go down as a good year for the European Union. As unemployment soared, demands for protection grew louder across the continent. State aid applications piled up in the commissioner's in-tray.

As the year ebbed away, worse spectres began to emerge. The nightmare scenario for Karel Van Miert is a progressive erosion of confidence in the principles upon which EU competition policy is based. It is unlikely this would affect the most entrenched prerogatives of the Commission – the control of cartels and abuse of market dominance under Articles 85 and 86 of the Treaty of Rome – but more recent elements of the *acquis communautaire*, the European Union's heritage, would be put at risk: state aids would multiply, to the detriment of the poorer EU member states, and the Commission's already tolerant attitude towards mergers would become downright supine in the face of stiff lobbying from member state governments.

Worst of all, though, the Union's forward momentum would be checked, to be regained only with great difficulty. Here we come to the third of Mr Overbury's predictions, that Mr Van Miert would be less tough on state-owned monopolies than Sir Leon Brittan had been. The commissioner's weapon, Article 90 of the Treaty of Rome, can cut deeply if wielded with determination: it entitles the Commission to apply the treaty's competition rules to some of the state's most cherished preserves, such as its monopolies in energy, telecommunications and postal services. The weapon has been little used, though. In June 1993, Mr Van Miert said he would use it 'with caution'.[11]

The break-up of these monopolies represents the biggest challenge facing Karel Van Miert. He says he wants to take the process step by step, to give the companies involved time to adjust.[12] The renewal of his mandate at the beginning of 1995 gives him much more time. However, a risk remains that Europe's deepening political malaise may rob him of his chance to make a lasting impression on the development of the European Union.

NOTES

1. The following information on Karel Van Miert's family background and early career draws upon research undertaken by the author for an article that appeared in *The Engineer*, 7 January 1993.
2. Cecilia Andersen, *Influencing the European Community: Guidelines for a successful business strategy*. Kogan Page, 1992, page 115.
3. Interview with the author, 3 June 1993.
4. *Ibid.*
5. *Financial Times*, 23 February 1993.
6. *Financial Times*, 26 March 1993.
7. *Les Echos*, 22 February 1993.
8. Interview with the author, 3 June 1993.
9. *Evening Standard*, 4 February 1993.
10. Interview with the author, 3 June 1993.
11. *Ibid.*
12. See, for example, Mr Van Miert's speech at the European Institute Club in Washington, D.C., 7 October 1993.

APPENDIX 1

TREATY OF ROME: ARTICLES 85 AND 86

Rules applying to undertakings

Article 85

1 The following shall be prohibited as incompatible with the common market: all agreements between undertakings, decisions by associations of undertakings and concerted practices which may affect trade between Member States and which have as their object or effect the prevention, restriction or distortion of competition within the common market, and in particular those which:

(a) directly or indirectly fix purchase or selling prices or any other trading conditions;
(b) limit or control production, markets, technical development, or investment;
(c) share markets or sources of supply;
(d) apply dissimilar conditions to equivalent transactions with other trading parties, thereby placing them at a competitive disadvantage;
(e) make the conclusion of contracts subject to acceptance by the other parties of supplementary obligations which, by their nature or according to commercial usage, have no connection with the subject of such contracts.

2 Any agreements of decisions prohibited pursuant to this Article shall be automatically void.

3 The provisions of paragraph 1 may, however, be declared inapplicable in the case of:

– any agreement or category of agreements between undertakings;
– any decision or category of decisions by associations of undertakings;
– any concerted practice or category of concerted practices;

which contributes to improving the production or distribution of goods or to promoting technical or economic progress, while allowing consumers a fair share of the resulting benefit, and which does not:

(a) impose on the undertakings concerned restrictions which are not indispensable to the attainment of these objectives;

(b) afford such undertakings the possibility of eliminating competition in respect of a substantial part of the products in question.

Article 86

Any abuse by one or more undertakings of a dominant position within the common market or in a substantial part of it shall be prohibited as incompatible with the common market in so far as it may affect trade between Member States.

Such abuse may, in particular, consist in:

(a) directly or indirectly imposing unfair purchase or selling prices or other unfair trading conditions;
(b) limiting production, markets or technical development to the prejudice of consumers;
(c) applying dissimilar conditions to equivalent transactions with other trading parties, thereby placing them at a competitive disadvantage;
(d) making the conclusion of contracts subject to acceptance by the other parties of supplementary obligations which, by their nature or according to commercial usage, have no connection with the subject of such contracts.

REGULATION 17

Regulation 17 was adopted in 1962 to enable the Commission to implement Articles 85 and 86 of the Treaty of Rome.

$$\star \quad \star \quad \star \quad \star \quad \star \quad \star$$

The Council of the European Community

Having regard to the Treaty establishing the European Economic Community, and in particular Article 87 thereof;

Having regard to the proposal from the Commission;

Having regard to the Opinion of the European Parliament;

Whereas, in order to establish a system ensuring that competition shall not be distorted in the common market, it is necessary to provide for balanced application of Articles 85 and 86 in a uniform manner in the Member States;

Whereas in establishing the rules for applying Article 85 (3) account must be taken of the need to ensure effective supervision and to simplify administration to the greatest possible extent;

Whereas it is accordingly necessary to make it obligatory, as a general principle, for undertakings which seek application of Article 85(3) to notify the Commission of their agreements, decisions and concerted practices;

Whereas on the one hand, such agreements, decisions and concerted practices are probably very numerous and cannot therefore all be examined at the same time and, on the other hand, some of them have special features which may make them less prejudicial to the development of the common market;

Whereas there is consequently a need to make more flexible arrangements for the time being in respect of certain categories of agreement, decision and concerted practice without prejudicing their validity under Article 85;

Whereas it may be in the interest of undertakings to know whether any agreements, decisions or practices to which they are party, or propose to become party, may lead to action on the part of the Commission pursuant to Article 85(1) or Article 86;

Whereas, in order to secure uniform application of Articles 85 and 86 in the common market, rules must be made under which the Commission, acting in close and constant liaison with the competent authorities of the Member States, may take the requisite measures for applying those Articles;

Whereas for this purpose the Commission must have the cooperation of the competent authorities of the Member States and be empowered, throughout the common market, to require such information to be supplied and to undertake such investigations as are necessary to bring to light any agreement, decision or concerted practice prohibited by Article 85(1) or any abuse of a dominant position prohibited by Article 86;

Whereas, in order to carry out its duty of ensuring that the provisions of the Treaty are applied, the Commission must be empowered to address to undertakings or associations of undertakings recommendations and decisions for the purpose of bringing to an end infringements of Articles 85 and 86;

Whereas compliance with Articles 85 and 86 and the fulfilment of obligations imposed on undertakings and associations of undertakings under this Regulation must be enforceable by means of fines and periodic penalty payments;

Whereas undertakings concerned must be accorded the right to be heard by the Commission, third parties whose interests may be affected by a decision must be given the opportunity of submitting their comments beforehand, and it must be ensured that wide publicity is given to decisions taken;

Whereas all decisions taken by the Commission under this Regulation are subject to review by the Court of Justice under the conditions specified in the Treaty; whereas it is moreover desirable to confer upon the Court of Justice, pursuant to Article 172, unlimited jurisdiction in respect of decisions under which the Commission imposes fines or periodic penalty payments;

Whereas this Regulation may enter into force without prejudice to any other provisions that may hereafter be adopted pursuant to Article 87;

Has adopted this Regulation:

Article 1
Basic provision

Without prejudice to Articles 6,7 and 23 of this Regulation, agreements, decisions and concerted practices of the kind described in Article 85(1) of the Treaty and the abuse of a dominant position in the market, within the meaning of Article 86 of the Treaty, shall be prohibited, no prior decision to that effect being required.

Article 2
Negative clearance

Upon application by the undertakings or associations of undertakings concerned, the

Commission may certify that, on the basis of the facts in its possession, there are no grounds under Article 85(1) or Article 86 of the Treaty for action on its part in respect of an agreement, decision or practice.

Article 3
Termination of infringements

1   Where the Commission, upon application or upon its own initiative, finds that there is infringement of Article 85 or Article 86 of the Treaty, it may by decision require the undertakings or associations of undertakings concerned to bring such infringement to an end.

2   Those entitled to make application are:
   (a) Member States;
   (b) natural or legal persons who claim a legitimate interest.

3   Without prejudice to the other provisions of this Regulation, the Commission may, before taking a decision under paragraph 1, address to the undertakings or associations of undertakings concerned recommendations for termination of the infringement.

Article 4
Notification of new agreements, decisions and practices

1   Agreements, decisions and concerted practices of the kind described in Article 85(1) of the Treaty which come into existence after the entry into force of this Regulation and in respect of which the parties seek application of Article 85(3) must be notified to the Commission. Until they have been notified, no decision in application of Article 85(3) may be taken.

2   Paragraph 1 shall not apply to agreements, decisions or concerted practices where:
   (1) the only parties thereto are undertakings from one Member State and the agreements, decisions or practices do not relate either to imports or to exports between Member States;
   (2) not more than two undertakings are party thereto, and the agreements only;
      (a) restrict the freedom of one party to the contract in determining the prices or conditions of business upon which the goods which he has obtained from the other party to the contract may be resold, or
      (b) impose restrictions on the exercise of the rights of the assignee or user of industrial property rights – in particular patents, utility models, designs or trade marks – or of the person entitled under a contract to the assignment, or grant, of the right to use a method of manufacture or knowledge relating to the use and to the application of industrial processes;
   (3) they have as their sole object:
      (a) the development or uniform application of standards or types; or
      (b) joint research and development;

(c) specialisation in the manufacture of products, including agreements necessary for achieving this,
- where the products which are the subject of specialization do not, in a substantial part of the common market, represent more than 15 per cent of the volume of business done in identical products or those considered by consumers to be similar by reason of the characteristics, price and use, and
- where the total annual turnover of the participating undertakings does not exceed 200 million units of account.

These agreements, decisions and practices may be notified to the Commission.

Article 5
Notification of existing agreements, decisions and practices

1 Agreements, decisions and concerted practices of the kind described in Article 85(1) of the Treaty which are in existence at the date of entry into force of this Regulation and in respect of which the parties seek application of Article 85(3) shall be notified to the Commission before 1 November 1962. However, notwithstanding the foregoing provisions, any agreements, decisions and concerted practices to which not more than two undertakings are party shall be notified before 1 February 1963.

2 Paragraph 1 shall not apply to agreements, decisions or concerted practices falling within Article 4(2); these may be notified to the Commission.

Article 6
Decisions pursuant to Article 85 (3)

1 Whenever the Commission takes a decision pursuant to Article 85(3) of the Treaty, it shall specify therein the date from which the decision shall take effect. Such date shall not be earlier than the date of notification.

2 The second sentence of paragraph 1 shall not apply to agreements, decisions or concerted practices falling within Article 4(2) and Article 5(2), nor to those falling within Article 5(1) which have been notified within the time limit specified in Article 5(1).

Article 7
Special provisions for existing agreements, decisions and practices

1 Where agreements, decisions and concerted practices in existence at the date of entry into force of this Regulation and notified within the time limits specified in Article 5(1) do not satisfy the requirements of Article 85(3) of the Treaty and the undertakings or associations of undertakings concerned cease to give effect to them or modify them in such manner that they no longer fall within the prohibition contained in

Article 85(1) or that they satisfy the requirements of Article 85(3), the prohibition contained in Article 85(1) shall apply only for a period fixed by the Commission. A decision by the Commission pursuant to the foregoing sentence shall not apply as against undertakings and associations of undertakings which did not expressly consent to the notification.

2 Paragraph 1 shall apply to agreements, decisions and concerted practices falling within Article 4(2) which are in existence at the date of entry into force of this Regulation if they are notified before 1 January 1967.

Article 8
Duration and revocation of decisions under Article 85(3)

1 A decision in application of Article 85(3) of the Treaty shall be issued for a specified period and conditions and obligations may be attached thereto.

2 A decision may on application be renewed if the requirements of Article 85 (3) of the Treaty continue to be satisfied.

3 The Commission may revoke or amend its decision or prohibit specified acts by the parties:

    (a) where there has been a change in any of the facts which were basic to the making of the decision;

    (b) where the parties commit a breach of any obligation attached to the decision;

    (c) where the decision is based on incorrect information or was induced by deceit;

    (d) where the parties abuse the exemption from the provisions of Article 85(1) of the Treaty granted to them by the decision.

In cases which subparagraphs (b), (c), or (d) apply, the decision may be revoked with retroactive effect.

Article 9
Powers

1 Subject to review of its decision by the Court of Justice, the Commission shall have sole power to declare Article 85(1) inapplicable pursuant to Article 85(3) of the Treaty.

2 The Commission shall have power to apply Article 85(1) and Article 86 of the Treaty; this power may be exercised notwithstanding that the time limits specified in Article 5(1) and in Article 7(2) relating to notification have not expired.

3 As long as the Commission has not initiated any procedure under Articles 2, 3 or 6, the authorities of the Member States shall remain competent to apply Article 85(1) and Article 86 in accordance with Article 88 of the Treaty; they shall remain competent in this respect notwithstanding that the time limits specified in Article 5(1) and in Article 7(2) relating to notification have not expired.

Article 10
Liaison with the authorities of the Member States

1   The Commission shall forthwith transmit to the competent authorities of the Member States a copy of the application and notifications together with copies of the most important documents lodged with the Commission for the purpose of establishing the existence of infringements of Article 85 or 86 of the Treaty or of obtaining negative clearance or a decision in application of Article 85(3).

2   The Commission shall carry out the procedure set out in paragraph 1 in close and constant liaison with the competent authorities of the Member States; such authorities shall have the right to express their views upon that procedure.

3   An Advisory Committee on Restrictive Practices and Monopolies shall be consulted prior to the taking of any decision following upon a procedure under paragraph 1, and of any decision concerning the renewal, amendment or revocation of a decision pursuant to Article 85(3) of the Treaty.

4   The Advisory Committee shall be composed of officials competent in the matter of restrictive practices and monopolies. Each Member State shall appoint an official to represent it who, if prevented from attending, may be replaced by another official.

5   The consultation shall take place at a joint meeting convened by the Commission; such meeting shall be held not earlier than 14 days after dispatch of the notice convening it. The notice shall, in respect of each case to be examined, be accompanied by a summary of the case together with an indication of the most important documents, and a preliminary draft decision.

6   The Advisory Committee may deliver an opinion notwithstanding that some of its members or their alternates are not present. A report of the outcome of the consultative proceedings shall be annexed to the draft decision. It shall not be made public.

Article 11
Request for information

1   In carrying out the duties assigned to it by Article 89 and by provisions adopted under Article 87 of the Treaty, the Commission may obtain all necessary information from the Governments and competent authorities of the Member States and from undertakings and associations of undertakings.

2   When sending a request for information to an undertaking or association of undertakings, the Commission shall at the same time forward a copy of the request to the competent authority of the Member State in whose territory the seat of the undertaking or association of undertakings is situated.

3   In its request the Commission shall state the legal basis and the purpose of the request and also the penalties provided for in Article 15(1)(b) for supplying incorrect information.

4   The owners of the undertakings or their representatives and, in the case of legal persons, companies or firms, or of associations having no legal personality, the persons authorised to represent them by law or by the constitution shall supply the information requested.

5   Where an undertaking or association of undertakings does not supply the information requested within the time limit fixed by the Commission, or supplies incomplete information, the Commission shall by decision require the information to be supplied. The decision shall specify what information is required, fix an appropriate time limit within which it is to be supplied and indicate the penalties provided for in Article 15(1)(b) and Article 16(1)(c) and the right to have the decision reviewed by the Court of Justice.

6   The Commission shall at the same time forward a copy of its decision to the competent authority of the Member State in whose territory the seat of the undertaking or association of undertakings is situated.

Article 12
Inquiry into sectors of the economy

1   If in any sector of the economy the trend of trade between Member States, price movements, inflexibility of prices or other circumstances suggest that in the economic sector concerned competition is being restricted or distorted within the common market, the Commission may decide to conduct a general inquiry into that economic sector and in the course thereof may request undertakings in the sector concerned to supply the information necessary for giving effect to the principles formulated in Articles 85 and 86 of the Treaty and for carrying out the duties entrusted to the Commission.

2   The Commission may in particular request every undertaking or association of undertakings in the economic sector concerned to communicate to it all agreements, decisions and concerted practices which are exempt from notification by virtue of Article 4(2) and Article 5(2).

3   When making inquiries pursuant to paragraph 2, the Commission shall also request undertakings or groups of undertakings whose size suggests that they occupy a dominant position within the common market or a substantial part thereof to supply to the Commission such particulars of the structure of the undertakings and of their behaviour as are requisite to an appraisal of their position in the light of Article 86 of the Treaty.

4   Article 10(3) to (6) and Articles 11, 13 and 14 shall apply correspondingly.

Article 13
Investigation by the authorities of the Member States

1   At the request of the Commission, the competent authorities of the Member States shall undertake the investigations which the Commission considers to be necessary under Article 14(1), or which it has ordered by decision pursuant to Article 14(3). The officials of the competent authorities of the Member States responsible for conducting these investigations shall exercise their powers upon production of an authorization in writing issued by the competent authority of the Member State in whose territory the investigation is to be made. Such authorization shall specify the subject matter and purpose of the investigation.

2   If so requested by the Commission or by the competent authority of the Member State in whose territory the investigation is to be made, the officials of the Commission may assist the officials of such authorities in carrying out their duties.

Article 14
Investigating powers of the Commission

1   In carrying out the duties assigned to it by Article 89 and by provisions adopted under Article 87 of the Treaty, the Commission may undertake all necessary investigations into undertakings and associations of undertakings. To this end the officials authorized by the Commission are empowered:

(a) to examine the books and other business records;
(b) to take copies of or extracts from the books and business records;
(c) to ask for oral explanations on the spot;
(d) to enter any premises, land and means of transport of undertakings.

2   The officials of the Commission authorized for the purpose of these investigations shall exercise their powers upon production of an authorization in writing specifying the subject matter and purpose of the investigation and the penalties provided for in Article 15(1)(c) in cases where production of the required books or other business records is incomplete. In good time before the investigation, the Commission shall inform the competent authority of the Member State in whose territory the same is to be made of the investigation and of the identity of the authorized officials.

3   Undertakings and associations of undertakings shall submit to investigations by decision of the Commission. The decision shall specify the subject matter and purpose of the investigation, appoint the date on which it is to begin and indicate the penalties provided for in Article 15(1)(c) and Article 16(1)(d) and the right to have the decision reviewed by the Court of Justice.

4   The Commission shall take decisions referred to in paragraph 3 after consultation with the competent authority of the Member State in whose territory the investigation is to be made.

5   Officials of the competent authority of the Member State in whose territory the investigation is to be made may, at the request of such authority or of the Commission, assist the officials of the Commission in carrying out their duties.

6   Where an undertaking opposes an investigation ordered pursuant to this Article, the Member State concerned shall afford the necessary assistance to the officials authorized by the Commission to enable them to make their investigation. Member States shall, after consultation with the Commission, take the necessary measures to this end before 1 October 1962.

Article 15
Fines

1 The Commission may by decision impose on undertakings or associations of undertakings fines of from 100 to 5,000 units of account where, intentionally or negligently:

(a) they supply incorrect or misleading information in an application pursuant to Article 2 or in a notification pursuant to Articles 4 or 5; or
(b) they supply incorrect information in response to a request made pursuant to Article 11(3) or (5) or to Article 12, or do not supply information within the time limit fixed by a decision taken under Article 11(5); or
(c) they produce the required books or other business records in incomplete form during investigations under Articles 13 or 14, or refuse to submit to an investigation ordered by decision issued in implementation of Article 14(3).

2 The Commission may by decision impose on undertakings or associations of undertakings fines from 1,999 to 1,000,000 units of account, or a sum in excess thereof but not exceeding 10 per cent of the turnover in the preceding business year of each of the undertakings participating in the infringement where, either intentionally or negligently:

(a) they infringe Article 85(1) or Article 86 of the Treaty; or
(b) they commit a breach of any obligation imposed pursuant to Article 8(1).

In fixing the amount of the fine, regard shall be had both to the gravity and to the duration of the infringement.

3 Article 10(3) to (6) shall apply.

4 Decisions taken pursuant to paragraphs 1 and 2 shall not be of criminal law nature.

5 The fines provided for in paragraph 2(a) shall not be imposed in respect of acts taking place:

(a) after notification to the Commission and before its decision in application of Article 85(3) of the Treaty provided they fall within the limits of the activity described in the notification;
(b) before notification and in the course of agreements, decisions or concerted practices in existence at the date of entry into force of this Regulation, provided that notification was effected within the time limits specified in Article 5(1) and Article 7(2).

6 Paragraph 5 shall not have effect where the Commission has informed the undertakings concerned that after preliminary examination it is of opinion that Article 85(1) of the Treaty applies and that application of Article 85(3) is not justified.

Article 16
Periodic penalty payments

1 The Commission may by decision impose on undertakings or associations of undertakings periodic penalty payments of from 50 to 1,000 units of account per day, calculated from the date appointed by the decision, in order to compel them:

(a) to put an end to an infringement of Articles 85 to 86 of the Treaty, in accordance with a decision taken pursuant to Article 3 of this Regulation;

(b) to refrain from any act prohibited under Article 8(3);

(c) to supply complete and correct information which it has requested by decision taken pursuant to Article 11(5);

(d) to submit to an investigation which it has ordered by decision taken pursuant to Article 14(3).

2 Where the undertakings or associations of undertakings have satisfied the obligation which it was the purpose of the periodic penalty payments to enforce, the Commission may fix the total amount of the periodic penalty payment at a lower figure than that which would arise under the original decision.

3 Article 10(3) to (6) shall apply.

Article 17
Review by the Court of Justice

The Court of Justice shall have unlimited jurisdiction within the meaning of Article 172 of the Treaty to review decisions whereby the Commission has fixed a fine or periodic penalty payments; it may cancel, reduce or increase the fine or periodic penalty payments imposed.

Article 18
Unit of account

For the purposes of applying Articles 15 to 17 the unit of account shall be that adopted in drawing up the budget of the Community in accordance with Articles 207 and 209 of the Treaty.

Article 19
Hearing of the parties and of third persons

1 Before taking decisions as provided for in Articles 2, 3, 6, 7, 8, 15 and 16, the Commission shall give the undertakings or associations of undertakings concerned the opportunity of being heard on matters to which the Commission has taken objection.

2 If the Commission or the competent authorities of the Member States consider it necessary, they may also hear other natural or legal persons. Applications to be heard on the part of such persons shall, where they show sufficient interest, be granted.

3 Where the Commission intends to give negative clearance pursuant to Article 2 or take a decision in application of Article 85(3) of the Treaty, it shall publish a summary of the relevant application or notification and invite all interested third parties to submit their observations within a time limit which it shall fix being not less than one month. Publication shall have regard to the legitimate interests of undertakings in the protection of their business secrets.

Article 20
Professional secrecy

1 Information acquired as a result of the application of Articles 11, 12, 13 and 14 shall be used only for the purpose of the relevant request or investigation.

2 Without prejudice to the provisions of Article 19 and 21, the Commission and the competent authorities of the Member States, their officials and other servants shall not disclose information acquired by them as a result of the application of this Regulation and of the kind covered by the obligation of professional secrecy.

3 The provisions of paragraphs 1 and 2 shall not prevent publication of general information or surveys which do not contain information relating to particular under-takings or associations of undertakings.

Article 21
Publication of decisions

1 The Commission shall publish the decisions which it takes pursuant to Articles 2, 3, 6, 7 and 8.

2 The publication shall state the names of the parties and the main content of the decision; it shall have regard to the legitimate interest of undertakings in the protection of their business secrets.

Article 22
Special provisions

1 The Commission shall submit to the Council proposals for making certain cat-egories of agreement, decision and concerted practice falling within Article 4(2) or Article 5(2) compulsorily notifiable under Article 4 or 5.

2 Within one year from the date of entry into force of this Regulation, the Council shall examine, on a proposal from the Commission, what special provisions might be made for exempting from the provisions of this Regulation agreements, decisions and concerted practices falling within Article 4(2) or Article 5(2).

Article 23

Transitional provisions applicable to decisions of authorities of the Member States

1   Agreements, decisions and concerted practices of the kind described in Article 85(1) of the Treaty to which, before the entry into force of this Regulation, the competent authority of a Member State has declared Article 85(1) to be inapplicable pursuant to Article 85(3) shall not be subject to compulsory notification under Article 5. The decision of the competent authority of the Member State shall be deemed to be a decision within the meaning of Article 6; it shall cease to be valid upon expiration of the period fixed by such authority but in any event not more than three years after the entry into force of this Regulation. Article 8(3) shall apply.

2   Applications for renewal of decision of the kind described in paragraph 1 shall be decided upon by the Commission in accordance with Article 8(2).

Article 24

Implementing provisions

The Commission shall have the power to adopt implementing provisions concerning the form, content and other details of applications pursuant to Articles 2 and 3 and of notifications pursuant to Articles 4 and 5, and concerning hearings pursuant to Article 19(1) and (2).

Article 25

1   As regards agreements, decisions and concerted practices to which Article 85 of the Treaty applies by virtue of accession, the date of accession shall be substituted for the date of entry into force of this Regulation in every place where reference is made in this Regulation to this latter date.

2   Agreements, decisions and concerted practices existing at the date of accession to which Article 85 of the Treaty applies by virtue of accession shall be notified pursuant to Article 5(1) or Article 7(1) and (2) within six months from the date of accession.

3   Fines under Article 15(2)(a) shall not be imposed in respect of any act prior to notification of the agreements, decisions and practices to which paragraph 2 applies and which have been notified within the period therein specified.

4   New Member States shall take measures referred to in Article 14(6) within six months from the date of accession after consulting the Commission.

5   The provisions of paragraphs 1 to 4 above shall apply in the same way in the case of accession of the Hellenic Republic, the Kingdom of Spain and the Portuguese Republic. This regulation shall be binding in its entirety and directly applicable in all Member States.

Done at Brussels, 6 February 1962

Amendments

Article 25 was added by the Act of 1972 concerning the conditions of accession and the adjustments to the treaty, annex I.

Paragraph 5 was added by the Act of the Hellenic Republic 1979, annex I(V)1 and subsequently replaced by the Act of Accession of the Kingdom of Spain and the Portuguese Republic 1985, annex I(IV)(5).

APPENDIX 3

THE 1989 MERGER REGULATION

Council Regulation (EEC) No. 4064/89
of 21 December 1989
on the control of concentrations between undertakings

The Council of the European Communities,

Having regard to the proposal from the Commission.[1]

Having regard to the opinion of the European Parliament.[2]

Having regard to the opinion of the Economic and Social Committee.[3]

1 Whereas, for the achievement of the aims of the Treaty establishing the European Economic Community, Article 3(f) gives the Community the objective of instituting 'a system ensuring that competition in the common market is not distorted';

2 Whereas this system is essential for the achievement of the internal market by 1992 and its further development;

3 Whereas the dismantling of internal frontiers is resulting and will continue to result in major corporate reorganizations in the Community, particularly in the form of concentrations;

4 Whereas such a development must be welcomed as being in line with the requirements of dynamic competition and capable of increasing the competitiveness of European industry, improving the conditions of growth and raising the standard of living in the Community;

5 Whereas, however, it must be ensured that the process of reorganization does not result in lasting damage to competition; whereas Community law must therefore include provisions governing those concentrations which may significantly impede effective competition in the common market or in a substantial part of it;

[1] OJ No. C 130, 19 May 1988, page 4.
[2] OJ No. C 309, 5 December 1988, page 55.
[3] OJ No. C 208, 8 August 1988, page 11.

6 Whereas Articles 85 and 86, while applicable, according to the case-law of the Court of Justice, to certain concentrations, are not, however, sufficient to control all operations which may prove to be incompatible with the system of undistorted competition envisaged in the Treaty;

7 Whereas a new legal instrument should therefore be created in the form of a Regulation to permit effective control of all concentrations from the point of view of the effect on the structure of competition in the Community and to be the only instrument applicable to such concentrations;

8 Whereas this Regulation should therefore be based not only on Article 87 but, principally, on Article 235 of the Treaty, under which the Community may give itself the additional powers of action necessary for the attainment of its objectives, including with regard to concentrations on the markets for agricultural products listed in Annex II of the Treaty;

9 Whereas the provisions to be adopted in this Regulation should apply to significant structural changes the impact of which on the market goes beyond the national borders of any one Member State;

10 Whereas the scope of application of this Regulation should therefore be defined according to the geographical area of activity of the undertakings concerned and be limited by quantitative thresholds in order to cover those concentrations which have a Community dimension; whereas, at the end of an initial phase of the application of this Regulation, these thresholds should be reviewed in the light of the experience gained;

11 Whereas a concentration with a Community dimension exists where the combined aggregate turnover of the undertakings concerned exceeds given levels worldwide and within the Community and where at least two of the undertakings concerned have their sole or main fields of activities in different Member States or where, although the undertakings in question act mainly in one and the same Member State, at least one of them has substantial operations in at least one other Member State; whereas that is also the case where the concentrations are effected by undertakings which do not have their principal fields of activities in the Community but which have substantial operations there;

12 Whereas the arrangements to be introduced for the control of the concentrations should, without prejudice to Article 90(2) of the Treaty, respect the principle of non-discrimination between the public and the private sectors; whereas, in the public sector, calculation of the turnover of an undertaking concerned in a concentration needs, therefore, to take account of undertakings making up an economic unit with an independent power of decision, irrespective of the way in which their capital is held or of the rules of administrative supervision applicable to them;

13 Whereas it is necessary to establish whether concentrations with a Community dimension are compatible or not with the common market from the point of view of the need to maintain and develop effective competition in the common market; whereas, in so doing, the Commission must place its appraisal within the general framework of that achievement of the fundamental objectives referred to in Article 2 of the Treaty, including that of strengthening the Community's economic and social cohesion, referred to in Article 130a;

14   Whereas this Regulation should establish the principle that a concentration with a Community dimension which creates or strengthens a position as a result of which effective competition i.e. the common market or in a substantial part of it is significantly impeded is to be declared incompatible with the common market;

15   Whereas concentrations which, by reason of the limited market share of the undertakings concerned, are not liable to impede effective competition may be presumed to be compatible with the common market; whereas, without prejudice to Articles 85 and 86 of the Treaty, an indication to this effect exists, in particular, where the market share of the undertakings concerned does not exceed 25 per cent either in the common market or in a substantial part of it;

16   Whereas the Commission should have the task of taking all the decisions necessary to establish whether or not concentrations with a Community dimension are compatible with the common market, as well as decisions designed to restore effective competition;

17   Whereas to ensure effective control undertakings should be obliged to give prior notification of concentrations with a Community dimension and provision should be made for the suspension of concentrations for a limited period, and for the possibility of extending or waiving a suspension where necessary; whereas in the interest of legal certainty the value of transactions must nevertheless be protected as much as necessary;

18   Whereas a period within which the Commission must initiate proceedings in respect of a notified concentration and periods within which it must give a final decision on the compatibility or incompatibility with the common market of a notified concentration should be laid down;

19   Whereas the undertakings concerned must be afforded the right to be heard by the Commission when proceedings have been initiated; whereas the members of the management and supervisory bodies and the recognized representatives of the employees of the undertakings concerned, and third parties showing a legitimate interest, must also be given the opportunity to be heard;

20   Whereas the Commission should act in close and constant liaison with the competent authorities of the Member States from which it obtains comments and information;

21   Whereas, for the purposes of this Regulation, and in accordance with the case-law of the Court of Justice, the Commission must be afforded the assistance of the Member States and must also be empowered to require information to be given and to carry out the necessary investigations in order to appraise concentrations;

22 Whereas compliance with this Regulation must be enforceable by means of fines and periodic penalty payments; whereas the Court of Justice should be given unlimited jurisdiction in that regard pursuant to Article 172 of the Treaty;

23 Whereas it is appropriate to define the concept of concentration in such a manner as to cover only operations bringing about a lasting change in the structure of the undertakings concerned; whereas it is therefore necessary to exclude from the scope of this Regulation those operations which have as their object or effect the coordination of the competitive behaviour of undertakings which remain independent, since such operations fall to be examined under the appropriate provisions of the Regulations implementing Articles 85 and 86 of the Treaty; whereas it is appropriate to make this distinction specifically in the case of the creation of joint ventures;

24 Whereas there is no coordination of the competitive behaviour within the meaning of this Regulation where two or more undertakings agree to acquire jointly control of one or more undertakings with the object and effect of sharing amongst themselves such undertakings or their assets.

25 Whereas this Regulation should still apply where the undertakings concerned accept restrictions directly related and necessary to the implementation of the concentrations;

26 Whereas the Commission should be given exclusive competence to apply this Regulation, subject to review by the Court of Justice;

27 Whereas the Member States may not apply their national legislation on competition to concentrations with a Community dimension, unless this Regulation makes provisions therefor; whereas the relevant powers of national authorities should be limited to cases where, failing intervention by the Commission, effective competition is likely to be significantly impeded within the territory of a Member State and where the competition interest of that Member State cannot be sufficiently protected otherwise by this Regulation; whereas the Member States concerned must act promptly in such cases; whereas this Regulation cannot, because of the diversity of national law, fix a single deadline for the adoption of remedies;

28 Whereas, furthermore, the exclusive application of this Regulation to concentrations with a Community dimension is without prejudice to Article 223 of the Treaty, and does not prevent the Member States from taking appropriate measures to protect legitimate interests other than those pursued by this Regulation, provided that such measures are compatible with the general principles and other provisions of Community law;

29 Whereas concentrations not covered by this Regulation come, in principle, within the jurisdiction of the Member States; whereas, however, the Commission should have the power to act, at the request of a Member State concerned, in cases where effective competition could be significantly impeded within that Member State's territory;

30   Whereas the conditions in which concentrations involving Community undertakings are carried out in non-member countries should be observed, and provision should be made for the possibility of the Council giving the Commission an appropriate mandate for negotiations with a view to obtaining non-discriminatory treatment for Community undertakings;

31   Whereas this Regulation in no way detracts from the collective rights of employees as recognized in the undertakings concerned,

HAS ADOPTED THIS REGULATION:

Article 1
Scope

1   Without prejudice to Article 22 this Regulation shall apply to all concentrations with a Community dimension as defined in paragraph 2.

2   For the purpose of this Regulation, a concentration has a Community dimension where:

(a) the combined aggregate worldwide turnover of all the undertakings concerned is more than ECU 5000 million; and
(b) the aggregate Community-wide turnover of each of at least two of the undertakings concerned is more than ECU 250 million, unless each of the undertakings concerned achieves more than two-thirds of its aggregate Community-wide turnover within one and the same Member State.

3   The thresholds laid down in paragraph 2 will be reviewed before the end of the fourth year following that of the adoption of this Regulation by the Council acting by a qualified majority on a proposal from the Commission.

Article 2
Appraisal of concentrations

1   Concentrations within the scope of this Regulation shall be appraised in accordance with the following provisions with a view to establishing whether or not they are compatible with the common market.

In making this appraisal, the Commission shall take into account:

(a) the need to maintain and develop effective competition within the common market in view of, among other things, the structure of all the markets concerned and the actual or potential competition from undertakings located either within or outwith the Community;
(b) the market position of the undertakings concerned and their economic and financial power, the alternatives available to suppliers and users, their access to suppliers or markets, any legal or other barriers to entry, supply and demand trends for the relevant goods and services, the interests of the intermediate and ultimate consumers, and the development of technical and economic progress that is to consumers' advantage and does not form an obstacle to competition.

2   A concentration which does not create or strengthen a dominant position as a result of which effective competition would be significantly impeded in the common market or in a substantial part of it shall be declared compatible with the common market.

3   A concentration which creates or strengthens a dominant position as a result of which effective competition would be significantly impeded in the common market or in a substantial part of it shall be declared incompatible with the common market.

Article 3
Definition of concentration

1   A concentration shall be deemed to arise where:

(a) two or more previously independent undertakings merge, or

(b) one or more persons already controlling at least one undertaking, or – one or more undertakings acquire, whether by purchase of securities or assets, by contract or by any other means, direct or indirect control of the whole or parts of one or more undertakings.

2   An operation, including the creation of a joint venture, which has as its object or effect the coordination of the competitive behaviour of undertakings which remain independent shall not constitute a concentration within the meaning of paragraph 1(b).

The creation of a joint venture performing on a lasting basis all the functions of an autonomous economic entity, which does not give rise to coordination of the competitive behaviour of the parties amongst themselves or between them and the joint venture, shall constitute a concentration within the meaning of paragraph 1(b).

3   For the purposes of this Regulation, control shall be constituted by rights, contracts or any other means which, either separately or in combination and having regard to the considerations of fact or law involved, confer the possibility of exercising decisive influence on an undertaking, in particular by:

(a) ownership or the right to use all or part of the assets of an undertaking;

(b) rights or contracts which confer decisive influence on the composition, voting or decisions of the organs of an undertaking.

4   Control is acquired by persons or undertakings which:

(a) are holders of the rights or entitled to rights under the contracts concerned; or

(b) while not being holders of such rights or entitled to rights under such contracts, have the power to exercise the rights deriving therefrom.

5   A concentration shall not be deemed to arise where:

(a) credit institutions or other financial institutions or insurance companies, the normal activities of which include transactions and dealing in securities for their own account or for the account of others, hold on a temporary basis securities which they have acquired in an undertaking with a view to reselling them, provided that they do not exercise voting rights in respect of those securities with a view to determining the competitive behaviour of that undertaking or provided that they exercise such voting rights only with a view to preparing the disposal of all or part of that undertaking or of its assets or the disposal of those securities and that any such disposal takes place within one year of the date of acquisition; that period may be extended by the Commission on request where such institutions or companies can show that the disposal was not reasonably possible within the period set;

(b) control is acquired by an office-holder according to the law of a Member State relating to liquidation, winding up, insolvency, cessation of payments, compositions or analogous proceedings;

(c) the operations referred to in paragraph 1(b) are carried out by the financial holding companies referred to in Article 5(3) of the Fourth Council Directive 78/660/EEC of 25 July 1978 on the annual accounts of certain types of companies,[1] as last amended by Directive 84/569/EEC,[2] provided however that the voting rights in respect of the holding are exercised, in particular in relation to the appointment of members of the management and supervisory bodies of the undertakings in which they have holdings, only to maintain the full value of those investments and not to determine directly or indirectly the competition conduct of those undertakings.

Article 4
Prior notification of concentrations

1   Concentrations with a Community dimension defined in this Regulation shall be notified to the Commission not more than one week after the conclusion of the agreement, or the announcement of the public bid, or the acquisition of a controlling interest. That week shall begin when the first of those events occurs.

2   A concentration which consists of a merger within the meaning of Article 3(1)(a) or in the acquisition of joint control within the meaning of Article 3(1)(b) shall be notified jointly by the parties to the merger or by those acquiring joint control as the case may be. In all other cases, the notification shall be effected by the person or undertaking acquiring control of the whole or parts of one or more undertakings.

3   Where the Commission finds that a notified concentration falls within the scope of this Regulation, it shall publish the fact of the notification, at the same time indicating the names of the parties, the nature of the concentration and the economic sectors involved. The Commission shall take account of the legitimate interest of undertakings in the protection of their business secrets.

Article 5
Calculation of turnover

1   Aggregate turnover within the meaning of Article 1(2) shall comprise the amounts derived by the undertakings concerned in the preceding financial year from the sale of

---

[1] OJ No. L 222, 14 August 1978, page 11.
[2] OJ No. L 314, 4 December 1984, page 28.

products and the provision of services falling within the undertakings' ordinary activities after deductions of sales rebates and of value added tax and other taxes directly related to turnover. The aggregate turnover of an undertaking concerned shall not include the sale of products or the provision of services between any of the undertakings referred to in paragraph 4.

Turnover, in the Community or in a Member State, shall comprise products sold and services provided to undertakings or consumers, in the Community or in that Member State as the case may be.

2 By way of derogation from paragraph 1, where the concentration consists in the acquisition of parts, whether or not constituted as legal entities, of one or more undertakings, only the turnover relating to the parts which are the subject of the transaction shall be taken into account with regard to the seller or sellers.

However, two or more transactions within the meaning of the first subparagraph which take place within a two-year period between the same persons or undertakings shall be treated as one and the same concentration arising on the date of the last transaction.

3 In place of turnover the following shall be used:

(a) for credit institutions and other financial institutions, as regards Article 1(2)(a), one-tenth of their total assets.

As regards Article 1(2)(b) and the final part of Article 1(2), total Community-wide turnover shall be replaced between loans and advances to credit institutions and customers in transactions with Community residents and the total sum of those loans and advances.

As regards the final part of Article 1(2), total turnover within one Member State shall be replaced by one-tenth of total assets multiplied by the ratio between loans and advances to credit institutions and customers in transactions with residents of that Member State and the total sum of those loans and advances;

(b) for insurance undertakings, the value of gross premiums written which shall comprise all amounts received and receivable in respect of insurance contracts issued by or on behalf of the insurance undertakings, including also outgoing reinsurance premiums, and after deduction of taxes and parafiscal contributions or levies charged by reference to the amounts of individual premiums or the total volume of premiums; as regards Article 1(2)(b) and the final part of Article 1(2), gross premiums received from Community residents and from residents of one Member State respectively shall be taken into account.

4 Without prejudice to paragraph 2, the aggregate turnover of an undertaking concerned within the meaning of Article 1(2) shall be calculated by adding together the respective turnovers of the following:

(a) the undertaking concerned;

(b) those undertakings in which the undertaking concerned, directly or indirectly:
  - owns more than half the capital or business assets, or
  - have the power to exercise more than half the voting rights, or

- have the power to appoint more than half the members of the supervisory board, the administrative board or bodies legally representing the undertakings, or
- have the right to manage the undertakings' affairs;

(c) those undertakings which have in the undertaking concerned the rights or powers listed in (b);

(d) those undertakings which an undertaking as referred to in (c) have the rights or powers listed in (b);

(e) those undertakings in which two or more undertakings as referred to in (a) to (d) jointly have the rights or powers listed in (b).

5   Where undertakings concerned by the concentration jointly have the rights or powers listed in paragraph 4(b), in calculating the aggregate turnover of the undertakings concerned for the purposes of Article 1(2):

(a) no account shall be taken of the turnover resulting from the sale of products or the provision of services between the joint undertaking and each of the undertakings concerned or any other undertaking connected with any one of them, as set out in paragraph 4(b) to (e);

(b) account shall be taken of the turnover resulting from the sale of products and the provision of services between the joint undertaking and any third undertakings. This turnover shall be apportioned equally amongst the undertakings concerned.

Article 6
Examination of the notification and initiation of proceedings

1   The Commission shall examine the notification as soon as it is received.

(a) Where it concludes that the concentration notified does not fall within the scope of this Regulation, it shall record that finding by means of a decision.

(b) Where it finds that the concentration notified, although falling within the scope of this Regulation, does not raise serious doubts as to its compatibility with the common market, it shall decide not to oppose it and shall declare that it is compatible with the common market.

(c) If, on the other hand, it finds that the concentration notified falls within the scope of this Regulation and raises serious doubts as to its compatibility with the common market, it shall decide to initiate proceedings.

2   The Commission shall notify its decision to the undertakings concerned and the competent authorities of the Member States without delay.

Article 7
Suspension of concentrations

1   For the purposes of paragraph 2 a concentration as defined in Article 1 shall not be put into effect either before its notification or within the first three weeks following its notification.

2 Where the Commission, following a preliminary examination of the notification within the period provided for in paragraph 1, finds it necessary in order to ensure the full effectiveness of any decision taken later pursuant to Article 8(3) and (4), it may decide on its own initiative to continue the suspension of a concentration in whole or in part until it takes a final decision, or to take other interim measures to that effect.

3 Paragraphs 1 and 2 shall not prevent the implementation of a public bid which has been notified to the Commission in accordance with Article 4(1), provided that the acquirer does not exercise the voting rights attached to the securities in question or does so only to maintain the full value of those investments and on the basis of a derogation granted by the Commission under paragraph 4.

4 The Commission may, on request, grant a derogation from the obligations imposed in paragraphs 1, 2 or 3 in order to prevent serious damage to one or more undertakings concerned by a concentration or to a third party. That derogation may be made subject to conditions and obligations in order to ensure conditions of effective competition. A derogation may be applied for and granted at any time, even before notification or after the transaction.

5 The validity of any transaction carried out in convention of paragraph 1 or 2 shall be dependent on a decision pursuant to Article 6(1)(b) or Article 8(2) or (3) or on a presumption pursuant to Article 10(6).

This Article shall, however, have no effect on the validity of transactions in securities including those convertible into other securities admitted to trading on a market which is regulated and supervised by authorities recognized by public bodies, operates regularly and is accessible directly or indirectly to the public, unless the buyer and seller knew or ought to have known that the transaction was carried out in contravention of paragraph 1 or 2.

Article 8
Powers of decision of the Commission

1 Without prejudice to Article 9, all proceedings initiated pursuant to Article 6(1)(c) shall be closed by means of decision as provided for in paragraphs 2 to 5.

2 Where the Commission finds that, following modification by the undertakings concerned if necessary, a notified concentration fulfils the criterion laid down in Article 2(2), it shall issue a decision declaring the concentration compatible with the common market.

It may attach to its decision conditions and obligations intended to ensure that the undertakings concerned comply with the commitments they have entered into *vis-à-vis* the Commission with a view to modifying the original concentration plan. The decision declaring the concentration compatible shall also cover restrictions directly related and necessary to the implementation of the concentration.

3   Where the Commission finds that a concentration fulfils the criterion laid down in Article 2(3), it shall issue a decision declaring that the concentration is incompatible with the common market.

4   Where a concentration has already been implemented, the Commission may, in a decision pursuant to paragraph 3 or by separate decision, require the undertakings or assets brought together to be separated or the cessation of joint control or any other action that may be appropriate in order to restore conditions of effective competition.

5   The Commission may revoke the decision it has taken pursuant to paragraph 2 where:

   (a) the declaration of compatibility is based on incorrect information for which one of the undertakings is responsible or where it has been obtained by deceit; or
   (b) the undertakings concerned commit a breach of an obligation attached to the decision.

6   In the cases referred to in paragraph 5, the Commission may take a decision under paragraph 3, without being bound by the deadline referred to in Article 10(3).

Article 9
Referral to the competent authorities of the Member States

1   The Commission may, by means of a decision notified without delay to the undertakings concerned and the competent authorities of the other Member States, refer a notified concentration to the competent authorities of the Member State concerned in the following circumstances.

2   Within three weeks of the date of receipt of the copy of the notification a Member State may inform the Commission, which shall inform the undertakings concerned, that a concentration threatens to create or to strengthen a dominant position as a result of which effective competition would be significantly impeded on a market, within that Member State, which presents all the characteristics of a distinct market, be it a substantial part of the common market or not.

3   If the Commission considers that, having regard to the market for the products or services in question and the geographical reference within the meaning of paragraph 7, there is such a distinct market and that such a threat exists, either:

   (a) it shall itself deal with the cases in order to maintain or restore effective competition on the market concerned; or
   (b) it shall refer the case to the competent authorities of the Member State concerned with a view to the application of that State's national competition law.

If, however, the Commission considers that such a distinct market or threat does not exist it shall adopt a decision to that effect which it shall address to the Member State concerned.

4   A decision to refer or not to refer pursuant to paragraph 3 shall be taken:

(a) as a general rule within the six-week period provided for in Article 10(1), second subparagraph, where the Commission, pursuant to Article 6(1)(b), has not initiated proceedings; or

(b) within three months at most of the notification of the concentrations concerned where the Commission has initiated proceedings under Article 6(1)(c), without taking the preparatory steps in order to adopt the necessary measures under Article 8(2), second subparagraph, (3) or (4) to maintain or restore effective competition on the market concerned.

5   If within the three months referred to in paragraph 4(b) the Commission, despite a reminder from the Member State concerned, has not taken a decision on referral in accordance with paragraph 3 nor has taken the preparatory steps referred to in paragraph 4(b), it shall be deemed to have taken a decision to refer the case to the Member State concerned in accordance with paragraph 3(b).

6   The publication of any report or the announcement of the findings of the examination of the concentration by the competent authority of the Member State concerned shall be effected not more than four months after the Commission's referral.

7   The geographical reference market shall consist of the area in which the undertakings concerned are involved in the supply and demand of products or services, in which the conditions of competition are sufficiently homogeneous and which can be distinguished from neighbouring areas because, in particular, conditions of competition are appreciably different in those areas. This assessment should take account in particular of the nature and characteristics of the products or services concerned, of the existence of entry barriers, of consumer preferences, of appreciable differences of the undertakings' market shares between the area concerned and neighbouring areas or of substantial price differences.

8   In applying the provisions of this Article, the Member State concerned may take only the measures strictly necessary to safeguard or restore effective competition on the market concerned.

9   In accordance with the relevant provisions of the Treaty, any Member State may appeal to the Court of Justice, and in particular request the application of Article 186, for the purpose of applying its national competition law.

10   This Article will be reviewed before the end of the fourth year following that of the adoption of this Regulation.

Article 10
Time limits for initiating proceedings and for decisions

1   The decisions referred to in Article 6(1) must be taken within one month at most. That period shall begin on the day following that of the receipt of a notification or, if the information to be supplied with the notification is incomplete, on the day following

that of the receipt of the complete information. That period shall be increased to six weeks if the Commission receives a request from a Member State in accordance with Article 9(2).

2   Decisions taken pursuant to Article 8(2) concerning notified concentrations must be taken as soon as it appears that the serious doubts referred to in Article 6(1)(c) have been removed, particularly as a result of modifications made by the undertakings concerned, and at the latest by the deadline laid down in paragraph 3.

3   Without prejudice to Article 8(6), decisions taken pursuant to Article 8(3) concerning notified concentrations must be taken within not more than four months of the date on which proceedings are initiated.

4   The period set by paragraph 3 shall exceptionally be suspended where, owing to circumstances for which one of the undertakings involved in the concentration is responsible, the Commission has had to request information by decision pursuant to Article 11 or to order an investigation by decision pursuant to Article 13.

5   Where the Court of Justice gives a Judgement which annuls the whole or part of a Commission decision taken under this Regulation, the periods laid down in this Regulation shall start again from the date of the Judgement.

6   Where the Commission has not taken a decision in accordance with Article 6(1)(b) or (c) or Article 8(2) or (3) within the deadlines set in paragraphs 1 and 3 respectively, the concentration shall be deemed to have been declared compatible with the common market, without prejudice to Article 9.

Article 11
Requests for information

1   In carrying out the duties assigned to it by this Regulation, the Commission may obtain all necessary information from the Governments and competent authorities of the Member States, from the persons referred to in Article 3(1)(b), and from undertakings and associations of undertakings.

2   When sending a request for information to a person, an undertaking or an association of undertakings, the Commission shall at the same time send a copy of the request to the competent authority of the Member State within the territory of which the residence of the person or the seat of the undertaking or association of undertakings is situated.

3   In its request the Commission shall state the legal basis and the purpose of the request and also the penalties provided for in Article 14(1)(c) for supplying incorrect information.

4   The information requested shall be provided, in the case of undertakings, by their owners or their representatives and, in the case of legal persons, companies or firms, or of associations having no legal personality, by the persons authorized to represent them by law or by their statutes.

5 Where a person, an undertaking or an association of undertakings does not provide the information requested within the period fixed by the Commission or provides incomplete information, the Commission shall by decision require the information to be provided. The decision shall specify what information is to be required, fix an appropriate period within which it is to be supplied and state the penalties provided for in Articles 14(1)(c) and 15(1)(a) and the right to have the decision reviewed by the Court of Justice.

6 The Commission shall at the same time send a copy of its decision to the competent authority of the Member State within the territory of which the residence of the person or the seat of the undertakings or associations of undertakings is situated.

Article 12
Investigations by the authorities of the Member States

1 At the request of the Commission, the competent authorities of the Member States shall undertake the investigations which the Commission considers to be necessary under Article 13(1), or which it has ordered by decision pursuant to Article 13(3). The officials of the competent authorities of the Member States responsible for conducting those investigations shall exercise their powers upon production of an authorization in writing issued by the competent authority of the Member State within the territory of which the investigation is to be carried out. Such authorization shall specify the subject matter and purpose of the investigation.

2 If so requested by the Commission or by the competent authority of the Member State within the territory of which investigation is to be carried out, officials of the Commission may assist the officials of that authority in carrying out their duties.

Article 13
Investigative powers of the Commission

1 In carrying out the duties assigned to it by this Regulation, the Commission may undertake all necessary investigations into undertakings and associations of undertakings.

To that end the officials authorized by the Commission shall be empowered:

    (a) to examine the books and other business records;
    (b) to take or demand copies of or extracts from the books and business records;
    (c) to ask for oral explanations on the spot;
    (d) to enter any premises, land and means of transport of undertakings.

2 The officials of the Commission authorized to carry out the investigations shall exercise their powers on production of an authorization in writing specifying the subject matter and purpose of the investigation and the penalties provided for in Article 14(1)(d) in cases where production of the required books or other business records is incomplete. In good time before the investigation, the Commission shall inform, in writing, the competent authority of the Member State within the territory of which the investigation is to be carried out of the investigation and of the identities of the authorized officials.

3   Undertakings and associations of undertakings shall submit to investigations ordered by decision of the Commission. The decision shall specify the subject matter and purpose of the investigation, appoint the date of which it shall begin and state the penalties provided for in Articles 14(1)(d) and 15(1)(b) and the right to have the decision reviewed by the Court of Justice.

4   The Commission shall in good time and in writing inform the competent authority of the Member State within the territory of which the investigation is to be carried out of its intention of taking a decision pursuant to paragraph 3. It shall hear the competent authority before taking its decision.

5   Officials of the competent authority of the Member State within the territory of which the investigation is to be carried out may, at the request of that authority or of the Commission, assist the officials of the Commission in carrying out their duties.

6   Where an undertaking of association of undertakings opposes an investigation ordered pursuant to this Article, the Member State concerned shall afford the necessary assistance to the officials authorized by the Commission to enable them to carry out their investigation. To this end the Member States shall, after consulting the Commission, take the necessary measures within one year of the entry into force of this Regulation.

Article 14
Fines

1   The Commission may by decision impose of the persons referred to in Article 3(1)(b), undertakings or associations of undertakings fines of from ECU 1,000 to 50,000 where intentionally or negligently:

(a) they fail to notify a concentration in accordance with Article 4;
(b) they supply incorrect or misleading information in a notification pursuant to Article 4;
(c) they supply incorrect information in response to a request made pursuant to Article 11 or fail to supply information within the period fixed by a decision taken pursuant to Article 11;
(d) they produce the required books or other business records in incomplete form during investigations under Article 12 or 13, or refuse to submit to an investigation ordered by decision taken pursuant to Article 13.

2   The Commission may by decision impose fines not exceeding 10 per cent of the aggregate turnover of the undertakings concerned within the meaning of Article 5 on the persons or undertakings concerned where, either intentionally of negligently, they:

(a) fail to comply with an obligation imposed by a decision pursuant to Article 7(4) or 8(2), second subparagraph;

(b) put into effect a concentration in breach of Article 7(1) or disregard a decision taken pursuant to Article 7(2);

(c) put into effect a concentration declared incompatible with the common market by decision pursuant to Article 8(3) or do not take the measures ordered by decision pursuant to Article 8(4).

3 In setting the amount of a fine, regard shall be had to the nature and gravity of the infringement.

4 Decision taken pursuant to paragraphs 1 and 2 shall not be of criminal law nature.

Article 15
Periodic penalty payments

1 The Commission may by decision impose on the persons referred to in Article 3(1)(b), undertakings or associations of undertakings concerned periodic penalty payments of up to ECU 25,000 for each day of delay calculated from the date set in the decision, in order to compel them:

(a) to supply complete and correct information which it has requested by decision pursuant to Article 11;

(b) to submit to an investigation which it has ordered by decision pursuant to Article 13.

2 The Commission may by decision impose on the persons referred to in Article 3(1)(b) or on undertakings periodic penalty payments of up to ECU 100,000 for each day of delay calculated from the date set in the decision, in order to compel them:

(a) to comply with an obligation imposed by decision pursuant to Article 7(4) or Article 8(2), second subparagraph, or

(b) to apply the measures ordered by decision pursuant to Article 8(4).

3 Where the persons referred to in Article 3(1)(b), undertakings or associations of undertakings have satisfied the obligation which it was the purpose of the periodic penalty payment to enforce, the Commission may set the total amount of the periodic penalty payments at a lower figure than that which would arise under the original decision.

Article 16
Review in the Court of Justice

The Court of Justice shall have unlimited jurisdiction within the meaning of Article 172 of the Treaty to review decisions whereby the Commission has fixed a fine or periodic penalty payments; it may cancel, reduce or increase the fine or periodic penalty payments imposed.

Article 17
Professional secrecy

1   Information acquired as a result of the application of Articles 11, 12, 13 and 18 shall be used only for the purposes of the relevant request, investigation or hearing.

2   Without prejudice to Articles 4(3), 18 and 20, the Commission and the competent authorities of the Member States, their officials and other servants shall not disclose information they have acquired through the application of this Regulation of the kind covered by the obligation of professional secrecy.

3   Paragraphs 1 and 2 shall not prevent publication of general information or of surveys which do not contain information relating to particular undertakings or associations of undertakings.

Article 18
Hearing of the parties and third persons

1   Before taking any decision provided for in Article 7(2) and (4), Article 8(2), second subparagraph, and (3) to (5) and Articles 14 and 15, the Commission shall give the persons, undertakings and associations of undertakings concerned the opportunity, at every stage of the procedure up to the consultation of the Advisory Committee, of making known their views on the objections against them.

2   By way of derogation from paragraph 1, a decision to continue the suspension of a concentration or to grant a derogation from suspension as referred to in Article 7(2) or (4) may be taken provisionally, without the persons, undertakings or associations of undertakings concerned being given the opportunity to make known their views beforehand, provided that the Commission gives them that opportunity as soon as possible after having taken its decision.

3   The Commission shall base its decision only on objections on which the parties have been able to submit their observations. The rights of the defence shall be fully respected in the proceedings. Access to the file shall be open at least to the parties directly involved, subject to the legitimate business interests of undertakings in the protection of their business secrets.

4   In so far as the Commission or the competent authorities of the Member States deem it necessary, they may also hear other natural or legal persons. Natural or legal persons showing sufficient interest and especially members of the administrative or management bodies of the undertakings concerned or the recognized representatives of their employees shall be entitled, upon application, to be heard.

Article 19
Liaison with the authorities of the Member States

1   The Commission shall transmit to the competent authorities of the Member States

copies of the notifications within three working days and, as soon as possible, copies of the most important documents lodged with or issued by the Commission pursuant to this Regulation.

2   The Commission shall carry out the procedures set out in this Regulation in close and constant liaison with the competent authorities of the Member States, which may express their views upon those procedures. For the purposes of Article 9 it shall obtain information from the competent authority of the Member State as referred to in paragraph 2 of that Article and give it the opportunity to make known its views at every stage of the procedure up to the adoption of a decision pursuant to paragraph 3 of that Article; to that end it shall give it access to the file.

3   An Advisory Committee on concentrations shall be consulted before any decision is taken pursuant to Articles 8(2) to (5), 14, 15, or any provisions are adopted pursuant to Article 23.

4   The Advisory Committee shall consist of representatives of the authorities of the Member States. Each Member State shall appoint one or two representatives; if unable to attend they may be replaced by other representatives. At least one of the representatives of a Member State shall be competent in matters of restrictive practices and dominant positions.

5   Consultation shall take place at a joint meeting convened at the invitation of and chaired by the Commission. A summary of the case, together with an indication of the most important documents and a preliminary draft of the decision to be taken for each case considered, shall be sent with the invitation. The meeting shall take place not less than 14 days after the invitation has been sent. The Commission may in exceptional cases shorten that period as appropriate in order to avoid serious harm to one or more of the undertakings concerned by a concentration.

6   The Advisory Committee shall deliver an opinion on the Commission's draft decision, if necessary by taking a vote. The Advisory Committee may deliver an opinion even if some members are absent and unrepresented. The opinion shall be delivered in writing and appended to the draft decision. The Commission shall take the utmost account of the opinion delivered by the Committee. It shall inform the Committee of the manner in which its opinion has been taken into account.

7   The Advisory Committee may recommend publication of the opinion. The Commission may carry out such publication. The decision to publish shall take due account of the legitimate interest of undertakings in the protection of their business secrets and of the interest of the undertakings concerned in such publication's taking place.

Article 20
Publication of decisions

1   The Commission shall publish the decisions which it takes pursuant to Article 8(2) to (5) in the Officials Journal of the European Communities.

2 The publication shall state the names of the parties and the main content of the decision; it shall have regard to the legitimate interest of undertakings in the protection of their business secrets.

Article 21
Jurisdiction

1 Subject to review by the Court of Justice, the Commission shall have sole jurisdiction to take the decisions provided for in this Regulation.

2 No Member State shall apply its national legislation on competition to any consideration that has a Community dimension.

The first subparagraph shall be without prejudice to any Member State's power to carry out any enquiries necessary for the application of Article 9(2) or after referral, pursuant to Article 9(3), first subparagraph, indent (b), or (5), to take the measures strictly necessary for the application of Article 9(8).

3 Notwithstanding paragraphs 1 and 2, Member States may take appropriate measures to protect legitimate interests other than those taken into consideration by this Regulation and compatible with the general principles and other provisions of Community law.

Public security, plurality of the media and prudential rules shall be regarded as legitimate interests within the meaning of the first subparagraph.

Any other public interest must be communicated to the Commission by the Member State concerned and shall be recognized by the Commission after an assessment of its compatibility with the general principles and other provisions of Community law before the measures referred to above may be taken. The Commission shall inform the Member State concerned of its decision within one month of that communication.

Article 22
Application of the Regulation

1 This Regulation alone shall apply to concentrations as defined in Article 3.

2 Regulations No. 17, (EEC) No. 1017/68, (EEC) No. 4056/86 and (EEC) No. 3975/87 shall not apply to concentrations as defined in Article 3.

3 If the Commission finds, at the request of a Member State, that a concentration as defined in Article 3 that has no Community dimension within the meaning of Article 1 creates or strengthens a dominant position as a result of which effective competition would be significantly impeded within the territory of the Member State concerned it may, in so far as the concentration affects trade between Member States, adopt the decisions provided for in Article 8(2), second subparagraph, (3) and (4).

4 Articles 2(1)(a) and (b), 5, 6, 8 and 10 to 20 shall apply. The period within which proceedings may be initiated pursuant to Article 10(1) shall begin on the date of the receipt of the request from the Member State. The request must be made within one month at most of the date on which the concentration was made known to the Member State or effected. This period shall begin on the date of the first of those events.

5 Pursuant to paragraph 3 the Commission shall take only the measures strictly necessary to maintain or restore effective competition within the territory of the Member State at the request of which it intervenes.

6 Paragraphs 3 to 5 shall continue to apply until the thresholds referred to in Article 1(2) have been reviewed.

Article 23
Implementing provisions

The Commission shall have the power to adopt implementing provisions concerning the form, content and other details of notification pursuant to Article 4, time limits pursuant to Article 10, and hearings pursuant to Article 18.

Article 24
Relations with non-member countries

1 The Member States shall inform the Commission of any general difficulties encountered by their undertakings with concentrations as defined in Article 3 in a non-member country.

2 Initially not more than one year after the entry into force of this Regulation and thereafter periodically the Commission shall draw up a report examining the treatment according to Community undertakings, in the terms referred to in paragraphs 3 and 4, as regards concentrations in non-member countries. The Commission shall submit those reports to the Council, together with any recommendations.

3 Whenever it appears to the Commission, either on the basis of the reports referred to in paragraph 2 or the basis of other information, that a non-member country does not grant Community undertakings treatment comparable to that granted by the Community to undertakings from that non-member country, the Commission may submit proposals to the Council for an appropriate mandate for negotiation with a view to obtaining comparable treatment for Community undertakings.

4 Measures taken under this Article shall comply with the obligation of the Community or of the Member States, without prejudice to Article 234 of the Treaty, under international agreements, whether bilateral or multilateral.

Article 25
Entry into force

1 This Regulation shall enter into force on 21 September 1990.

2 This Regulation shall not apply to any concentration which was the subject of an agreement or announcement or where control was acquired within the meaning of Article 4(1) before the date of this Regulation's entry into force and it shall not in any circumstances apply to any concentration in respect of which proceedings were initiated before that date by a Member State's authority with responsibility for competition.

This Regulation shall be binding in its entirety and directly applicable in all Member States.

Done at Brussels, 21 December 1989.

For the Council

The President

E. Cresson

CALCULATING THRESHOLDS FOR BANKS AND INSURANCE COMPANIES UNDER THE 1989 MERGER REGULATION

Instead of attempting to calculate a worldwide turnover figure for banks and other financial institutions, the regulation stipulates that one-tenth of total assets will be the benchmark. Therefore, if two banks were contemplating a merger and their combined total assets amounted to Ecu 50 billion or more, they would be deemed to meet the Ecu 5 billion worldwide turnover criterion.

The EC (EU) turnover criterion is also different for banks and other financial institutions. It is calculated by multiplying one-tenth of the institutions' combined total assets by the ratio of loans to EU residents as a proportion of total loans.

For example, let us suppose that two banks, or a bank and a building society, have total assets of Ecu 60 billion and their combined loan portfolios amount to Ecu 40 billion. Half of the Ecu 40 billion has been lent to EU residents.

The EU turnover of the two institutions would be calculated thus:

$$\frac{\text{Total assets (Ecu 60 billion)}}{10} \times \tfrac{1}{2} = \text{Ecu 3 billion}$$

Since the EU turnover threshold is Ecu 250 million, these two institutions easily qualify for investigation.

In fact this formula works on the same lines as the formula for other companies. The combined EU turnover threshold of Ecu 250 million is exactly one-twentieth of the combined worldwide turnover threshold of Ecu 5 billion. Assuming two banks hit the
global turnover threshold exactly, their EU loans will have to exceed one-twentieth of total loans in order to meet the EU turnover threshold.

As banks' worldwide turnovers grow (measured as one-tenth of total assets), the fraction required to meet the EU turnover threshold will shrink. Two banks with worldwide turnover calculated at Ecu 10 billion would only have to have one-fortieth of their loan portfolio dedicated to EU residents in order to meet the EC turnover threshold, thus:

$$\frac{\text{Ecu 100 billion}}{10} \times \frac{1}{40} = \text{Ecu 250 million}$$

The last test that the Commission applies in assessing whether a merger has a

Community dimension is also subtly different for banks. This is the so-called two-thirds test: if one or other of the parties to a merger derives more than two-thirds of its EU turnover in one member state, the merger may be a matter for that member state, but not for the Commission. For banks and other financial institutions the two-thirds test is satisfied if loans to the residents of one member state account for more than two-thirds of loans to all EU residents.

For insurance companies, the thresholds are rather simpler. Instead of turnover, the Commission uses gross written premiums. This applies to all three thresholds.

THE STRUCTURE OF DGIV: CONTACT NAMES AND NUMBERS

At the beginning of 1993, Directorate General IV was divided into three main sections. The first section, under Philip Lowe, was charged with the investigation of 'concentrations' under the 1989 merger control regulation – it is better known as the merger task force. Lowe's telephone and facsimile numbers respectively are: Brussels (32–2) 296 5040 and Brussels (32–2) 296 4301.

The second section was responsible for 'general competition policy' and co-ordination with other Community institutions. It was divided into four directorates, as follows.

Directorate A. General competition policy and co-ordination

Director. Rafael Garcia Palencia. Tel: Brussels (32–2) 295 0253. Fax: Brussels (32–2) 295 0128.

Unit 1: General policy and international aspects – relations with the European parliament and the Economic and Social Committee. Unit head: Anke Haagsma. Tel: Brussels (32–2) 296 5826.

Unit 2: Procedural and juridical issues relating to infraction proceedings and intracommunity dumping. Unit head: Helmuth Schroter. Tel: Brussels (32–2) 295 1196.

Unit 3: Economic studies. Unit head: David Deacon. Tel: Brussels (32–2) 295 5905.

Unit 4: Co-ordination of decisions in applying the competition rules. Unit head: vacant (but Sebastiano Guttoso heads the main operating section within this unit charged with intellectual property rights and research and development). His telephone number is Brussels (32–2) 295 1102.

Unit 5: Public enterprises and state monopolies. Unit head: Claude Rakovsky. This is the section charged with investigating offences against Article 90 of the Treaty of Rome, referred to above. Tel: Brussels (32–2) 295 5389. Fax: Brussels (32–2) 295 0128.

Directorate B. Cartels, abuses of dominant positions and other distortions of competition I

Director. Jean Dubois. Tel: Brussels (32–2) 295 1008. The units comprising Directorate B are industry-specific, thus:

Unit 1: Electrical and electronics industry, information technologies and telecommunications. Contact names: Fin Lomholt (Tel: (32–2) 295 5619), Mikael Suenson (Tel: (32–2) 295 5619).

Unit 2: Machine industries, textile industries, leatherwork, etc. Unit head: Franco Giuffrida. Tel: Brussels (32–2) 295 6084.

Unit 3: Banks, insurance companies and other financial services. Unit head: Gisele Vernimmen. Tel: Brussels (32–2) 295 3983.

Unit 4: The media, entertainment, distributive trades. Unit head: Norbert Menges. Tel: Brussels (32–2) 295 3936.

Directorate C. Cartels, abuses of dominant positions and other distortions of competition II

Director: Gianfranco Rocca. Tel: Brussels (32–2) 295 1152. Fax: Brussels (32–2) 296 4273. Again, the units are industry-specific.

Unit 1: Non-ferrous metals, non-metallic minerals; construction industry; wood, glass, paper, rubber industries. Unit head: Maurice Guerrin. Tel: Brussels (32–2) 295 1817.

Unit 2: Energy (except coal); basic chemical industry products. Unit head: Kurt Ritter. Tel: Brussels (32–2) 295 1155.

Unit 3: Processed chemical products; agricultural products; foodstuffs. Unit head: Jurgen Mensching. Tel: Brussels (32–2) 295 2224.

Directorate D. Cartels, abuses of dominant positions and other distortions of competition III

Director: John Temple Lang. Tel: Brussels (32–2) 295 5571. Fax: Brussels (32–2) 295 3615.

Unit 1: Steel and coal. Unit head: Juan Riviere Marti. Tel: Brussels (32–2) 295 1146.

Unit 2: Supervision of European Coal and Steel Community Treaty. Unit head: Pierre Duprat. Tel: Brussels (32–2) 295 3524.

Unit 3: Transport and tourism. Unit head: Jonathan Faull. Tel: Brussels (32–2) 295 8658.

Unit 4: Cars and other means of motorised transport. Unit head: Dieter Schwarz. Tel: Brussels (32–2) 295 1880.

The third section is, strictly speaking, a fifth directorate (Directorate E) but its business distinguishes it sharply from the other four. Headed by Asger Petersen (tel: (32–2) 295 5691), it is charged with monitoring state aids – one of DGIV's more delicate tasks in early 1993 as recession tightened its grip over Europe.

Directorate E's fax numbers are Brussels (32–2) 296 1242 and 296 6045. It is split into six units, as follows:

Unit 1: General state aids schemes. Unit head: vacant. Contact name: Paul Knaff. Tel: Brussels (32–2) 295 3584.

Unit 2: Research and development aid. Unit head: Serge Durande. Tel: Brussels (32–2) 295 7243.

Unit 3: Regional aids. Unit head: Gianluigi Campogrande. Tel: Brussels (32–2) 295 2767.

Units 4 and 5: Sectoral aids. Unit head: Francisco Esteve Rey. Tel: Brussels (32–2) 295 1140.

Unit 6: Inventory and analysis. Unit head: vacant.

It should be noted that staff move around DGIV quite rapidly in response to changes in the demands placed upon the directorate general. The telephone and facsimile numbers given above are certainly not set in stone: in 1992 the first three digits of the Commission's telephone number were changed from 235 to 295, to the horror of guidebook authors, but doubtless to the delight of the Commission's stationery suppliers.

If any of the above numbers fails to put you in touch with the person you need to talk to, the Commission's full postal address, telephone and telex numbers are as follows:

The Commission of the European Communities
Rue de la Loi 200
B–1049 Brussels
Belgium

Tel: Brussels (32–2) 295 1111
Telex: 21877 COMEU B

Faxes should be sent direct to DGIV on Brussels (32–2) 296 4298, or to the individual fax numbers of the directorate heads listed above.

The Commission's offices in London are tucked away in a side street near the Houses of Parliament, beside the Queen Elizabeth II Conference Centre. The postal address is:

Commission of the European Communities
Jean Monnet House
8 Storey's Gate
London SW1P 3AT

The telephone number was changed not so long ago to take advantage of the single market fever that was sweeping Europe. It is now 071–973 1992. The facsimile number is 071–973 1900.

BLOCK EXEMPTIONS

The following EEC block exemptions have been incorporated, with suitable but minor adaptations, into the EEA Agreement between the European Union and the European Free Trade Association countries (excluding Switzerland and Liechtenstein):

1. Exclusive distribution agreements (Reg. 1983/83)
2. Exclusive purchasing agreements (Reg. 1984/83)
3. Motor vehicle selective distribution agreements (Reg. 123/85)
4. Franchising agreements (Reg. 4087/88)
5. Patent licensing agreements (Reg. 2349/84)
6. Know-how licensing agreements (Reg. 556/89)
7. Specialisation agreements (Reg. 417/85)
8. Research and development agreements (Reg. 418/85)
9. Inland transport (Reg. 1017/68)
10. Maritime transport (Reg. 4056/86).

Block exemption regulations in the air transport sector have also come into effect throughout the European Economic Area since 1 July 1993, as have the block exemption rules governing insurance undertakings described in chapter 6.

Commission Regulation 151/93, which amends the patent, know-how, specialisation and R&D block exemptions and which was adopted after the EEA Agreement was signed, will be added to the list under the same procedure.

(I am indebted to Allen & Overy for the bulk of the above information.)

INDEX